THE PROFESSOR

The Life Story of Azumah Nelson

ASHLEY MORRISON

Strategic Book Publishing and Rights Co.

Cover Picture: Photographer Chris Smith. Source Hulton Archive.

Strategic Book Publishing and Rights Co.
12620 FM 1960, Suite A4-507
Houston, TX 77065
www.sbpra.com

ISBN: 978-1-62857-105-9

I dedicate this book to the former president of Ghana, J. J. Rawlings, for his guidance and support when I was starting out, and to Dave Harper for his friendship and support today.

I would also like to dedicate it to all the people of Ghana, my home, and the country I love. Hopefully, my story shows that as Africans, we can conquer the world.

Azumah Nelson

TABLE OF CONTENTS

ACKNOWLEDGMENTS

The writing of this book has been an absolute pleasure. I first became aware of Azumah Nelson when he knocked out Pat Cowdell in London, having watched the fight on television with my dad. It was a happy memory of growing up, watching boxing on television with him.

First of all, I must thank Azumah himself for trusting me to tell his remarkable story, especially for the treasured friendship that has resulted. I hope that I have done his life justice and have given people an insight into this special man. I must also thank Dave Harper for having the vision that Azumah's tale should be told and for entrusting me to be the one to tell it. I must also acknowledge the time and help Azumah's mother and brother afforded me.

Along the journey, there have been others who have contributed, and this book would not have been possible without their help. From the boxing fraternity, I would like to thank Brian Mitchell, Joe Cortez, Barry McGuigan, Jesse James Leija, Jeff Fenech, Johnny Lewis, Lawrence Cole, Carl King, Dr. Lou Moret, Jim McDonnell, and Charlie Magri.

My thanks also go to those outside of the ring. Former president of Ghana J. J. Rawlings, lifelong friend Obi Oblitey, Adriana Nelson, Nii Amakai Amarteifio, Peter and Jacob Zwennes, and Yaw Sakyi were more help than they will ever realise, especially in terms of relating what it was like living in Ghana in those times.

There were many old boxing magazines that helped me confirm certain details leading up to and following fights. I would like to acknowledge the work done by the writers and the publishers of *Boxing News*, *The Ring*, *Boxing Illustrated*, *KO*, *World Boxing*, *Boxing Monthly*, *Boxing Illustrated*, *Boxing Scene*, *The Fist*, and *Inside Boxing*.

Also, it would be remiss of me to not acknowledge the site that has become the first port of call when checking a fighter's record, www.boxrec.com.

Over the years, I have read many books on the noble art of boxing and would like to acknowledge the following books, which were useful sources of information:

I love youse all by Jeff Fenech with Terry Smith, published by Modern Publishing in 1993.

Johnny Lewis: The Biography: The Story of Australia's King of Boxing by Dave Kent, published by Allen & Unwin in 2010.

The Business of Pain by Araceli Martinez-Rose, published by RM Advisors Ediciones in 2011.

Cyclone by Barry McGuigan, published by Virgin Books in 2011.

Heroes Without a Country by Donald McRae, published by Harper Collins Publishers in 2002.

I hope that my words help portray the life of a remarkable man and encourage others to follow his example in and out of the ring.

Ashley Morrison

I

MADISON SQUARE GARDEN

A short, stocky man in a suit enters the convention centre at the Mandalay Bay Hotel in Las Vegas, searching the room for his table. As he snakes his way between the seemingly endless rows of tables, many former colleagues come up to warmly shake his hand. He smiles but maintains his thoughtful gaze into the distance, looking for that elusive table.

As he nears the front of the room, a waiter breaks away from his work and makes a beeline for the man; he stops in front of him and stretches out his hand. The man in the suit stops, takes his hand, and listens to the waiter, smiling. "Azumah Nelson, you were one of the greatest. I was there when you fought Salvador Sanchez—what a fight."

Azumah smiles and tells the waiter that Sanchez was one hell of a fighter, but before he can move forward, the waiter turns and gestures at some other waiters in the room to come and meet the man.

"This is Azumah Nelson," he tells them. "The greatest featherweight of them all. He fought Sanchez; he took him all the way."

"Yes, and at seventeen days' notice," Azumah reminds him with a smile on his face. "I wanted a rematch, but sadly he died, so it was not possible."

"It would have been some fight," the waiter says, finally letting go of Nelson's hand. With a respectful nod of his head, he and his fellow waiters return to their duties.

History never feels like history at the time, but when the unknown boxer, Azumah Nelson from Ghana, stepped into the ring at New York's

1

Madison Square Garden on July 21, 1982, his name became a part of boxing folklore.

Mexican Salvador Sanchez had been twenty-three years old. He was the World Boxing Council featherweight champion of the world, with an impressive professional record of forty-three wins—thirty-one by knock-out—one loss, and one draw. Remarkably he had turned professional at the tender age of sixteen, reportedly after just four amateur bouts. His only defeat came in his nineteenth fight, at the hands of fellow Mexican Antonio Becerra, the bantamweight champion.

He didn't look back after that day, and many believed him to be the best featherweight champion the world had ever seen.

He was due to defend his title against Mario Miranda in 1982, but the Argentinean had to withdraw after he was injured in training.

Promoter Don King needed to find a replacement at late notice. Telephone calls were made, and in the United Kingdom, promoter Mickey Duff said he had just the man.

Duff picked up the phone in his London office and called a number in the West African country of Ghana. Azumah Nelson's manager, John Kermeh, answered the phone in Accra, the capital city. As Azumah's life-long friend Obi Oblitey recalls, "At that time, Azumah had fought a Nigerian at the Kaneshie Sports complex. When the phone call came, he was not in the house. Kermeh, his manager, answered and then came to see Ashikwei Tetteh and me. He told us we were going to fight for the world championship. For three days, we had not seen Azumah. We thought he may be at his father's place in Mamprobi, so we looked there."

Azumah had fought Mukaila Bukare in Accra on June 26, and, having won by technical knockout in the sixth round, was taking some time out for himself.

So why Azumah Nelson?

Scouts in Africa had witnessed his impressive victory over Zambian Charm Chiteule in Lusaka for the Commonwealth Featherweight title, and that was how Mickey Duff had come to put Azumah forward for the fight against Sanchez. Azumah had won that fight by technical knockout in the tenth round of fifteen.

It was thought that Nelson would come out with all guns blazing in the opening rounds and that the champion would toy with him before disposing of him in round five or six.

When his management found Azumah and told him of the chance to fight for the World title, despite having only seventeen days to prepare, he knew that he had to take up the challenge.

When he jumped into the ring in Madison Square Garden for the fifteen-round World title fight, few outside Ghana had ever heard of Azumah Nelson. It was thought that he had little or no chance against a champion many regarded as one of the greatest fighters of all time in his division, and certainly of his era.

Azumah knew this was his chance. He had no intention of letting the opportunity slip. As he waited in the ring for his opponent, he looked focused and far from nervous. Few knew or understood that he carried the hopes of a nation desperate for success. His trunks reflected that hope and that nation.

With both boxers in the ring, the announcer began his introductions: "The man in charge of this scheduled fifteen-round World Boxing Council Featherweight Championship is referee Tony Perez. And now, boxing fans, introducing the principals: First, in the blue corner, wearing the yellow trunks with the red and green trim, he is weighing in at an even 124 pounds. He is undefeated in thirteen professional fights with ten knockouts. He is the Commonwealth champion from Accra, Ghana, Africa. He is Azumah Nelson."

A roar goes up and the challenger raises his arms above his head. The ringside bell began to strike.

The announcer continues. "His opponent in the red corner, wearing the red trunks with the white trim, is weighing in at an even 126 pounds. This young man has a record of forty-two wins, one loss, one draw, and thirty knockouts. From Mexico City, Mexico, the WBC featherweight champion is Salvador Sanchez."

A massive roar followed the announcement of Sanchez's name as the Mexicans inside "The Garden" make it clear who they are supporting.

The referee brings the two together in the centre of the ring for their final instructions. Both boxers then return to their respective corners, and the bell sounds for the fight to begin.

The ringside commentators on the Don King Sports and Entertainment Network had never seen Azumah Nelson fight and are evaluating him as the fight progresses.

Azumah is compact and dominates the centre of the ring in the opening round, landing some telling blows early on. One minute and twenty seconds into the opening round, however, he worries Sanchez with a right hand.

World Heavyweight Champion Larry Holmes, commentating ringside, makes a telling point: "We have a fight on our hands. Nelson has no fear—he's come to fight."

The challenger then throws in an "Ali Shuffle." Was this showboating or trying to show he has dominated the opening three minutes? Whatever it was, the crowd loved it.

Sanchez knows he has a fight on his hands, and in an effort to emphasise that fact, Azumah does not sit down in his corner straightaway, trying to stir up the crowd.

Round two starts almost as round one had finished, with another Ali Shuffle from Azumah, followed by a fast exchange of punches.

Azumah waits for Sanchez to throw and then counters effectively. In five minutes, he has shown he is a very competent fighter who does not fear Sanchez, or his reputation. The challenger is forcing the fight, making Sanchez reach for him, and the touch of gloves at the end of the round, shows that both boxers know this is going to be a tough fight, and that they already respect each other.

Commentator John Condon, despite the opening salvo from Nelson, believes the challenger has to get lucky early to win, as Sanchez has been fifteen rounds before and that experience will tell as the fight goes on.

Azumah stops and smiles at Sanchez in the third as Sanchez thrusts his jab into the face of the challenger, but he keeps coming forward. No one had seen Azumah fight before; none of his fights were on film. Sanchez can only attempt to work him out, round by round, while trying to avoid getting hurt at the same time. At the end of the round, Sanchez lands two good rights over the top of Azumah's left, revealing a possible chink in the Ghanaian's armor.

Sanchez sits in his corner, waiting for the bell for round four. When it sounds, he crosses himself as he does before every round and rises to his feet.

Once again, though, it is Azumah who takes the lead, landing a good flurry of punches at the start of the round. After another Ali Shuffle, he manages to avoid most of Sanchez's punches. At the end of the round, both boxers stand toe-to-toe, belting each other with blows to the body and to the head, prompting the commentator Holmes at ringside to say, "He is the champion in his country, and the way he is fighting, he's trying to prove he is the best in all countries."

When the bell sounds, Azumah smiles at Sanchez, and once again, the two touch gloves. Azumah is raring to go at the start of round five, so much so that he comes out from his corner early, and referee Tony Perez sends him back to wait until the bell sounds. Once it does, he chases Sanchez around the ring and lands four or five good blows, including a telling right. "A warrior down to his toes" was how commentator John Condon saw the challenger.

Azumah lands a series of good body punches and is starting to hurt Sanchez. His expression has changed and he is beginning to take more blows than in previous rounds. Early in round six, Azumah is caught by a left hook as Sanchez starts to move and jab, attempting to control the fight. He circles Azumah, holding him off with his jab and restricts him from being able to move forward and get in close. As good as Sanchez is, he cannot avoid being caught with a right in the dying seconds as Azumah keeps plugging away.

The seventh round sees Sanchez continue to jab, and when he unleashes a powerful left hook, he has Azumah stumbling backwards. He manages to stay on his feet, but Sanchez moves in for the kill. Azumah tries to fight back but eventually hits the canvas when another short left hook lands flush on the side of his head. He is up at the count of five, and standing in front of Tony Perez, taking the mandatory eight-count.

Azumah comes forward, knowing the best form of defence is to attack. Sanchez is patient and not prepared to risk being caught by one of Azumah's powerful hooks. That caution gives Azumah time to recover, but at the end of the round, it is apparent that all is not well with the challenger when he goes to a neutral corner, rather than to his own.

Early in the eighth round, a left hook rocks Azumah, and he wobbles as if drunk. As he tries to steady himself, a right hook catches him. He stumbles again but somehow manages to stay on his feet.

There is no doubt that Azumah is hurt, but when a warrior is hurt, pride kicks in and he comes forward rather than retreats. Azumah throws a flurry of punches that lets Sanchez know he isn't finished yet. The salvo has the desired effect. Sanchez eases up the attack, deciding that caution is the best option rather than getting caught by one of Azumah's powerful swinging punches. Sanchez then plays a patient game, knowing there are still plenty of rounds left to take out the challenger. The courageous Azumah keeps fighting, but the momentum of the fight is starting to shift, and Sanchez's experience is starting to win out.

Again, Azumah is up early and out of his corner, waiting for the bell to start the ninth. Sanchez, however, remains seated in his and doesn't rise until he hears the bell. A close exchange of blows sees Azumah rocked again when the champion lands a left hook over the top of his guard. A minute into the round, Sanchez circles his opponent and neither boxer throws any punches. Suddenly, Azumah launches an attack, but unlike in the early rounds, Sanchez fights back. Both fighters land a flurry of punches, and when they are separated, Azumah is bleeding from his mouth. But being the warrior that he is, he can only go one way: He continues to move forward. At the end of the round, the evidence is clear that Sanchez has again troubled the challenger when Azumah bizarrely goes to Sanchez's corner rather than his own.

As the bell sounds for the tenth, many are surprised that Azumah is still there, especially after accepting the fight at the eleventh hour, but the ascendancy is definitely with Sanchez. Azumah keeps moving forward, but Sanchez is picking him off and manages to slip in his dangerous, swinging right hook. Azumah keeps forcing the champion back, concentrating his attack to the body and landing some hard, powerful blows. When the bell sounds, Azumah does a little dance, but rather than showboating, he looks to be trying to reinvigorate his undoubtedly tired body.

Between rounds, World Champion Larry Holmes announces that the fighters are now entering championship territory. "This is where the champions show their class and overpower the challenger," he declared.

Azumah is up from his stool early again, ready to get on with the fight. Sanchez lands a good right, but Azumah continues to move forward. The Mexicans in the crowd start to find their voice, hoping to cheer their champion home in the last five rounds. The two stand toe-to-toe, head-to-head, as Sanchez begins to throw to the body, Azumah to the head. Azumah then backs Sanchez into the corner and lands two powerful left hooks, which hurt the champion.

Suddenly, questions are being asked as to whether the challenger can really take the fight and the title from the champion. With less than thirty seconds left in the round, Azumah is knocked off-balance. He stumbles but then throws a left hook that visibly hurts Sanchez, who looks to be hanging on in the final seconds of the round. This time, it is Sanchez who dances at the bell, but it is a dance to try and convince his fans that he still has control of his legs. The determined Azumah is still standing, and in unknown territory in terms of rounds fought. But as he proved in that round, if he can land his punches, he can hurt the champion.

Azumah is again up early from his corner, wanting to get down to business. He starts the twelfth as the aggressor, throwing punches from all angles, while Sanchez keeps snapping his jab into Azumah's face.

The challenger is looking for a knockout and is trying to set Sanchez up for a right hook. He manages to force Sanchez into the corner, but cannot land a telling right. As they come back out into the centre of the ring, Azumah forces his opponent back again and lands a left hook that skims off Sanchez. But as the champion backs away, his right foot slips in the wet patch in his corner. He takes a right as he tries to get up. Meanwhile, Azumah keeps landing punches and scoring points, and ringside observers consider the fight even at this point, with just three rounds to go. For once, Azumah is not out before the bell, and his corner have worked hard on the swelling around his left eye. Both boxers are fighting like champions.

Still, the two fighters go at it, with referee Perez peripheral. Azumah is still forcing Sanchez back and lands most of his punches. With one minute and thirty seconds to go, a left and then a great right hook rock Sanchez, as does another combination seconds later. The champion looks tired and is suddenly taking a lot of punches. As the round comes to a close, Azumah staggers by him with a right, followed by an uppercut, and then a right hook. It looks to be Azumah's round—that is, until a left hook rocks him just after the bell sounds. Courageously, he dances in the ring to say, "I'm okay."

The left hook appears to be the one weapon Sanchez has to save himself from defeat. There are two rounds to go, and there was little doubt his corner has told him he has to step it up. Sanchez is more purposeful at the start of the fourteenth; he is constantly thrusting his jab into Azumah's face. He then lands two jabs in a row, followed by a good right. Halfway through the round, though, Azumah starts chasing Sanchez and lands some good blows. Once again, the two stand toe-to-toe and both land powerful punches.

At the end of the round, both boxers are still standing there, throwing punches with little movement, and fail to hear the bell. For the first time in the fight, referee Perez has to step in and separate them. As they break apart, Azumah looks like he is out on his feet, while Sanchez slumps heavily onto his own stool.

No one had expected the fight to go the distance. Sanchez was regarded as one of the truly great champions, and no one had heard of the Ghanaian Azumah Nelson. But one thing was sure: Few were going to forget him.

Again, Azumah is up and ready before the bell, while Sanchez waits on his stool until it sounds. The two warriors come to the centre of the ring and touch gloves as the crowd shows its appreciation of a great fight. Azumah goes on the attack early; many still believing he needs a knockout to win.

His opening flurry looks impressive. However, in looking for that much-needed knockout, he opens himself up and is caught by a right hook, and then another follow-up right. Azumah keeps fighting back, the right side of his jaw is visibly swollen and blood is pouring out of his mouth. His breathing has become difficult and his mouth is hanging open. He is noticeably tired, and his punches have become wilder.

With just under two minutes left, Azumah finds himself on the ropes in his corner. Suddenly, a short right and two follow-up punches force his legs to buckle. He falls to the canvas. As he did in round seven, though, he bounces up and takes a standing eight-count, but the spring in his step has gone. Perez lets the fight continue with just under a minute-and-a-half left. Two swinging lefts from Sanchez and Azumah's resistance is non-existent; his legs wobble and the referee moves in to stop the fight.

The fight ended after one minute and forty-nine seconds of the final round. Azumah had lost in cruel circumstances. He had tried to stay on his feet and fight back, but the lack of time to prepare for a fight against a great world champion had taken its toll in the very last round.

Commentator John Landon showed his respect for Azumah when he summed up the fight by saying, "I salute you for a great performance. You're a great fighter, and you are going to be greater as you go on." Prophetic words, indeed.

As it turned out, the judges all had Azumah behind when the fight was stopped, and only a knockout would have seen him take the WBC featherweight championship from Salvador Sanchez. The judges' scores were: Castelano 135–131, Reid 132–133, Aidala 134–131.

They say that life is about seizing opportunities when they come your way, and Azumah Nelson certainly did that against the great Salvador Sanchez. No one had given the young unknown from Ghana a hope of lasting the distance, but he had stood toe-to-toe with the champion, and even dominated him at times. With just seventeen days' notice, he had almost weathered fifteen rounds with one of the greats.

He woke up that day unknown outside of Africa, but his name was now indelibly stamped in the minds of fight fans the world over.

II

THE HUSTLER

Very few outside his native Ghana knew much about Azumah Nelson before he fought Salvador Sanchez for the world title. This was emphasised when fight commentator, John Condon, informed viewers that "Azumah Nelson does not come from a poor family. His father was a millionaire in the tailoring business and fishing business."

The truth, as is often the case, was very different.

Azumah Nelson was born on July 19, 1958, in Timber Market, a suburb in the old port area of Accra, the capital of Ghana, and his heritage goes deep into the past of this region. He is directly descended from the Tabon people. Back in 1829, seven families made up of seventy-five individuals from Bahia, Brazil, bought their freedom and were the first slaves to make their way back to the lands from which they had been taken. They landed in Accra and were led by Kangidi Asuman, who later changed his name to Azumah Nelson.

West African slaves had been shipped to Brazil since 1550. This trading in human life between Africa and Brazil would not be abolished until 1851, and it wouldn't be until 1871 that the children of slaves would be deemed to have been born free. Today, the state of Bahia has the highest number of Afro descendants in Brazil, with 80 per cent of the state having African ancestors.

Now free, these former slaves returned to their homelands, determined to rebuild their lives. They were the first tailors and architects of the region and were experienced farmers who mastered basic irrigation techniques.

11

Rather than being threatened by the new arrivals in Accra's Jamestown area, the locals welcomed them home. They were respected by the Ga Chiefs, who themselves had originally come from Chad and Benin. The *mantse* (king), Nii Ankrah, granted them a place in his territory, the Otublohum.

Accra, at this time, was divided between three powers: the English, the Danes, and the Dutch. The Otublohum fell under the control of the Danes, who were none too pleased with Nii Ankrah's decision but accepted it.

Nearly two hundred years later, there is still harmony, as the Tabon *mantse* has placed himself under the protection of the Otublohum *mantse*, one of the seven chieftains under the Ga *mantse*.

The Tabon lived in Old Accra, which was made up of Ussher Town, or Kinka, and Jamestown, which was regarded as the heart of the city and was where the independence movement began in the 1930s.

The Nelson family, the leaders of the Tabon, left a lasting mark on the people by forming the first Scissors House in 1854. The building was a centre for training master tailors in modern, Western-style clothing. It is still standing and occupied by tailors today.

Azumah Nelson was the firstborn son of Emmanuel Teilo Nelson, who was, not surprisingly, a tailor. His mother, Madam Comfort Atswei Quarcoo, was a trader. Azumah would be the eldest of seven children.

This was a time of new beginnings, as when Azumah was born the new nation of Ghana was itself only just over a year old. Formerly called the Gold Coast, it was among the wealthiest and most socially advanced areas in Africa, with schools, railways, hospitals, Social Security, and an advanced economy. The British had established the Gold Coast Crown colony in 1874 over part, but not all, of the country. The Gold Coast achieved independence from the United Kingdom at midnight on March 6, 1957, becoming the first sub-Saharan African nation to do so.

The name Ghana was chosen for the new nation to reflect the ancient Empire of Ghana, which had once extended throughout much of West Africa. Aptly, the name means "warrior king." Independence brought with it a new identity, and with that identity came a new flag of red, gold, and green, with a black star set in the middle. Designed by Theodosia Salome

Okoh, the red represents the blood that was shed in the fight for independence; the gold represents the mineral wealth of the region; and the green symbolizes Ghana's rich agriculture. The strategically placed black star symbolizes African emancipation.

Little did the newborn Azumah Nelson know that his future success would give this fledgling nation an identity on the world stage and its people a belief that they could compete internationally and step out of the shadows of colonialism.

Timber Market was and still is a typical African suburb, overcrowded and made up of a kaleidoscope of multicoloured, low-cost, self-constructed huts of wood and corrugated metal. Most are simply one room occupied by many. The narrow and uneven avenues between these wooden huts are unpaved, heavily rutted, and always busy with locals, children, chickens, and goats.

At the time of Azumah's birth, there were no modern-day amenities such as electricity and sewage systems; the only running water was one communal tap, shared by many. Life was undoubtedly tough. When it rained, it was crowded and wet; the dusty avenues soon turned to mud, and water snaked among the dwellings. When it didn't rain, it was crowded, dusty, and hot. Privacy was scarce and poverty persistent. Yet there was a spirit of togetherness, of community, as people looked out for each other.

"Timber Market was very beautiful back then, as there were not so many people living there. It was similar to the way it is today, but the houses were beautiful because they were new and painted. Now they are old," lifelong friend Obi Oblitey recalls. "Formerly, it was a cemetery. Then they stopped burying people, and people moved into the area. There were so many trees there then, but they have all gone now. It was very beautiful. Then people came from Niger and Mali and started trading there in timber and cola nuts. But when our second president, Major General Joseph Arthur Ankrah, came to power, he made the aliens go back to their countries. We Ghanaians did not know much about trading, so when they came back, they reclaimed their land and started trading again."

As Timber Market falls away down a small hill, it almost slips into

Korley Lagoon. Today, the lagoon is full of rubbish and is heavily polluted, but it was a very different place in the early 1960s.

"It was very beautiful. It was green, and the blue seawater came into the lagoon. The water was very clear. There was green grass, and coconut trees grew around the edge of the lagoon. It was so beautiful. Our first president, Nkrumah, planted the coconut trees. In the lagoon, the water was so clean we could see the fish swimming—it was so clear and there were so many fish," Obi remembers. "Then the Dagoma people came from the north of Ghana with the Nanumbe and Komkobas people. They came to Accra because of a quarrel. They were traders, too, and they came to sell yams. It is because of them the lagoon became polluted. They became so many, as they kept coming from the north, and they were the ones who put rubbish in there. Formerly, it was so beautiful."

For children, there was a freedom few can imagine. Barefoot and smiling, the children would run, laughing up and down the dried mud boulevards, while their parents worked hard to feed and clothe them. Well, most did. The young Azumah was a boy who never smiled much, as Obi Oblitey remembers. "He was too serious; he never smiled."

His mother confirms this. "He didn't smile when he was small. He would just give you a look—he would lower his head and glare at you, and if he saw you coming and did not want to see you, he would turn away. You knew he did not want to talk to you or see you. He was a very serious boy, very serious."

Obi has been a friend of Azumah since the two were just ten years old. "It was then that we started as friends, best friends, doing everything together. There were about eight to ten of us who stayed together. We did everything together. Before he entered into boxing, we were best friends," he recalls.

Azumah remembers those days. "When I was young, it was difficult to see me laughing, as I was always thinking about where the next meal or money was coming from. I knew when I was very young that I had to work to help put food on the table for my family."

Azumah was not an only child for long. He soon found himself with two brothers, Aruna and Joseph, and four sisters, Beatrice Abiana, Theresa Louisa, Lakia Felecia, and Oboshie Susana. "I remember when they were young, I looked after them and felt it was up to me to make sure that they had eaten."

His mother agrees that from a young age he always wanted to try and help his family. "He tried to look after his sisters, and he used to give me something to care for the children. When he was growing up in Timber Market, I sold fish. When I went to buy fish at the seaside, I would take him with me to carry the fish to the market. He was always happy to help. We were not a very poor family, but also we were not rich," she recalls. "He was always trying to help. There was a time he would go to the seaside and buy coconuts and sell them. He was a good hustler. He would always manage to make money and bring it back to the house."

Tragedy, though, struck Azumah at a young age. "My second brother, Aruna, who was two years younger, died when he was five years of age, but I don't really remember it," he says. "He was taken ill and was rushed to the hospital, but regrettably, he passed away a week later."

A sense of duty to provide for and look after his younger siblings was very strong in the young Azumah, and that feeling of helping others extended well beyond his immediate family. He cared for everyone. However, the young Azumah did not enjoy going to school.

"I sent him to school but he did not want to go," his mother reminisces. "I wanted him to learn, but he did not go. He wanted to box. So in the end, I left him to do what he wanted. Now he is a scholar. He is a professor, so he has done well. He has learned English and can speak it, and he has had God's help along the way. If you give yourself to God, he will live with you, and he lives with Azumah.

"He fought a lot as a little boy. I sent him to school, and he was wearing his uniform, and instead he went to the lagoon. He came home with no uniform. He said that this boy had taken it after a fight. I tried to get him to go to school, but he did his own thing. He was very determined."

During those formative years, Azumah's life was spent between his mother's family home in Timber Market and the family house in Mamprobi, two suburbs on either side of the Korley Lagoon and close to the coast.

"I used to wake up at five o'clock in the morning and go and cut down coconuts before I went to school," he recalls. "Some days I had to walk a long way to find them; some days I did not go to school at all. If I didn't have money to buy coconuts to sell, or could not find any to cut down, I would find some coconuts on a man's land and I knocked on the door. I would ask if I could cut them down and tell them that I would give them some money after I sold them. When they said yes, I would take a cutlass and a pan and I would find a tree with big coconuts. I would climb the tree, cut them down, and sell the coconuts. I would take some money for myself and then go back and offer them the remaining money. They would then take some and leave some for me."

School was in Mamprobi and would start at seven o'clock in the morning. The children would arrive and sweep the classroom before school began. At eight, the classes would start and they would go until four in the afternoon. It was a quarter of a mile walk, and in those days, there was not much traffic.

School was not a place that Azumah enjoyed. He would often fall asleep in class. When he entered middle school, the teachers asked him to bring his father. They wanted to talk about why he was so tired. By the age of thirteen, he had stopped going to school altogether. "I stopped going to school because I was too tired to learn when I got there," he says. "I was always thinking of where the next money was going to come from. I stayed at my mother's house, and every day would go out and hustle for money and food. Often I never went home. I would stay with my grandmother and work to find money for my friends to feed them. My dad would come looking for me and take me home. If I saw him coming, I would run away, as I knew he would be angry. My dad loved me so much. I never knew how much until I was older. He wanted what was best for me. If he caught me, he would tie my hands around a coconut tree and beat me. He loved me so much that he did not want me to be in trouble with the police."

Even before he opted to leave school, Azumah was hustling on the streets with his friends, finding ways to make money so that they could all eat and to help provide for his family as well. "We were hustlers," he says. "We had parents but we did not rely on our parents to get food—we used to hustle to get food. We would find anything we could to sell. We sold empty bottles for my great-grandmother to an old lady in the area.

We would sell timber. We would sell anything."

He adds, "The chickens would go to the lagoon next to Timber Market to have chicks. I thought about it, and then went to the lagoon to claim chickens that no longer belonged to people—ones that no one could prove they owned. I would take some and sell them. I would only catch a chicken once its chick could fend for itself. I would then sell them at the market and share the money with my friends. It was not like the Rocky films as I was younger. I would walk low down—like Groucho Marx—and then drop on the chicken to catch it," he says, laughing at the memory.

"Sometimes we would go to the market, and if we saw a stray white chicken walking around, we would ask the men if they had seen my white chicken. They would say, 'Yes, it walked past earlier,' and then they would help me catch him. 'Poor little boy has lost his chicken,' they would say.

"One day a man grabbed me and said the chicken was his. 'Stop, stop!' he shouted. I did not run away, and a crowd started to form. He took hold of me and started pulling me, saying, 'I will show you where this chicken comes from.' People asked what had happened, and he said that I was a thief. I did not let him speak. I had my hand around the throat of the chicken, and I started hitting him in the face with it.

"'He says this chicken is his,' I said. 'It's okay. I will take him to my house and prove that this chicken is mine. Go home, you bad man.' The crowd was on my side, and he let me go. I walked as if I was going home, and then I turned around and sold the chicken in the market."

Obi recalls these days of hustling as well and smiles as he tells of what these young boys would do to eat or to earn money to eat. "We used to go and steal fowl in Timber Market," he remembers. "The people from Niger and Mali sold wood for building in Timber Market, and they would always sit together, four or five people sitting and conversing. So Azumah would go around the back of them, and I would stand nearby. He would then shoo the chickens, and they would pass in front of the people who were sitting and talking. After five minutes, we would say, 'Have you seen our black or red chickens?' and they would say yes. Azumah would say, 'My grandmother is very worried. We must catch them.' So then we would go and round them up, and they would help us catch them. Then we would take them to Katamanton to sell.

"Sometimes we would get coconuts. We would then go and sell them. There is a place in Mamprobi where his father's house was, Akoshie Junction—*akoshie* means coconut in our language. All the taxis and small buses would pass by there, and they would stop and buy some from us. It is because of that they named it Akoshie Junction."

Even Azumah's great-grandmother fell prey to his hustling, as Obi recalls. "His great-grandmother, Afio-Aba—his mother's mother's mother—she loved Azumah very much. This old lady was very short. She had started selling cassava, and they used the money to build a house in Timber Market, called Cassava House.

"When he was hungry and there is no food to eat, Azumah would go to her house and ask the old lady, 'Have you bathed?' 'Oh I haven't bathed,' she would say. Azumah would say, 'I will fetch water so that you can bathe.' She would then say, 'I love you, Azumah. You are a good boy, my great-great-grandson. You are the only one who cares for me, always.'

"The house was open all around. When you entered the main gate, you would pass through the back of the house. So he would put the water and the sponge and the towel in the bathroom, and he would then fetch the water from a pipe. He would call her when it was ready. He would help her there. When she closed the door—there was no door, no cover, really; it was just a piece of cloth—she would remove her clothes and put them on the wall.

"The old ladies make a scarf that they put money in and keep it tied to their waists or thighs and sew the money in the handkerchief or scarf. When you see an old lady with that, you know she has money. So while she puts the clothes on the wall, I am standing at the gate, waiting and watching. When she starts her bath and puts soap on her face, Azumah would grab the handkerchief with the money, take some money, and then put it back. Then we would go off and buy some food. She was very short and very strong and lived to ninety or a hundred."

The lagoon nearby was a source of not only food but also money.

"The lagoon was full of crabs, so we used to find empty Milluti containers and make traps," Azumah remembers. "We would make plenty and then go to the riverside and spread them over the crab holes at around four or five o'clock in the afternoon and leave them there until daybreak. The next day, we would go early in the morning to see whether we have caught any crabs. We caught plenty. We would then go selling them house to house, and the old ladies loved the crabs. Through that, we became very popular."

However, not all of his memories of the lagoon have a happy ending. Construction was underway at the lagoon, which meant that there was an opportunity to remove some of the building materials and make some money. Azumah watched the building site for a number of days, casing the joint just as a bank robber would. He came up with a plan. They would take the steel rods from the site, put them in a boat, and then cross the river and sell them. But there was a problem early on.

"We couldn't find a boat. There was a security guard sitting there, and the rods were at his feet and a spear by his side. He was sleeping. The rods were right in front of him. There were three of us and one was very afraid, so I told him to go keep a lookout. I said that I would go to the guard and the other person must do as I say. I needed someone with experience.

"I went there and counted the rods. They were very long. I would pick up one end, and once I raised it up, the other person would grab the other end. Just as we did that, the third boy told us that he saw men running across the bridge on the other side of the river. We had been spotted.

"So we took the rods to the edge of the river and slid them into the water and pretended that we were looking for crabs. When one of the men saw the rods in the water, he sounded the alarm, and we all ran off in different directions.

"I ran home the long way, running about three miles. It would have only been about one mile if I ran straight there. When we got home, I told my friends to go into their homes and change clothes quickly. This would mean that the men couldn't tell who we were. Twenty minutes later, the men appeared, and when they asked if we had seen boys wearing what we had been wearing, we sent them somewhere else. I had run barefoot through all sorts of areas to get home. When I got home, I had all these needles in my feet, but I just kept running because I could not get caught. The men could not understand how we managed to get the rods from right in front of the guard. But we never managed to get them away," he recalls with a hint of regret that his well-planned manoeuvre had come to nothing.

Another occasion when the hustler was outhustled was when he was asked to help a shoemaker in Timber Market. "One of the shoemakers sent me to buy some leather because someone had brought him business," he recalls. "I got to the top of Timber Market and two guys called me, saying that they wanted to make something for me. They asked how much money I was holding. They said that they wanted to double it for me, so I said, 'How?'

"I was sitting down with them in a bar, and the one who was drinking told me I should count the telegraph poles after the junction. When I have counted them, I should come back and the money would be doubled. So I left my bag and I counted the telegraph poles, but before I got back, they ran away. This was when I started stealing leather—because I had to. I went to the man who sold the leather with a friend and asked him about some leather behind him. When he turned away, I stuffed the leather I needed into my bag."

There are many who will find it hard to reconcile the fact that a young boy who so revered his God could behave in such a way, but desperate times require desperate measures.

In Germany, this would be called *fringsen*. *Fringsen* is a verb which literally translated means "to Frings," an expression that became synonymous with stealing food or other consumables out of need. The expression dates back to the sermon given by Cardinal Josef Frings on New Year's Eve in 1946 in the St. Engelbert Church in Cologne-Riehl. He was at the time referring to the looting of coal trains during a grim winter in Germany.

"We live in times where the single individual, in his need, ought to be allowed to take what he needs to preserve his life and health if he cannot obtain it through other means, work or bidding," he said.

Azumah was always looking to provide for his friends and his family before himself, and would frequently make sure that they ate before he did. Despite his small stature, he was fit and strong and was never afraid of hard work. He would do whatever it took to make a dollar to put food on the table.

"One day, I bought a box of mangoes with money I had earned the day before and was planning to sell them, but my mum saw them. She took them to sell and ended up selling them at the beach. She saw a fisherman and used the money from the mangoes to buy fish. She bought the fish for six *cedis* and sold them for nine *cedis*. She told my dad it was a good day. The next day, she went to the beach again to buy fish and sell it. She would then buy a daily carton of fish to sell.

"When I started boxing and made some money [when he became Commonwealth champion], I had a boat made for her so she could send a fisherman out to get her own fish. She paid the fisherman to fish and then sold all of the fish."

Having left school, he had to work, and like many fellow Ghanaians in those tough economic times, he would be up before sunrise and would head off to building sites to offer his services as a labourer for the day.

"Each day, you went there to see if there was work. If there was, you stayed, and at the end of the day, they paid you. Then the next day, you came back and tried again," he remembers.

Sometimes there was no work to be had on the building sites, so it was then a case of finding other places where they needed people to work for a day. There was never any security: It was first come, first served. But if you had established a reputation as a hard and reliable worker, you stood more of a chance of being selected on a daily basis than the other hopefuls. This was what happened to Azumah when he went to work at the quarry.

"I worked in the quarry and broke stones there with a hammer. We would then load the stones in the truck and they paid us," he recalls.

One group of workers at the quarry would sit there, breaking rocks into stones and drop them into bowl-like baskets. Other workers would carry the baskets to a waiting truck, where they would lift the baskets onto their shoulders and throw them onto to the truck. Another worker would catch and empty the basket and then they would go and get another. It was tough, grueling work, and only the fit and the strong were able to perform these duties from dawn to dusk on a daily basis.

"I remember when we were breaking the stones. They thought I was too small to load the tipper trucks and so they sacked me," he recalls. "But then one day, a tipper came and the driver was in a hurry. Everyone else was busy, so they called me from the quarry. They asked if I felt I could do it, and I said that I could. Because there was no one else and the driver wanted to have his truck filled and then go, the manager said, 'Go ahead. If you can do it, we will see what we can do for regular work.' I started loading and I loaded more than the big boys because I had the power.

"They would load the baskets with stones, and I would get to the truck and push with my legs and arms and tip them into the truck. I loaded it so well, and loaded more than the bigger people. The driver was so surprised that someone so small could load so much and so fast. So when he left, he told everyone, 'When you go, if you want your load to be fast, you need to look for Small.' So they called me Small, and then I had regular work. Whenever the drivers came, they asked, 'Are you Small? Can you load fast?' I said yes and off I would go. So my nickname became Small.

"After that first truck, everyone came looking for Small. 'I am in a hurry. I want Small,' they used to say. No one could believe I could load the truck because I was so small, but I was very strong. The power and the stamina I had surprised everyone. If I was not there, they knew the loading would be slow. Then the next time I was there, they would complain when they saw me.

"Moving the stones was a hard job, but I needed the money and I would do anything to earn money—as long as you paid me, I would do it. If you asked me to write, it would be very hard because I did not do much at school, but if you asked me to break things or do physical work, that was easy.

"I think that this helped me later with my boxing—this and *fufu*. When you have to pound the *fufu* with a stick until it is soft, that, too, helped give me strength. I used to pound the *fufu* and it was very hard physical work."

Fufu is pounded cassava, or yam, mixed with pounded plantain, and it originated in Ghana. The word *fufu* comes from the Twi language—the language spoken by more than half of Ghana's population—and it is usually eaten with a light tomato soup, groundnut soup, or *abenkwan* (palm nut) soup. It is also eaten with other types of soups made with vegetables or different kinds of meat and fish, fresh or smoked.

Azumah still has a love of *fufu* today and remembers one occasion from his youth when another local dish, jollof rice, never tasted so good.

"One day, I was at Mamprobi, at my father's place, and I was so hungry. I had been working, and I went out from the house. I was thinking, *If I don't get food in five minutes, I will die.* There is a school park nearby, and the church people had come for a convention. In those days, people used to leave their homes and come for a few days, maybe a week, for the church convention. They would stay together, and they would cook food and everything for you.

"I was so hungry. I didn't know what to do, and something said to me to go there. I was heading towards the school buildings and all the people are at the back of the school, praying. As I was passing, I smelled some food, and when I smelled it, I went, 'Wow!' I walked back again and slowly moved nearer to the school. The smell was driving me crazy.

"I saw a lot of pans with different food in them through the window. So I made a plan as to how I could get some food. I jumped through the open window and entered the room. The first pan lid I lifted was a pan with jollof rice. I ate some while I stood there, and it tasted so sweet. I took some more. Holding out the dress that I was wearing, I dropped it in there.

"I have never eaten sweet jollof like that, even today. I went and sat under a tree and ate it. Ever since then, I am always praying to find whoever made the jollof that day and say thank you. It was the best I have ever tasted—the best I have ever had in all my life. I want to meet the person and physically say thank you. I am sure when she went to the kitchen, she said, 'Who ate my rice?' But she will not know what happened.

"God directed me to the rice. Everything I do, I pray. When I was hungry, I prayed. When I found the food, I said thank you to God, and then I prayed for forgiveness after taking it. I did not do wrong to that lady; I did wrong to God; and I prayed to him to forgive me. We were young guys and we are different. We are living a very different life than people in homes.

"Looking back, I hated no job. It was all about money, making money to get food. This is the beginning of your life and you are small—it is better to struggle when you are young than when you are old. I am happy that these things happened when I was young. It was God who planned my life for me, so I was not worried. I knew everything in my life and I knew one day I would be big, so I was not worried.

"I knew I would be a world champion, so when I did become a champion, I was not surprised. I knew it already. All the struggling I was going through did not worry me because I knew that God was going to deliver me. In this world, good things do not come easy. I had to struggle, pray to God, and do everything that could bring success. You can't stop or quit. If you stop, you cannot be a champion, and quitters can never become winners."

It was not all hard graft and searching for food and money. Sometimes Azumah's father would take him to the movies and, if times were good, buy him an ice cream. "I loved going to the movies in and around Timber Market, especially at the Opera Palladium. I went to the movies, but I did not understand the language, English. If they said something, I didn't understand it. I wanted action. With action, I understood the story.

"I could explain the movie if there was action, like King Kong. I could not understand what people said, and so if someone was going to hit someone, I only could see the hitting. I did not understand what was happening before they were hit and why they were being hit. I liked cowboy films. I loved them.

"I still love *The Good, the Bad, and the Ugly*. I love Indian films now, Bollywood. The man will hold the girl and then they start singing—I love it." Azumah even knows many of the songs from Bollywood films. With a smile spreading across his face, he breaks into song.

There was also time for a little romance. Azumah Nelson was well known in Timber Market, as were his friends. They had a reputation. They were not bad boys, but likeable street urchins—African versions of Charles Dickens's Artful Dodger. They were cheeky, resourceful, and capable of obtaining food and money by whatever means possible, but they would never willfully hurt anyone. They would be up at the crack of dawn, picking coconuts and doing whatever they could to make money as people made their way to work.

Timber Market was a close-knit community then, and everyone knew everybody else, which is still very much the case today. So Azumah would have been well aware of the family living in the tall stone house two hundred metres from his grandmother's Cassava House.

It was here that the Tanoh family lived. The father and mother had a store selling building materials, and in that family were two young girls. Azumah had grown up seeing them pass by on many occasions; he knew who they were and where they lived, and they knew who he was and where he lived. What he failed to notice, because his mind was always focused on the task of bringing in money each day, was that Beatrice watched him much more closely than the other boys he hung out with.

It was never obvious, just a glance that lingered a little longer than it normally would. He intrigued her. There was something about this boy who rarely smiled that she found appealing, and every day as she walked past him, she would look at him and try and work out what it was. Sometimes she would smile as she went by the boys with her sister or her friends. Obi would shout hello, but Azumah, the quiet one, would smile softly, his lips never parting. It was with his eyes that his face lit up. She noticed this sparkle in his eyes, something that no one else could see. It was unspoken, and each day she looked forward to seeing him leaning against a wall or sitting atop it and having his eyes meet hers … and smile.

No one noticed the glances between the two, and they both went on without saying a word until one day when he was sitting on the wall outside Cassava House and all his friends were messing around. His eyes followed her as she walked towards them. His eyes never left her. As most young girls would, she found it nice to be looked at, but also embarrassing. She lowered her head and kept walking, but could feel his eyes upon her.

As soon as she was level with him, she raised her head slightly and looked up at him as he sat on the wall, looking at her and swinging his legs. He smiled and his mouth opened for the first time. She didn't look away. He gave a slight upward movement of his head and said, "I like you." She returned his smile and, feeling herself blush, quickened her step and hurried off on her way to school. With a smile on her face and a spring in her step, she knew it was going to be a good day.

Boys, especially fifteen-year-old boys, usually rib one of their own for such an open display of affection to a girl, but Azumah's friends all looked up to him. He was the provider, the leader, and so rather than teasing him, they fell into silence as Beatrice continued on her way to school.

According to Azumah, despite letting her know he liked her, she gave the impression that she was not very interested. For several days, she did not say anything as she walked past him on her way to school.

Then one day, he spoke to her again with no one around, and after that day, they became friends. The glances no longer needed to be surreptitious, and they were happy to be seen talking together. In fact, when they were talking to each other, they were often oblivious to anyone else.

Obi Oblitey remembers the day that Azumah first spoke to Beatrice, as he was friends with her family. "I remember him saying to her when she was going to school that he liked her, but she was not interested in a hustler. Beatrice was going to Bishops Elementary Accra High Secondary School, and her parents were very proud of their daughter. She was going to be a graduate, so they did not want her to be with a hustler."

Azumah recalls their early days together. "Her father was not happy that she was friends with me. 'How can you follow someone who did not go to school?' he would say to her. He wanted her to be a doctor. Her people gave my father a warning that they did not want to see me with their daughter.

"But we became friends, longtime friends, before becoming boyfriend and girlfriend. One day, we were walking on the street, and her father saw us. He came up and started beating me. I just stood there and took it. I did not want to hit him back, as I could have hurt him and he was her father. Beatrice was telling him to stop, but he kept going. I was nineteen and she said to him, 'Okay, I am not going to school,' and she came to my father's house in Mamprobi.

"Beatrice was annoyed that he came and beat me, so she left home and came to me. I said, 'Hey, you can't stay here. Your father will be mad.' She refused to go, so I went and told my daddy. He said, 'Okay, I will go and see her father.'

"So my father told him to come and collect his daughter, and he came with her mother. 'Your daughter is here so come and take her. She is your daughter. I do not want to beat her if she does wrong in my house,' he told her father.

"I was in a wooden house, a shanty house, and we slept on the floor. So the mother and father came, and Beatrice said she was not going. The mother and the father were surprised: 'Are you stupid? How can you stay here? You say you are not going home?'

"Beatrice said she would leave school if they made her go home. She said she would stop everything. She was a very clever girl, and her parents wanted her to be a doctor or a teacher. They argued, and one hour later, they were scared she would not come home and stay in school.

"They looked at my face, and the father said to her, 'When you finish school, you can marry him, so now you can go to school.' But she was not happy and she asked him, 'Why did you beat him?'

"Oh, she was tough, very tough! The father apologised for beating me, and the mother was shocked. Beatrice still said she is not going, and they started begging her to go home. They were looking at me to tell her to go home.

"She said, 'I am not going.' I went and got my daddy to talk to her. She made her parents sign a piece of paper to say that she could marry me when she left school. She was sixteen when she did this. Her father said no problem, so then they said to her, 'Okay, let's go.' She said we would follow and told me I should walk her home. I was afraid—if the father saw me, what would he say? Already, they did not like it. So when they left, she got up and said, 'Okay, let's go. You can walk me home.'

"I was like, 'No, no, no.' So we followed them and she held my hand. I was scared that her father would look back and see and then come and beat me up again, but she said we had to hold hands. I told her okay, and when we got to her house, she said, 'I will see you tomorrow,' and I walked away and left her. The next day, I saw her. Gradually, her parents began to like me.

"Walking home, I am so happy and I am thinking about how this girl is very strong. How can I be like that? I cannot stand firm like that—how she stands for what she thinks. She wanted her rights and she got them. I realised then through her that you can get it if you really want it.

"The father looked very unhappy whenever he saw me and would not speak to me. But after a while, he said, 'How are you, my son-in-law?' I smiled and said I was well, and then he was good to me, but her mum took longer to like me.

"Did she make me stronger? Yes, she was a very strong girl. You see, she had true love; she loved me with everything she had. She got money, food, everything. I remember one day we travelled and when we came back, my friends bought some alcohol. I never drank, so when I drank it I got so drunk and I went downstairs to the park, and I was walking and I had no idea of where I was going.

"So someone went and told her, 'Your boyfriend is drunk. You must come.' My people were calling me and trying to pull me home. I was not happy—no one could touch me. I took my jacket off and threw it; I have no idea where. They did not know what to do. I was just walking around. They went and got her and told her I was drunk. 'No one can control him,' they told her.

"So she was with her mum and dad upstairs. She ran downstairs and chased me and came and held me. 'Where are you going? Where is your jacket?' She found it and she took me home, and we sat down and she started crying. 'Why should you do that? Why did you get drunk?' she asked me. Then I came to myself; the drink cleared.

"I was sorry and she asked why? She prepared some food and I ate, and then I went in and had a bath. After that, I lay down and she was sitting beside me. When I woke up, I could not find her and it was the morning. She said, 'How are you? I am going to school.' She took me to my house in Timber Market before she went to school. She loved me so much.

"She went to school, and when she came home, she came straight to me and checked that I was okay. She cooked me dinner. Her parents didn't like the idea, but she said, 'This is the one I want, and if you say no, I will not talk to my father again.' She finished school and I kept fighting."

III

GOD WILL LOOK AFTER ME

Despite its newly gained independence, Ghana was far from stable in the 1960s, Azumah's formative years. In 1966, the first republic was overthrown in a military coup, and just three years later, that government was also toppled. Unemployment was high, and the country was in a precarious economic situation: Foreign debt was an astronomical $580 million. To add to the country's woes, its leading export, cocoa, was under serious threat from foreign competition.

Like many of his fellow countrymen, Azumah approached his teenage years unsure of the future and, due to his circumstances, mature beyond his years. He was a rough, tough nobody: a boy with very little education, doing what he could to earn money to buy food for his friends and family in a hard, unforgiving environment, but one that was inhabited by a strong and loyal community.

He so easily could have been sucked into unlawful behaviour. He so easily could have ended up in trouble with the police and entered a spiral from which he may well have never recovered, but there was a reason why he never trod this path. During his formative years, doing whatever he had to in order to help his friends on the street and his family, there were two key events that would have a massive impact on the man he would become. The first involved his mother and the second his father, but neither could have known when they took their son along to these two events that they would change his life forever.

"I tried to take him to church when he was young," his mother recalls.

29

"He changed from that first day he went to church. It was I who introduced him to God. From the first day he went, he loved the stories in the Bible and now he is a prophet. He cannot miss church. If you have a child and you teach them to know God, it is better than sending them to school, as they learn and know right from wrong."

After that first time, Azumah was happy to attend church every week. Being the son of a tailor, his father always made sure that his son looked smart when he entered God's house. "I remember that when I was six or seven years old, I went to church—mostly with my mother and father—and we would pray," Azumah remembers. "My father would come to our house and read the Bible to us. It was then that I learned that God is the most powerful. Apart from him, there is no one. He taught us how to live and that we have to feel for people and help our brothers and sisters. We would go to church in our best clothes, and as a tailor, he would make some dresses for me to wear. He would hold my hand as we walked to church. I know he loved me so much. Now that I have children, I see how much he loved me. I love my son, Dalvin, so much. I see him as me, and the way I love him is was how my father loved me."

It was, however, his mother who saw to it that the church played an important role in his life. "He and Obi were bad boys. There were four or five of them. I did not see them a lot, but I knew they were bad. They never did hurt anyone. They were fighting with understanding at that time, and I am glad they have found their own place in the world," Madam Comfort reflects.

Obi, too, remembers when Azumah first started to go to church, as he saw an immediate change in his young friend. "I remember in our infancy, his parents used to take him to a church convention, Brema-Asikuma. It was during that time, I think, that he became a prophet, a priest. He knows the Bible very well. He was young when he changed, but it was at this time that the things that he said would happen started to happen. It was at that time I began to fear him. I started to fear him, as then I did not know the kind of person he was."

In those early days, Azumah would fight on the street like many children in Bukom, and as long as no weapons were used, it was acceptable. Fighting was often a form of protection and self-preservation, but

Azumah, who according to his mother was quick-tempered as a child, was probably involved in more than most. Bukom had a reputation for breeding tough children: It backed onto Timber Market and was full of fishermen, fishmongers, and small-time traders; life was competitive there, and as a result, fights were sure to break out, and did.

At around the same time that he was finding God, Azumah was also discovering boxing. "My father always wanted to be a boxer, but my grandfather would not let him. So sometimes he would hide and then go boxing. When I was young, he took me to boxing, and I was about ten years old when I saw two boys my own age fighting. The boxers were covered in sweat, but I thought that one of them was crying. I do not like to see anyone crying or upset, and I do not want to see anyone cheating anyone, so I said to my father, 'I want to fight the other boy, the bigger of the two.' He said, 'Okay, no worries,' but started to walk to the door. I tugged at his arm and stood my ground. I said, 'No, I want to fight him now.' But before I knew it, my father had taken me home.

"Every day, I am putting pressure on him. I said he should take me somewhere where I can become a boxer. I want to be a boxer. I went to my mother's family house, and I saw a coach with a small boy. He was getting some boxing shoes made by my father. I asked the coach, 'Is this boy a boxer?' and the coach said 'Yes.' So I said, 'I want to fight him.' He was very small—he was six years old and I was eight—and the coach said, 'You cannot fight him,' and I said, 'Why not? I will beat him.'

"He looked at me and then at the boy and finally said okay. He told me to come to the gym and what time I had to be there. So the time came, and I went to the gym. When I arrived the coach did not recognise me. I stood there with my friends for a while waiting, but when he did not say hello I went over to him and I said, 'Coach, I am here,' and he asked, 'Who are you?' I told him, 'I am the boy you met at the tailor's,' and then he remembered me."

There was no ring in which the boys could fight; there was just a square marked on the floor, which the boxers would walk inside and fight once ready. "Now he remembered me," Azumah recalls. "He put the gloves on me and led us to the square marked on the floor and we started to fight. I threw a punch, and the boy ducked and I missed. I threw another and

I missed again. I could not hit him, and in the end, he beat me so bad.

"I had gone with all my friends to the gym, and it looked like I disgraced my friends. They believed in me and I had disappointed them, so we all went home very quietly. That night, I went to bed but I couldn't sleep. I was thinking about the mistakes I had made and why I could not hit the other boy. The more I thought about it, the more I thought I understood why I had lost, so I decided in the morning that I would go back and fight him again. This time, I went alone without my friends. I did not want them to be disgraced again.

"I fought the same guy and I did better than the day before, but I still lost. On my way home, I thought, *I did well today,* so I went back every day for three days. On the third day, the fight was a draw, and then after that day, I started to beat him. I then fought the other small boys, and I became champion in the gym. That was how I started to become a boxer. My father always wanted me to be a boxer, as he had wanted to be one. One thing we always shared was boxing."

Azumah was captivated by his first few trips to the gym, and with his fights on the street, he believed he had what was required to be a boxer: the strength, the skill, the power, and the aggression. Even at that young age, he was able to analyse his opponent, spot a weakness, and then find a way to exploit that weakness.

One person who was not so keen on him following a career in the ring was his mother. "We lived at Timber Market, and he grew up there before he started boxing. The first time he started to fight, I said to him that I did not like it. I said I did not like it because if you don't try, you die. But he said he liked it, so I left him to it. He started fighting at Timber Market, and he took friends who joined him training—they did everything together. I cannot complain because he has always tried his best for me," Madam Comfort reflects, though her comments reveal that she would have preferred another career for her son, even after all his success.

Over the next few years, with a faith in God and a determination to succeed, as well as an undying belief in his ability, Azumah transformed himself from a disorderly street fighter into a disciplined boxer. Soon he was attracting attention around the small but heavily populated area of Bukom. He believed he could fight at the highest level, and it was not long before he joined the renowned Akotoku Academy, formed by the late Attuquaye Clottey.

This is where Azumah Nelson, strong and anxious to prove his ability, went to fine-tune the natural ability that he had already shown locally. His coach was "the best coach in the world, and he trained the first boxer in Ghana to become a world champion, D. K. Poison," Azumah recalls. Azumah undoubtedly blossomed under his tutelage.

The academy was a basic setup—extremely basic. It was a courtyard with a two-storey wooden building on two sides; a single-storey stone construction ran along one of the other walls, while the final side of the yard was simply a stone wall about three metres high. In the centre of the courtyard were two ramshackle boxing rings. Neither stood more than a few feet off the ground, and both were uncovered and unsheltered from the heat of the Ghanaian sun beating down on those who entered to train or fight. Speedballs and punch bags were attached to the walls and whatever else was strong enough to support them.

Most of the young potential boxers training at the academy would sleep outside on the wooden platforms of the two-storey buildings. Azumah remembers these times with great fondness, and it is clear that these formative years played a major part in making him the boxer he became. "I slept outside with the other young boxers, and when we woke up, we trained. After training, we would go out, and it was up to you and your God to find something to eat each day," he says.

Many boxers have come from the tough side of the street; many have always had that truculence and restlessness simmering beneath the surface. Many have had nowhere to sleep and no food on the table as they set off on their journey to fight for a world title. Many boxers who, when their time comes in the ring—a place where their aggression and sometimes vicious ruthless streak has won them plaudits—have struggled to handle that side of their personalities outside the ropes.

Azumah was never one of those. With God in his heart, he never wanted to hurt anyone. To him, it was a job, a sport that he enjoyed and was good at, one in which he enjoyed the physical challenges as well as the tactical. The ring was a place where he could show he was strong physically and where he could show he could outthink his opponent. It was where he could show he was not just some slugger, that there was a science to his art, and what greater acknowledgment could there be than eventually being dubbed "The Professor"?

"I started learning boxing when I was about eight or nine years old. I worked each day, as you needed to get money to feed yourself. You would go to training at four o'clock, finish work, and then run to training. It was the same every day until life started to change," recalls Azumah.

At age eleven, Azumah knew he was destined to become a world champion. "I knew I would be a champion, and I told my friends that I would be," he recalls with great confidence. "God told me that I would be a world champion. I was eleven years old and I had this vision. God took me to this place that was beautiful—it was so beautiful, unlike anywhere I have ever seen, and I was so happy. Then he said to me, *C'mon, we have to go.* I said, *I don't want to go.* It was then that he told me, *When you have finished the work I have for you, this is where you will come. You have to finish off things first.*

"From that day, I know where I am headed. I know that I will go there when I die, and I am happy about that. I no longer fear anything in my life because I know what lies ahead. I knew that I would be a world champion, and I know that this is so that I could help people, especially the people of Ghana. I have always wanted to help people and put a smile on their faces, and I knew then that that was my role in life. I know that everything happens at the right time and for a reason, and if you trust God, it will be all right. From that day on, I knew my destiny and I knew my future, and I was no longer scared."

When Azumah saw his future, those around him saw a change, and it was disconcerting. Obi still remembers the time in their lives when suddenly Azumah's whole personality changed. "He was always planning from our infancy, so that was nothing new, but at age eleven he told us, 'I will be a world champion. I will buy a fishing trawler. I will buy a shop …' I did not think he was crazy because he was my friend, my brother, but it made me wonder, *Who is this little guy?* I mean, did we know our future? But when we kept on growing up, and I saw the changes in his life and I realised that all the things that happened were things he said before, I thought it must be something from the Bible. It was like he was a prophet; he could see into the future. He knew what was going to happen. In Ghana, we say, 'Right now, you will not know, but later you will understand.' I did not understand then as a young boy, but I understand now that he could see his future, and everything he said has happened."

Azumah blossomed at the Akotoku Academy, and it was here that the foundations of his boxing career were laid. "When you went to the Akotoku Academy, you went there to learn. Early on, we are training with another coach, but he did not have the experience. If I stay with that coach, I know I would not be a champion. Attuquaye Clottey had transferred from Kumasi to coach in Accra. He was the best. Oh, was he the best—too good! May he rest in peace. I love him so much. Everything he taught me and others helped make me what I am today, and I know if it was not Attuquaye, it was my God who brought him from Kumasi to train me. He trained a lot of people, but I am lucky that I am the one who became the longest reigning world champion," Azumah remembers with emotion in his voice and in his eyes. It is as clear as daylight that this man had a massive influence on the young boxer with stars in his eyes, both inside and outside the ring.

"He was like a father to all of the boxers. We would train all week, and the older boys would fight on Saturday. Sunday would be our day off. I used to like these days, as he would show us films of old boxers and their fights. There were no videos or DVDs in those days, just film. He would show old fights and show us how good the boxers were and why. Joe Louis and Jersey Joe Walcott were two who stand out in my memory. As we all sat there and watched these films of their fights in black and white, it was so nice. Jersey Joe became my favourite."

It is interesting to ponder what it was about Jersey Joe Walcott that appealed to a young, impressionable Azumah. Walcott's career blossomed late, and maybe that was something that stuck in the young Azumah's mind: Patience would pay dividends. Also interesting is the fact that Walcott's real name was Arnold Cream, and that he took the name of Joe Walcott from a welterweight from Barbados, who had impressed him as a youngster and prefaced his name with the state he came from.

Walcott, who said he worked "at every filthy job, from cleaning cesspools on up, to earn a living," was always classed as a nearly man in boxing. His poverty saw him fight many bouts on an empty stomach, and experts at the time believed that starvation and a lack of energy was why he suffered three knockdowns. By 1944, his career had virtually dried up. He was on state welfare with a wife and six children to feed, and he went back into boxing to combat poverty. Incredibly, he started to win, and his wins came against fighters who were contenders for the light-heavyweight and heavyweight titles: boxers such as Joe Baksi, Lee Oma, Jimmy Bivins, and Joey Maxim.

Then he was offered a dream fight against World Heavyweight Champion Joe Louis. Unfortunately, the New York Commission said the bout could only be an exhibition with no title up for grabs, but pressure from Mike Jacobs, the promoter, and Joe Louis, who was also strapped for cash, made them relent.

A total of 18,194 spectators filed into Madison Square Garden in December 1947, paying what was then a house record of $216,477. Jersey Joe was supposed to be the fall guy, but he hadn't read the script: He dropped Louis twice, and many thought he had done enough to win a decision over the fifteen rounds. Louis, however, won on a split-decision. One wonders about the impact that watching such a fight had on Azumah; there is no doubt it resonated throughout his professional career. There was a rematch, and again Walcott floored Louis, but this time he was knocked out in round eleven.

Joe Louis retired but Walcott kept on boxing. He then lost two title fights with Ezzard Charles, who succeeded Louis. However, in Pittsburgh in 1951, more than twenty years after he started fighting for a living, Walcott carved his name in the annals of boxing history. At thirty-seven years of age, he became the oldest man to win the heavyweight crown, and he held that record until it was taken by George Foreman, who won the title at the age of forty-five in 1994.

Again, who knows whether the longevity of Walcott's career inspired Azumah? If it did, he is not letting on. He claims the reason he liked Jersey Joe Walcott was because "of the way he fights. He had moves; he had style; and his style was good. The way he hit, he always fights with his head."

This was a time when Azumah first tried to analyse other fighters and incorporate their styles into his own repertoire. Not only that, he also managed at that young age to remember styles used in certain fights by certain boxers when fighting against opponents with various different styles. To this day, he will recall a fight where a boxer changed his approach to negate an awkward opponent.

"You know, I am so lucky," he says today. "I am gifted in boxing circles. If I see someone do something that I like, I take it and use it. No one showed me how to do these things; I just watched and learned. All my coach showed me was how to throw the punches, how to move and bob. If I see someone throw a one-two and I like the way they have done it, they do not have to show me. I see it and then I remember it, learn it, and use it. I just add to it and it's perfect."

Azumah was soon showing his prowess as a boxer and his ability to watch and learn more quickly than most, as his good friend Obi recalls: "During his amateur days, no one could beat him. Even his first coach, Attuquaye Clottey, took D. K. Poison, who was the world featherweight boxing champion between 1975 and 1976 and was the first Ghanaian professional boxer to win a world title, and made Azumah fight with him, as he coached both of them."

D. K. Poison had his first professional bout on February 5, 1966, in Accra and became the national featherweight champion that same year. Although he fought once in neighbouring Togo in 1967, all his subsequent fights until 1971 were in Ghana. In 1972, he fought seven times in Australia, winning five and losing two. He won the African featherweight title in February 1974 when he knocked out Tahar Ben Hassen in the first round of a scheduled fifteen-round fight in Tunisia. In December 1974, thanks to a technical knockout in round ten against British boxer Evans Armstrong, he won the Commonwealth featherweight title; that victory gave Poison an opportunity to have a tilt at the World Boxing Council version of the world title. On September 20, 1975, in The Forum, Inglewood, California, he met Rubén Olivares and won on a split points decision after fifteen rounds to become the first Ghanaian world boxing champion.

Despite the Ghanaian government of the day giving him a house at

Teshie-Nungua, a suburb in Accra, in honour of this achievement in boxing, he is now very much a forgotten man in Ghana. However, when a young Azumah climbed in the ring with him, despite having lost his world title in 1976 to Danny "Little Red" Lopez, he was still a big name and still at his peak.

"D. K. Poison was the first champion from Ghana, and he was a good boxer. He made us all believe we could win a world title. To fight with him at that time was an honour, and I learned so much from him. I was lucky to have him train at the same academy," Azumah remembers with respect still very much apparent.

According to Obi, that respect was reciprocated. "D. K. liked him and respected him a lot. When his coach, Floyd Klutei Robertson, an ex-Commonwealth champion, was watching them spar, Azumah was punching D. K. hard. The coach would say, 'Azumah, don't punch hard.' Azumah would look at him and he would say, 'Hey, Coach, he is punching hard so I have to punch hard,' and he would continue to hit hard. Even then, Azumah was the better boxer."

Floyd Klutei Robertson certainly knew what he was talking about, as he, too, was a former featherweight; in fact, he was Ghana's first world championship contender. At the Accra Sports Stadium in 1964, he was part of an epic encounter against hall-of-famer Sugar Ramos, then the titleholder. He had the defending champion on the canvas in round thirteen only to lose to a controversial split-decision. The Ghanaian boxing commission, which was fuming at the decision, first ruled the fight a no contest, and then said Robertson had won. But it was Ramos who left the country with the championship belt in his baggage. He did fight for a second world title two years later against Vicente Saldivar in Mexico City, but was knocked out in round two by the great Mexican.

Like Azumah, D. K. Poison and Floyd Klutei Robertson were from the Ga Tribe, renowned for showing its superiority over its adversaries by means of sheer physical strength, so all knew that sparring was always going to be competitive between the youngster and the former champ.

Despite training at the Akotoku Academy under the watchful eye of Attuquaye Clottey, life was still a struggle for the young Azumah and his friends. Ghana's economy was far from prosperous; in fact, it was spiraling downward, and work and food were in short supply.

"During the period when he started learning boxing, I used to go everywhere with him. We would sleep together, eat together, everything," Obi remembers. "You know, my mother was his mother. As Africans, we live as a family—my mum calls you her son and she loves you like she loves me, as you are my brother. She loved Azumah; everyone loved Azumah, but these were tough times in our country, and food was hard to come by."

Azumah agrees. "Often we did not get food to eat for two to three days, and so during those days, we did not go training, as we were trying to find food or money to buy food. We hustled and did not have time to train. The coach was not happy, and when we showed up he asked, 'Why have you not been here for three days?' He was so angry he put his three sons in the ring to fight me, and he wanted his sons to beat me to teach me a lesson. But even though I had not eaten, I was too good for them and beat them."

The coach must have had mixed feelings about this turn of events. He wanted to teach the young Azumah about commitment to training, but at the same time, he had seen firsthand the talent the young boy had, even fighting on an empty stomach. There was no doubt this young boy was different, special.

At the academy, Azumah would often sleep outside with the other boys training there. On one particular morning, while sleeping on a patch of ground outside, Azumah noticed some rubber in a doorway. As soon as he saw it, he knew that if he could sell it, he would be able to eat and so, too, would his fellow boxers. He lay there looking at the rubber, taking in who was awake and how he could not only grab it, but also get away.

"The rubber belonged to someone; I did not know who. Grandma, who looked after us, made bread, so if hungry, a lot of the boys could get food. However, I knew that unless I managed to get money or food, I would not eat tomorrow. It is five a.m. and people are waking up. So I quietly stood up and, on tiptoe, went to the room and carefully took the rubber, being sure to make no noise or wake anyone. But a man on the balcony saw me. I suddenly heard him coming down the stairs. Before I could run, he grabbed me, and wagging his finger at me, told me I was a bad boy. I wanted to run because he called his friend, and they were going to take me to the police station, which was not very far away. 'Leave me,' I said. I wanted to punch him and run. I then saw a policeman coming up the street, having finished his night duty, so I changed and started speaking slowly. Then when he wasn't expecting it, I started punching him in the ribs. He let go and I ran away. I did not go back for a week because I was afraid that when I did, he would take me to the police."

If that man did go to the police, they never came looking for Azumah. By that time, he was becoming well known in the Bukom area, thanks to his boxing prowess. In Ghana, boxing was no longer just a sport for street-smart boys. Thanks to the likes of D. K. Poison, it was a sport in which Ghana could compete with the rest of the world, a sport that gave the nation pride and self-belief. Little was the young Azumah to realise how much his career would be linked to the emergence of Ghana from these tough, miserable times.

There was another key moment in Azumah's life, and this came in 1975, when Azumah was seventeen years old. At that time, he owned just one shirt. When it was being washed, he wore a traditional Ghanaian cloth wrapped around him until the shirt was dry and ready to wear again. It was New Year's Eve, and Azumah was with his friends, waiting to see the New Year dawn.

"I was waiting for midnight with my friends. They all had a ticket to a concert and were all going, but I had nothing to wear. I was happy, but I wanted to go. I walked with them, wearing my auntie's cloth, and when they came to the place, they went in and I waited around outside on my own until after midnight. It was at midnight when I heard all the celebrations that I started praying. I said, *God, I am happy with the way I look because that is the way you want me to look, but from today, I do not want to look like this again.* It was then that I started crying. I made my way home alone and did not wait for my friends. I knew from now on my life would be different. Five days after that night, I was called into the national camp for boxing. I was about to become a Black Bomber."

IV

THE BLACK BOMBERS

Becoming a Black Bomber, a member of the national team, was not quite as straightforward as it appeared. As was the case during most of his youth, Azumah had to fight to be heard and recognised; in fact, he had to fight in most aspects of his life to survive and to get ahead, inside and outside of the ring.

In order to become a Black Bomber, he had to win the national amateur title for his weight at the National Festival. Incredibly, Azumah struggled to find a team to box for so that he could compete at the festival. "I could not get a team to fight for. Military already had a fighter in my weight, so, too, did Greater Accra, Assante, and Police," Azumah remembers.

"Then I heard Ghana Prison Service might have a place, so I went to see their captain. When he saw me, he said I was too small and I cannot fight. I know if I don't get that chance to fight, I know I will never get a chance to fight. It was so important. He told me, 'I can't let you fight because if you get hurt, it will be my fault.' I told him, 'No one will see me. Please let me fight.' I was begging him; I was desperate. I kept telling him, 'I can fight,' and I was almost crying because he did not want to give me a chance. He still said no, so I went to see one of the big men—the bosses in the Prison Service—and I told him that the captain would not give me a chance to fight. I told him, 'I can beat them all but I need a chance. You have to give me a chance.' So he went to the captain and told him to give me a chance. The captain was not happy and told the boss he

41

would only let me box on the condition that if I was getting beaten, he could stop the fight. The boss asked me if I was okay with that, and I said, 'Okay, I don't care.'

"So they let me go and fight, and I fought for the Prison Service. The first fight I won. The second I won. Gradually, I am getting stronger and the people are starting to watch me, as they know that I can fight. It came to the semifinals and I won again. So then it was the finals, and I was supposed to fight a guy from the Military team. He was a big boy. He was twenty-five years old and I was only seventeen.

"Suddenly, the people, including my coach, are afraid that this boy will hurt me. He came to me and said that I should not fight. I said, 'I can. It will be okay. I can fight and I can beat him.' He called a meeting with the bosses, and they agreed that I could fight, but told me if I am losing, they will stop it. The reason they are scared is that the other boy is a national star and too experienced for me. They thought he would hurt me.

"His name was Ben Carl Loco, and when we went to the weigh-in, he was too heavy. So he had to go and lose the weight quickly before the final. I am sitting with the boxers from my gym, waiting for the time to pass, until it was time for us to fight. Then he came and sat with my gym's boxers.

"He looked at me and said I was a small boy, and I should not be fighting him; I will get hurt. I should go home now. I said nothing, as I knew he is going to have a tough time shedding the weight. He kept talking, saying he will show me what he was going to do to me, trying to put fear into me and threatening me. All my people are there, and they are starting to feel afraid for me. But he is talking too much, and so I said to him, 'Don't talk about what you are going to do to me. Wait until we are in the ring, and then show me what you are going to do. Don't talk anymore. Show me in the ring.'

"He was very angry and said to the other boxers, 'You see? He doesn't respect me. He should not talk to me like that.' I laughed and said, 'Why should I not talk? I am not afraid of you. Let's go to the ring and I will show you.'

"He then told me that once before he had to fight a small boy, a boy who wanted to be a soldier, and he was told to slow down and be easy with him. But when the fight started, the small boy went boom, boom, and hit him. So he said, 'No longer will I be kind to small boys. You will suffer. I am not going to play with you—I promise I will show you.'

"I replied, 'Okay, if you know how to do it, let's go to the ring and see.' He was so angry.

"When we got to the ring, my coach asked, 'Are you sure that you can fight?' I told him I was. I could see he was afraid for me and he was trying to protect me, as he was sure the guy would beat me. 'If you are not sure, I will stop the fight,' he said.

"No, I am fine,' I told him. In the end he said, 'Okay, you go for the first round, and we will see after that. If he is beating you, I will stop it. I will let the fight go for the first round, and if you get tired, I will throw in the towel.' I said, 'Okay, okay.' I just wanted to be allowed to climb into the ring and fight.

"We go to the ring and climb through the ropes for the first round. The bell sounded and my coach is shouting, 'Don't stand with him. Move, move!' He knows that I can box, so I start to move, and as I move, *boom, boom*, I hit and move. He tried to hit me, but whenever he did, I blocked his punches. He couldn't touch me, and I could feel his punches. I knew I could stand and fight with him, as I knew his punches lacked power and he was not strong. At the end of the first round when I get to the corner, my coach asks me, 'Are you tired? Should I stop the fight?' I said, 'No. I am not tired. I am fine. I can fight. Please don't stop the fight.' So he agreed to let me carry on, but told me not to stand and fight because he felt the boy would knock me out. He wanted me to box and move.

"So the bell goes for the second round, and we come out of our corners, and we are both throwing punches. I was bobbing and weaving, and he still couldn't touch me. I can see he is worried. Then something told me to stand with him and show him he is nobody. So I moved for a while and then I stopped and stood in the middle of the ring in front of him. *Boom, boom, boom.* I threw all these punches and I am hitting him in the body and on the head. I gave him a big cut above his eye, and the referee moved in to have a look. He took him to the corner for the doctor to look at it, and when the doctor saw the cut, he stopped the fight. I had won the national title by a TKO [technical knockout].

"When they stopped the fight, I raised my arms in the air to say, 'I am the winner,' and I told myself I had done well. I could see he was annoyed, and when I went across to him and tried to shake his hand, he said again, 'You don't respect me. Get out!' He had his head in a towel covered with blood, and he was still talking about how I should respect him, yet I had beaten him.

"I was happy, but after the fight my coach was so angry. 'I told you not to stand there and fight but you did!' he shouted at me. 'Sorry, I didn't know,' I told him. 'But I became the national amateur champion, and you said I should not fight like that, but I won. I showed you I can fight.'

"After that, I became a prison officer. They gave me a job, and I worked in the prison for three years, all thanks to my boxing. I say I worked there but we did not really go to work. We just went to the gym and trained. We were given jobs and I worked in the sewing department. I liked to sew, because my dad was a tailor, and so I worked in that area. They gave me the material to make my uniform, but I never put on the uniform all the time I worked there. I gave the material to my dad to use; they never asked where the material had gone. I think because I never went out, and as I was always training, no one ever asked why I never wore a uniform.

"It was funny how, after three years there, I became the boss; at one time, they did not want me because I was so small. Today, the young fighters there do not know me and that I fought for the Prison Services. It is only because of the fact that the old ones tell them Azumah Nelson used to fight for the Prison Service that anyone remembers those days."

Boxing, which for so long had been a well-supported sport in Ghana, had been going through the doldrums, and there was a desire to revive it. Azumah's arrival could not have come at a better time. After that victory over Ben Carl Loco, Azumah took his rightful place in the Black Bombers team and was about to leave Ghana for the very first time in his life. "We trained for a few weeks and then we travelled to Nigeria for a competition. It was my first time outside Ghana. I was excited, but I was not interested in sightseeing—I was there to represent my country and so I was focused on doing the best I could for Ghana. I did not want to let my people down.

"Lagos, in those days, was similar to Accra, so I felt comfortable. This

was my first time in Nigeria and the first time for some of the other boxers, so we went everywhere by bus. We did not walk around, so I did not
see very much of the city. But it was very different than Lagos today.

"In Nigeria, all of the boxers were given money for food, but I spent
my money buying presents for my family. I bought beautiful things for
my mother, my father, my brother, and sisters. I bought them all something; I was so happy. Later, one of the coaches called me over and asked
me what I bought for myself. I said nothing. He had been watching me
and wanted to know why I did not buy anything for myself. I told him I
had something I could wear, so I did not have to buy anything for myself.
I remember I was so happy. I just wanted to get home and give my family
their presents. I forget who I fought there, but I know that I won. Soon
after, we came home from Nigeria and were told we were going to Germany for another camp and some fights."

This would be Azumah's first trip outside the African continent. To
most, it would have been a huge adventure, but Azumah viewed it very
differently than his teammates. "I was happy to go to all these places, but
I knew that one day I would go to many places. When the time came, I
would be okay, as I knew God was guiding me and had a plan for me.
Therefore, I was happy to go where he has planned."

It was a one-month camp in Germany, but Azumah cannot recall
where the team was based. But the architecture is something that he
remembers vividly. "When we went there, it was very beautiful. The
buildings were very beautiful and big. I remember when we were in Germany, looking at the place, and I was thinking that it didn't matter to me
that Ghana is not developed like Germany; I was happy at home. We did
not need nice buildings to be happy—we had our friends and our families. It was very different for all of us, but I don't think many of us wanted
to live there. I know I didn't.

"A funny thing happened when we were in Germany. As I said, I was
always very serious, thinking, and so I didn't laugh too much. One day, I
was sitting quietly on my own, and some of the Germans were watching
me. They had noticed that they had not seen me laugh since we had got-
ten there. I am sitting there, thinking and minding my own business, and
they came across and asked me to laugh. I thought that they were crazy.

Then they said that they had never seen me laugh, and they wanted to know that I could. Then they offered me money to laugh, so I thought, *Okay.* I laughed and then I took the money. It was very funny.

"In Germany, we were given money for food, and again, I bought presents for my family. But when we arrived back in Accra, my luggage did not come. I had bought shoes for my brother, dresses for my sisters, and other gifts for my family. I never received my bag and all of the gifts. It pained me so much—I had bought a watch for my father, and I was so upset that I couldn't give it to him. It was so painful, but I didn't worry too much. I knew God would give me another opportunity, and hopefully my bag would not get lost again."

The next stop for Azumah and the Black Bombers was the Pan-African Games, also known as the All-Africa Games. What many people do not know is that Baron Pierre de Coubertin, founder of the modern Olympic Games, conceived the Pan-African Games as early as 1920. However, the colonial powers that ruled Africa during this period were very wary of the idea. They feared that the unifying aspect of sport among the African people would be a tool that would assist them in their push for independence.

Attempts were made to host the games in Algeria in 1925 and in Egypt in 1928, but both attempts failed, despite the International Olympic Committee's first African member, Greek-born Egyptian sprinter Angelo Bolanaki, donating funds to erect a stadium.

It would be three decades before the dream of an all-African games was realised. The Friendship Games were organised by the French-speaking countries of Africa as an annual event. In 1962, the African Ministers of Youth and Sport met in Paris, and because some English-speaking countries were participating, rechristened the games as the Pan-African Games. The International Olympic Committee gave the games official recognition alongside other continental games such as the Asian Games and the Pan-American Games.

In July 1965, the first games were held in Brazzaville, Congo, but they were now called the All-Africa Games. At the first event, thirty countries and around two thousand five hundred athletes competed. It was decided the games would be held every four years. The second games were awarded to Mali in 1969, but unfortunately, a military coup forced them to be cancelled. Nigeria stepped forward as host in 1971, but these games were not held until 1973 due to the Biafra War.

The third All-African Games, which Azumah was to attend with the Black Bombers, were scheduled to take place in 1977 in Algeria. However, due to technical reasons, the games had to be postponed for a year and were eventually held from July 13–28, 1978. This event was seen as a success, as forty-five countries attended the games to participate in twelve events.

Azumah remembers the games well. "After Nigeria and Germany, but before the All-Africa Games, I went to the West Africa Games. I was a flyweight then and I could not make the weight. I was so tired because I could not eat, but I made the weight. I won the fight—I know I won the fight—but they gave it to the other guy, and all the officials were mad with the judges. But I was relieved. If I had won, I would not have been able to make the weight for the next fight! So I was happy I lost, which is not how I feel very often. After this, I moved to bantamweight. I did not stay a bantamweight long. I soon moved to featherweight and went to the African games in Algeria as a featherweight. I won the gold medal there and I enjoyed that tournament.

"I remember I fought a Nigerian guy in Algeria, and I knew him from before, but I was not a featherweight then. When he realised I am a featherweight like him, he said to me, 'Small boy, featherweight, can you fight featherweight?' He remembered me from when I was a flyweight and he still thinks I am small and can't fight at featherweight. He was standing in my face, looking down at me, snarling. I stood there and I looked up at him and said, 'Don't worry. When the time comes, we will see if I am too small.'

"We met in the semifinal, and at the weigh-in, he shouted across to me when he was on the scales, 'Hey, small boy! Can you fight?' I smiled and said, 'Well, tonight we will see, but it will be war.' He was laughing because he thought I was joking. So the night came and we went out to the ring, and he was sure he would win. He thought he had a big punch and he will knock me out because I am so small.

"The bell goes and I am out of my corner quickly, jabbing and moving.

I am so fast he couldn't touch me. I am so fast with my hands. I threw five punches and he cannot see them. I beat him from corner to corner, and when in the corner, he wanted to get me on the ropes and try and keep me there. I would feign him and turn him, then boom, boom; I would hit him again. I beat him three to zero, and after the fight, I became champion. We hugged when the result was announced, and I said, 'You did well.' He said, 'Hey,' and looked at me with his head to one side. He still could not believe I had beaten him."

Ghana placed sixth in the medal tally at the third All-African Games. Azumah's gold medal was one of four that the country won along with four silver and seven bronze medals. Hannah Afriyie won two of the gold medals in the 100 metres and 200 metres.

One thing that the young Azumah may not have been aware of was that while these games were going ahead, the African nations associated with the Commonwealth were discussing the proposed boycott of the 1978 Commonwealth Games, which were to be held the following month in Edmonton, Canada. The discussions were based around whether the African nations should make a stand against New Zealand maintaining sporting contact with South Africa, which was still under apartheid rule. The African nations had taken a strong stance on South Africa, and so a very strong principle was on the table. The eventual outcome was that the boycott was not carried out; although, Nigeria stood alone on the issue and became the first country to boycott the Commonwealth Games.

The 1978 Commonwealth Games were the first to be held under that name. They were first known as the British Empire Games, and were first held in 1930. The Second World War interrupted the quadrennial schedule, and the games were not held again until 1950; in 1954, they were renamed the British Empire and Commonwealth Games. The 1970 and 1974 events were known as the British Commonwealth Games, and in 1978 in Edmonton, Canada, they were first held under the title of the Commonwealth Games.

The Edmonton games marked a new high in participation at that time, with almost one thousand five hundred athletes from forty-six countries taking part. Ghana was one of those countries, and Azumah Nelson was not only one member of their team, but also the newly crowned All-African champion, a serious medal hope.

"The Commonwealth Games was not good for Ghana—six of our boxers were beaten and so the team had not done well," Azumah recalls. "The coach was worried because our people expected us to do well, and he would be in trouble when we went home. Three of us went to the semi-finals—Kid Sumalia [light-flyweight], Adamah Mensah [heavy-weight], and me. Our coach was F. A. Moses, and I said to him, 'Don't worry. I will get the gold, and when we go home, they will reward you and promote you.' Every morning, he would ask me about the fight that day and I would say, 'Don't worry. I'll knock him out in the second round.' Then I would go to the fight and I did. It went like this all the way to the finals. In the semifinals, I met the captain of the Canadian team, Guy Boutin. He was a very good fighter. My coach came and asked me, 'How is the fight going to be?' I said it would be tough, but I will win on points, and he started celebrating.

"When we went to the ring and started fighting, the guy was good— pound for pound, he was very strong. We stood there, head-to-head fight-ing, and he was not going back. I could not make him move back. He was very strong. It was a very tough fight. There was no retreating. I loved that fight. He stood there and I stood there and we just threw punches at each other. In my life and when I am fighting, I pray, and I was praying then. We were standing toe-to-toe, throwing punches at each other—no one wanted to give any ground. No one wanted to move back. In the end, I moved back to get out of the way of a punch that was coming, and I called to God. I said to him, *Where are you? This fight is too tough. If you do not help me, I cannot continue.* Suddenly, I found the strength and I started fighting back, and he moved back across the ring and I followed him. The fight was very close, and he was a Canadian fighting in Canada, but I won three to two. It was very special to win. When I won, my coach was so happy."

In the final, Azumah went on to fight Zambian John Sichula, whom he defeated to win Ghana's only gold medal at the games. Adamah Men-sah also made the final, but was defeated by England's Julius Awome and had to settle for silver, while Kid Jumalia took home a bronze medal. These were Ghana's only medals of the games. Another winner, but in the bantamweight division, was a boxer whose name would come up again later in Azumah's career: Irishman Barry McGuigan.

Azumah remembers, "I was not surprised I won a gold medal, as I had always believed I would win it. Nothing surprises me. I was proud and I was happy to stand for Ghana and fight for the nation. I flew the flag for our nation, and I made the nation proud, the people proud. I made them happy and that was beautiful.

"When I have the medal around my neck and the flag went up, it made me very happy. It made me cry. I cried all the time while the anthem played—it was a very proud moment. Talking now, I can still feel it."

Azumah's eyes well up and he has to take his folded handkerchief out of his pocket to soak up the tears before they roll down his cheeks. It is still obviously a very special moment in a life, so rich with special moments. Once he has his composure back, he continues. "Any time I stand for Ghana, I have that feeling, but this was very special. Before the fight, I am in a place far from Ghana, alone, and I know that everyone back home is looking at me, wanting me to be the champion. I did not view it as pressure—I feel okay, but I feel I have to win for my people because I did not want to let them down.

"Edmonton was very different to from Accra. Every part of this world is different. In Canada, I appreciated the opportunity that God had given me, but I was thinking a lot about my fights and becoming Commonwealth Games champion. I was focused on that and so I did not go out and see the sights. I spent a lot of time on my own, praying and thanking God for this opportunity. The whole time you never saw me reading a book—the only book I read was the Bible. I remember reading the book of Samson and then tried to follow the word of God. The stories offered inspiration to me." One verse in particular was inspirational in his battle in the semi-final: "O Sovereign Lord, remember me. O God, please strengthen me just once more ..."

"I remember the opening ceremony to the games, as we all wore traditional African clothes. It was great to see all these countries in their traditional clothes—it was really special and something to remember. The closing ceremony was very different. It was much friendlier and everyone had a party. I was happy because everyone else was happy. I wish it could have lasted longer. I wore my medal to the closing ceremony so everyone could see I was the champion. You all aim for gold, but not everyone can get gold, so you can be proud of silver. Not everyone can get silver, so they can be proud of bronze. Some people were not fortunate to win medals because it was not their day, but they were happy to be there and to have taken part. It was a wonderful time," Azumah remembers.

When he returned home, Azumah was feted as the country's only gold medal winner. It was at this point that suddenly all the people of Ghana started to hear the name, Azumah Nelson. He had given the nation belief and hope at a time they needed it most. He embodied the fighting spirit of the nation.

He had also helped restore a nation's interest in boxing. Suddenly, it felt like the 1950s and '60s, when Ghana was very prominent in the world of boxing. People came rushing back to the sport, and the government took a keen interest in the developments. Azumah unwittingly became an ambassador for the country, and the government was keen to make sure that when he went outside of Ghana, he was promoting the country. The government put its weight behind him, and it proved to be a good marriage.

"Sportsmen generally contribute positively to the political health or the political climate of any country, and in his time, boxing was what was used to stimulate international interest," says the former president of Ghana, Flight Lieutenant Jerry Rawlings. "Ghana used to perform very well in the area of the featherweight. With the decline of the country politically and economically, it also led to the decline of sporting activity such as boxing, even though we were well known through the Roy Ankrahs and a lot of those who were in that weight division—the Floyd Pattersons, D. K. Poison, etc.

"It was a weight division that Ghana dominated internationally because of what I will call the intelligence-wisdom-age-weight factor. That was a weight division we dominated just as the heavyweight division has always belonged to the U.S., because of their sizes generally. In our case, the featherweight division belonged to us and South America, but we dominated it for a much longer time before they [South Americans] came onto the scene. The point I am trying to make is, putting together the IQ of the person, the age, the wisdom, experience, and size of the person, we struck the highest average. That was a weight division that we were at our best at that age. So it was a matter of course; it was a weight that belonged to Ghana. Let us not forget that the Ga-speaking people—the coastal fisher folk—have dominated that weight division. They loved boxing; they loved fighting. They are boisterous in their nature.

"The political and economic performance of the country had gone down pretty badly, and the corruption had eaten into the fabric of society. It was no wonder that our performance generally in international sports had also gone very low. Somehow, because of the intelligence-wisdom-age-weight factor I mentioned, it was no surprise that the area of boxing was an area that Ghana still dominated, but even that nearly suffered," he continues.

"Azumah, like his predecessors in that weight division, dominated that weight division by virtue of his physical prowess, as well as a positive mental and emotional disposition. But for him as a person, as an individual, he was a very highly disciplined person, and he had a strong fighting spirit. I could clearly see that the determination in his eyes reflected something beyond Ghana—a performance that was beyond Ghana. I could see it. So in effect, I did not want him to be held back by the standards in the military, even though most of the finest boxers in those days could be found in the military, and especially in the Air Force when I was in charge. That was how he used to come train with us," says Rawlings, who at that time was in charge of the Air Force Boxing Group and then became the head of the Ghana Armed Forces Boxing Group.

Azumah may have embodied the fighting spirit of the nation, but as J. J. Rawlings states, he was never a member of the armed forces. Incredibly, though, that would not prevent him from taking part in the Military Games in Nigeria. So how did a civilian end up representing his country at a sporting event supposedly restricted to military personnel?

"He used to train with us," Rawlings explains, "with my Air Force boys, and then from there to the Armed Forces group when we were preparing for the World Military Games. The boxing championship part took place in Ghana. We placed so high; I think we lost only to the U.S.

As he was training with us [the boxers in the Air Force], and still in a way, wanted to join the Air Force and was undecided, I did not see why not. If he was the best, I did not see why he should not be on the team."

Azumah remembers the games well, but not purely for boxing reasons. "There was one guy called Tony Santana, an American, and he had been beating everyone all the time. They realised that I could beat him, so they brought me onto the team. I trained with the soldiers and when the time came, I went with them to Nigeria. The big bosses said they were going to give us money, but when we got there, they would not give us the money they had promised. Now the military boxers, they could complain, but because I was not in the military, I could not. So I said that I would not fight. We are heading into the finals, and I am going to fight Tony Santana, the man I had come to beat. I said I couldn't fight. I told them that I am sick and I could not fight. They know that I am not sick, and they know it is about the money, so they come to see me. They said, 'If you fight, after the fight, we will give you the money.' 'No, no, no,' I said. 'If I do not have the money, I cannot fight.' So they went away and they collected the money, and then came back with it and showed it to me, but did not give it to me.

"But I had already disqualified myself. The fight was in the evening the next day, and that meant that I had to shed the weight [that night] to be able to make the weight at the weigh-in in the morning. So I went out and I ate *garri* and sardines." (*Garri* is made from cassava tubers that are peeled, washed, and grated or crushed to produce a mash. The mash is then placed in a porous bag and allowed to ferment for one or two days. Weights are placed on the bag to press the water out. It is then sieved and roasted by heating in a bowl.)

Azumah continues, "The word got to the bosses that I was not going to fight, and that I had eaten so much that I would not make the weight. They were panicking and said, 'No, we are depending on him. He must fight. We will be in trouble if he doesn't fight. It will cost us our jobs.' So they came and started talking. I said, 'Give me the money.' They refused and said, 'You went to eat—how can you fight?' I told them I was not feeling well and that was why I cannot fight. So they said I had to go to the clinic, and they took me to the hospital. The doctor was Ghanaian and he knew me. He said to me, 'Azumah, you can't be sick. We want you to beat Tony Santana. You are the only one who can.' He had seen me fight before. I told him I am sick; I have malaria. Even though he knew I wasn't sick, he gave me an injection so that I went to sleep.

"Later, they came and woke me up and gave me the money and asked me, 'Will you fight now?' I asked them, 'Where is the rest?' They looked at me surprised and asked what did I mean. So I said, 'Where is the money for the other boxers? Where is their money?' They tried to tell me that they had given them their money. I told them I knew they had not. Anyway, I took my money, and I raised the bed, and hid the money under my bed. I then waited until midnight for the food to settle and called one of the guys to come and help me train. We went jogging at midnight and I had to sweat after training. I went on the scales when we got back, and I still had one pound to lose. I took a bath and then for five hours I slept. At five a.m., I woke up again and I trained for one-and-a-half hours. I went for a run at six a.m. and shed the weight.

"We went to the weigh-in and the doctor examined us. It was the same doctor, and he looked at me and said, 'Champ, don't be sick. We know you can do it.' I was fine and made the weight. We went back to where we were staying and they found me something to eat. After eating, I went back to bed. They woke me up when it was almost my time to fight, so we went to the stadium and I dressed to get ready for my fight. Ten minutes before I was due in the ring, I entered the dressing room. I shut the door and I started praying. I said, *God, this is the time. I depend on you. Let me win this fight. If you let me win this fight, I will thank you and whatever you want, I will do for you.* I really wanted to win. While I was praying, I was interrupted. It was a Ghanaian who was living in Nigeria. He came in and said he was looking for me to wish me luck. He said that he saw me praying, so he waited and then he came in. He told me he was going to give me some money if I won. I can't remember how much, but he said, 'I see you will win so I will give you all the money now. I know you will win.'

"I went to the ring and Tony Santana is taller than me so I did not try to hit his face. I only hit his stomach. *Bam, bam, bam,* and then I moved. I keep kept hitting his body. I was so confident—I know I am fast and can hit hard, and I don't give him a chance to hit me. He fought a typical American-style fight and I put pressure on him. In the second round, I kept the pace up and he spent all of the time covering his stomach. When he did that, I went to his head. I was just too quick. He was brave and he kept coming forward, but the body punches were too much for him. After the fight, he told me no one had beaten him like this that before. I just smiled at him."

Azumah's next major boxing event was a historic one, and one that would stand him in good stead in the future. It was the first International Amateur Boxing Association (AIBA) World Cup held at the famous Madison Square Garden in New York in October 1979. Madison Square Garden is nowadays known for college basketball games, track meets, and rock concerts, but to people of a certain age, the first image it conjures up is of boxing. If you fought at "The Garden," you had arrived: It was what Wembley is to a footballer, the one place you wanted to showcase your skill.

To fight at The Garden meant more than simply climbing into the ring in a historic venue. The Garden reflected so much of boxing, not only the great fights such as Joe Frazier vs. Muhammad Ali in 1971, but some of the shadier moments, too, such as Jake "Raging Bull" LaMotta taking a dive there against middleweight Billy Fox in 1947. The magnitude of fighting at Madison Square Garden was not lost on the young Azumah. "Everyone in the world knows Madison Square Garden. If you fight there, you are tough. You have arrived in boxing if you fight there," Azumah says.

It was also the chance for Azumah to go to a place that he had only ever seen on a grainy black-and-white television. He had sat and watched film of the man he admired so much, Jersey Joe Walcott, fighting Joe Louis for the world heavyweight title at Madison Square Garden in 1947. Now he was going to be boxing in that very same arena. Regrettably, his memories of that fight are not what they should have been, and the events of the World Cup were to change his outlook and his career.

However, before he went, he faced a problem convincing his girlfriend, Beatrice, that he would be safe. All the trouble started when one rival boxer failed to be selected for the Black Bombers trip to the U.S. Akwei

"Razor" Addo, whose punches were supposed to be as sharp as razor blades, was not selected for the team.

"He told my girlfriend, Beatrice, that I was going to fight in New York, and I had not had any training, that I am going to get badly beaten up. So she comes running to find me and she is in tears. She said I shouldn't go because I will get hurt. She begged me to stay. 'We can manage,' she told me. 'You do not need to fight.' I said, 'It is okay. I can fight. If I get there and I find I cannot fight, I will stop. I promise I won't get hurt. No one can force me to fight.'

"He had been to see her because he did not want me to go—he wanted to go in my place. It was true; we were not in training at that time. We were told very late we had to go, so we trained for five days and then we left. They told us there was a lot of money for us if we went, so we said yes. He told Beatrice, 'Your boy is not in training and they will hurt him.' Beatrice said, 'I love you. I don't want you to be hurt.' She cried so much. I told her, 'I won't get hurt. Boxing is not by force if you can't fight, you stop.' I told her I was going for the money. When she stopped crying she was okay and knew I would be okay."

However, when Azumah and the rest of the Black Bombers arrived in New York, the money that they were promised failed to appear. "We were amateurs when we went to the World Cup, and they [the Ghana boxing authorities] had said that they would give us money. But when we got to New York, they did not give it to us. We knew that something was going on in the first few days, as the Nigerian people, the Togo people, and the Algerian people were all going shopping. Meanwhile, we Ghanaians were sitting quietly, doing nothing. These other Africans told us we should go and get our money, but at that time, we had not seen any money.

"So we had a meeting, and it was after this meeting we decided we would not fight. We were not in training now; we were in America. We were all heavy and we were forcing ourselves to make the weight. They told us we had to fight the next day. But having decided that we would not fight, we went to a restaurant and ate as much as we could. We ate until our tummies hurt.

"I was supposed to fight as a featherweight. When they weighed me, I was one pound over lightweight! [The maximum weight for a featherweight was 126 pounds/57.2 kilograms and for a lightweight 135 pounds/ 61.2 kilograms.] The managers said I should go and lose the weight, but I said, 'No, I will fight junior welterweight instead [140 pounds/ 63.5 kilograms—this is now classed as super lightweight]. They were still angry and said to me, 'You are a small boy. How can you fight at that weight?' I told them that I could, and so they finally agreed and put me in that division.

"We were all overweight. The only one who was not overweight was the heavyweight! That night where we were staying, we planned that everybody would go to the ring to fight. When they were hit, they would raise their hand and say they could not fight anymore, that they were hurt. In other words, everyone would disqualify themselves. This was, of course, all because of the money they were trying to take from us. Unfortunately for me, I had to go first, and once I entered the ring and the first round started, I did not know how to stop.

"My team was in the front row, and they are whistling to tell me to stop, to remind me that I was meant to stop fighting. But I kept fighting. The reason was that I was thinking I want to be sure that they will all stop, too, once they got in the ring. I did not want to give away my fight unless I knew everyone would give away theirs as well.

"Because I was overweight, I was very small as a junior welterweight. But I was 'smoking' in the ring. It was the second or third round and I hit the other guy. He was so tall and I remember he was from Australia. I hit him with a left hook, and he went down and didn't wake up. So I won the fight. As I climbed out of the ring, I can see my people were very angry with me. They told me we made a plan and you are so stupid not sticking to it. 'Why did you not stick to it? You went and fought. You think you are strong and you want to show off?' they shouted at me. They were so angry. I said, 'Sorry, sorry. It will not happen again.'

"When it was their turn to fight, they all went and retired. One threw a punch and jumped back and held his hand up to say, 'No more.' Another took a punch and went down and did not get up. People started to say, 'Oh, what happened to him?' They knew that the Black Bombers were a strong team and could not understand why we were losing.

"When my second fight came, I was not happy. It was difficult for me to do what they did. After I beat the guy in the first round and knocked him out, people were 'dashing' me money. I had to go and fight again, and people expected me to win. How could I simply not fight? I was so confused. Then my people came to me and said, 'You go ahead and fight and see what we do to you!'

"So I went into the ring and I start fighting. I was throwing punches in the first round and doing the same in the second, and then when the bell went for the third round, I raised my hand. My corner started begging me to fight. Suddenly, they are offering me money. But I shook my head and I said, 'No, no, I cannot go on.' I retired in the third round. When I did not go out for the third, they knew I was lying, but they could do nothing.

"After the fight, we realised that our money was with the Togo people. If we had known this earlier, we would have fought well and we would have won. After we got our money, they could not take it from us. What had happened was the organisers did not give the money to our people. They gave it to the Togo people to give to us. They wrote the names of each boxer on the Black Bombers team on an envelope with the money in it and gave it to us.

"We were surprised when a man from Togo said he wanted to talk to us. He asked to see us and so we went to his room. When we got there, he did not answer, so we left. The next day he called us and we went again, and he apologised to us for not being there and gave us our envelopes.

"The Ghana people were annoyed that he had given us our money. The next day, they called us to a meeting and asked us to hand over the money to them. They told us it was government money and not ours. They wanted us to apologise, but we said to them, 'We are sportsmen representing our country. We should be respected. We are in training and you said you would pay us. Now you are saying you will pay us when we get home after the games, but you will not pass the money on to us. Why should we trust you?' We told them that the money belonged to us. We had been told by the man from Togo that if our people asked for it, we did not have to give it to them. It was our money, so we refused.

"We became very angry and we told them, 'Your children are at school in London, and you are taking our money to pay for their education. We are the ones who go in the ring and get hit and get hurt, and then we have a problem. Then we take our sickness and our problems back to our families, while you enjoy life with your children and families with our money!' We told them that when they do that—take things when there is no blessing—they put a curse on themselves and their children.

"The managers were very angry and did not speak to us again. When we got to the airport, ready to leave America, my luggage was overweight, and so were the bags of the other boys. We were told that we had to pay. This was another thing that made the managers annoyed with us. All the bags were meant to be weighed together, as we were a group, but the managers made them weigh each one separately, so we all had to pay. But what happened was I checked in, and they gave me my ticket and the boarding pass. The money I had to pay was shown on the boarding pass, and they had to stamp this to show that I had paid before they let us through onto the plane. So I was thinking, *How can I get through without paying this money?*

"I was thinking and thinking, and then one of the annoyed managers came and said, 'Why did you spend all of your money on so many things? Now you have no money left to pay.' They knew we had the money, but he said, 'Okay, take twenty dollars,' and gave me some money. I had to pay about a hundred to a hundred and twenty dollars so I was still left with a lot to pay. While he was talking to me, some guy came over—a Ghanaian living in America—and he told me to listen to how I could get through without paying. He told me to take the boarding pass and tear it and go back to the check-in and ask them to change it because it had ripped. He told me to say I was playing with a baby and that the baby ripped it. 'They will give you a new one,' he told me.

"I was shaking; I was so scared. As I went to the desk, I was so nervous. I told the lady the story the man told me to say, and she looked at my boarding pass, checked my ticket, and then gave me a new one. This one didn't have the amount of money to be paid on it. I was so scared that I left my passport on the counter. I went and sat down and I was thinking we must get on board. I was sure they would come and get me and find me. I was sitting there nervous, waiting and just wanting to get on board the plane.

"Then I heard my name called out. I was in a panic. I thought, *Oh, no! Now they will not let me board.* 'Mr. Nelson, please report …' I knew that my people would not be pleased that I had been caught. I was sure they had caught me. One of the managers said he would take me. We went forward and the man said, 'Mr. Nelson, here is your passport. You left it on the counter.'

"I said, 'Thank you, thank you.' My hands were shaking. When they finally said we could board, I was on that plane as quickly as possible. Then I sat there, waiting to take off. All the time, I was saying to myself, *Please take off. Please take off.* When we did, I gave a huge sigh. I had got away with it, and I still had the twenty dollars the manager gave me.

"Of course, at this time, there was a revolution in Ghana. When we got home, they said we had to pay for our luggage. But we stood as a group and said, 'No, we have been away representing the nation. You cannot bill us for doing that.' We argued for a while, and then one of the big people came forward and told them to let us go.

"Sadly, it did not end there. They wanted to suspend us when we got back, as they said we owed the nation money. The Olympic Games were coming up, less than a year away, and they threatened us, saying that they would not pick us. So several started to look at turning professional. That was when they called us and told us that they would not give us a license to turn pro. As the Commonwealth Games gold medal winner, I was the favourite to win Ghana's first gold medal at the Olympic Games in Moscow, so the government did not want me to turn professional.

"The former minister for sport seized my passport so that I could not turn pro. The government wanted to keep me happy and have me fight at the Olympics, so they were giving me money to stay an amateur. They warned me that if I turned pro, that money would stop. It was a funny time. If I didn't have any money, I would tell someone to say that I was turning pro, and more money would come. They would go and see the minister, and they would come and give me some money. The minister would send his driver in a Mercedes, and we would sit in the back and he would give me some money. He would also tell my dad to talk to me and convince me not to turn pro with the Olympic Games coming up."

On Christmas Eve 1979, the Soviet Union under leader Leonid Brezhnev invaded Afghanistan. It was a war that would last nine years. On January 20, 1980, the then-U.S. President Jimmy Carter issued his Cold War adversaries an ultimatum: The U.S. would boycott the Moscow Olympics if Soviet troops did not withdraw from Afghanistan within one month.

The deadline passed and there was no withdrawal of troops. Debate raged, and the Bilderberg meeting was held in Aachen, Germany, to discuss the boycott and its impact. The minutes of this meeting have since become available, yet the speakers' names have been withheld. The report quotes an African representative at the event who stated that, "A boycott would be an effective symbolic protest because of its magically dramatic visibility to the citizens of the Soviet Union, regardless of whether or not the action provoked a response."

The boycott did take place; although, many countries allowed their athletes to participate if they wished and left the final decision to participate in the games to their respective National Olympic Committees and the individual athletes. As a result of this, sixteen nations participated in the games, but paraded into the Olympic stadium without their national flags. Instead, they marched behind the Olympic flag.

Ghana was one of the sixty-five nations that chose not to participate in the games. Most of these nations bowed out due to the war in Afghanistan, but some were unable to attend for economic reasons. Of those sixty-five, nineteen nations were from the African continent.

Former sports minister Nii Amakai Amarteifio remembers this time well. "In 1980, [Azumah] had the chance of becoming an Olympic champion, but then at the insistence of the Americans, the Moscow Olympics were boycotted. We had a very fine crop of boxers at that time to unleash on the world. I took them to Montreal, but we did not throw a punch. We walked out because of South Africa and New Zealand playing each other [in rugby) during the apartheid era ... and so we lost the opportunity to fight in the Olympics of 1976 and 1980. That is why Azumah never became an Olympic champion. He should have been in Moscow; he was ready. He could not wait another four years, so he turned professional. I would have loved to have seen him as an Olympic champion."

The decision to not travel to Moscow meant that Azumah's chance to become the first Ghanaian to win an Olympic gold medal had evaporated. It would be the only title he craved that was outside his grasp and, due to circumstances, beyond his control. "I would have fought as a featherweight at the Olympics," Azumah says. "I believed I would win the gold because I would then have become the national champion, African champion, and Commonwealth champion, and the Olympics would have been the last medal for me to win. If I did not win it, the one who beat me would have taken the gold.

"I don't feel annoyed. It was my aim to go and become an Olympic champion and then turn pro. It would have made me happy, as Ghana had never had a gold medal winner, and it could have been me. I think I could have won. I would have liked that. But it was obviously God's will. I do not feel I was definitely going to win—I mean, the plane could have crashed on the way there. I was never guaranteed to win the gold medal, but it would have been nice. I wanted to win it and I think I could have won it."

It was Rudi Fink of West Germany (the two nations were separate in 1980) who won the gold, defeating Adolfo Horta of Cuba in the final. Also in the featherweight division at the Moscow Olympics was a man who Azumah would in due course meet, Sidnei Dal Rovere from Brazil, and one who there would be much talk of him meeting, Irishman Barry McGuigan.

With Ghana no longer going to the Olympics, there was no reason for Azumah not to turn professional. But still, the power brokers in Ghanaian boxing at the time wanted him to remain an amateur. This obstinance, according to friend Obi, led to an incredible possibility. "Because they did not go to the Olympics, he decided to turn professional," Obi recalls. "But they started deceiving him and trying to stop him turning pro. They refused to give him a Ghana boxing license. We had a friend, Ray Moss Akwei, who was a boxer. We were with him and we planned to take Azumah to Nigeria because the people wanted him to go there and fight for them. They were offering a professional license.

"After all he had done for Ghana, winning gold medals, they did not want to give him a license. It was terrible. It was then that Samir Captan came in and said to Azumah that he would be his manager. He did all he could to get Azumah a license, and eventually he managed to get him one and became Azumah's manager. Samir Captan's company was called Sikaprix Promotions. He was a good guy, and Azumah was lucky to have him because a lot of the managers were not honest."

When Azumah is asked if he ever genuinely considered boxing under the flag of Ghana's archrival Nigeria, a wry smile spreads across his face, a steely look comes to his gaze, and he quietly says, "I don't think so." It may well have been the perfect ruse to make the Ghanaian power brokers relent, as they would never have been forgiven had Azumah fought under the flag of Nigeria.

With no hope of attending the 1980 Olympic Games, there was no longer any need for Azumah to stay an amateur. He had taken his time, and the only prize that had eluded him was the Olympic gold medal. Unlike many young men, Azumah was never in a hurry; he knew the path he wished to follow and would walk that path for as long as it took. "I know you have to train hard to focus. If you want something, you have to find a way to get it. I had to focus and concentrate on what I was doing when I went professional. I wanted to be a champion, and I knew I had to work."

Unlike many modern-day boxers, he had been in no hurry to turn professional, as his goal had been to win an Olympic gold medal. "It was not frustrating those days as an amateur. As a young guy, you do not see anything as difficult. You needed something to eat so you had to plan. What am I going to eat? What am I going to do to get food to eat? Let me get some coconuts to sell. If not, how about a chicken? If not, I will go and do some work to earn money. One day, you do construction and then you work as a labourer to get money. After work, you eat, and after that, you go straight to training because you know that boxing is what you want to do. It is what you are focused on. The other things you do to get food and to keep yourself going.

"When you went to the Akotoku Academy, first you learned how to stand. The foundations need to be strong. Without the foundations, you cannot build a boxer; it's just like building a house. If you cannot stand properly, you will never stay on your feet in a fight. From standing, we moved onto 'springing,' then to a jab, or parrying. Then we learned how to defend, and gradually it all came together. As you are learning, you put on gloves and see how much you have learned. Only when you get the gloves on do you find out how much you have learned. If you get hit, you go away and look at why you were hit, and then the next time you do well to not make the same mistake. The next day, you are more cautious and make sure that punch does not hit you again.

"The coach, Attuquaye Clottey, was there, but you had to learn yourself. Like with a teacher in school, you will not learn unless you are focused. You are not the only child, so you have to pay attention to what the teacher tells others, as well as you. If you are not paying attention and the teacher asks you a question, if you have not been listening, you will not know the answer. If you are listening, it is easier. If you are not focused, he would ask you to throw a jab, and you would use an uppercut because you have not paid attention.

"I have always had a good left hook, even when I was young. No one could understand why being so small I could hit so hard, but I had to pound the *foo-foo*, so that helped get my shoulders strong. Then the quarry work, lifting the stones into the truck, gave me power. Even climbing the coconut trees, I needed strong hands to climb. All these things helped me get strong and have a good left hook.

"When I was growing up, I knew I would be a champion. But you have to follow the path. You have to become national champion, African champion, Commonwealth champion, and Olympic champion. Then you turn professional and start all over again as national champion, African champion, and Commonwealth champion, and only then do you get a chance to become world champion.

"I was turning pro now, but I had the same belief: that was I made sure that anybody I fought I can beat. I knew boxing very well; I studied it for so many years. That is why when I fought, I believe I know more than my opponent and I will beat him. That is why, gradually, I climbed the ladder. All the time, I am praying to my God and I am reminding him that he told me I would be a world champion. At the same time, I am showing him I am doing all the work to get there. Everything that has been good in my life has been down to hard work.

"A handful of rice can be difficult to find, and opportunities are limited. But if you are prepared to work hard and you respect God, you can survive and you can succeed."

V

TURNING PROFESSIONAL

One other thing that could have hampered Azumah's goal of turning professional was following what he thought was a good career path: joining the armed services. It was in fact the then-future president of Ghana, Flight Lieutenant J. J. Rawlings, who talked him out of such a move.

"The spirit of determination in him was so impressive that I was afraid if he joined the forces, he would lose that fighting urge," Rawlings explains. "There is something about the military—it can lift your standards, but at the same time, in taking you through the military routine and rituals, it could step down certain performances. In other words, the military could provide for your basic needs in life, but it could easily affect a boxer's performance. A boxer who wants to reach international standards really must have a fighting spirit that is possibly beyond most armed forces institutions. What I saw in him was a spirit that should stay alive— that should still be burning inside him to want to achieve something.

"The dream I saw in him was not necessarily to join the forces. Some had that dream—they wanted the security of the armed forces. The security that he was fighting for could not be found in the armed forces, and I needed it to remain burning, so it meant that his existence would not be altered. His everyday life should not be altered. Wherever the fighting spirit was coming from, it should be kept ablaze. If it was in his environment, then it needed to stay that way. I did not want to see it altered to the extent that it would kill some of the fighting spirit in him." Rawlings's insight into Azumah's personality proved to be intuitive.

With fifty wins to his name and just two losses, and with no hope of going to the Olympic Games to complete his collection of amateur titles, Azumah Nelson turned professional in the latter half of 1979. He still vehemently defends the two blemishes on his amateur career, reminding everyone that he retired from the World Cup as part of the Black Bombers' solidarity pact in New York, and the other he still believes he won. It would be a brave man who decides to argue with him over the fact.

Azumah was sure he was destined to one day be the world champion, and his best friend, Obi, did not need a lot of convincing to share that belief. He remembers, "I was the one who called Azumah 'Terrible Terror.' He was the Terrible Terror because he was a warrior. He became a different man before a fight. I would be in the same room, and he would become a different man before my eyes. He scared me. He did not want to speak to anyone—he wanted to concentrate on the fight. He started punching the dressing room wall, shadowboxing, and I asked myself, *What kind of man is this?* During his amateur times, it was the same, but when he became a professional, it was worse. When he was an amateur, they were terrified of him. Now when I saw him, I knew he would be great.

"When he was not boxing, we still were friends, and his other nickname was 'Lord Mayebo,' which literally translated means 'Lord, I will win you.' We gave him this name because when we are playing cards, he always wins. Everything he does, he is the champion, even in draughts. He is wonderful at everything. He was even a very good goalkeeper when we play football."

Although, according to Azumah, "Football was not my talent."

Azumah was twenty-one years old when he turned professional, thanks to the intervention of Samir Captan, who was at the time the chairman of the Ghana Boxing Authority. With his father and brother, Mensah, alongside him, he signed professional forms that saw John Kermeh and Seth Ansah as his new managers.

Most young men at that age would have an eye for the ladies, but Azumah still only had eyes for Beatrice, as Obi recalls. "When we started growing up, at around twenty, we started to recognise beautiful women. At times, I would go to our family's house and try and pick some of my cousins for him, or sometimes we would go into town and get girls, but he was always very wary of the girls."

Azumah is very clear on this time in his life. "No girls liked me then. But I know one day they will like me. My father told me that women like champions, so when you are a champion, they will like you. They do not even need to know what champion you are. If you are the champion of whatever, they will like you. I never forgot him telling me that."

With that in mind, and the promise that Beatrice's parents made to her, he married his childhood sweetheart after she left school. It was a traditional Ghanaian wedding. Azumah and his father went to see Beatrice's father, who was by now well aware of his daughter's intent to marry. Once at her house, they poured a drink and started talking business. Azumah talked about how the two had met and how her smile was the light that eclipsed all others in his life. The whole discussion was aimed to persuade her father to part with his beloved daughter. Once he finally agreed, drinks were passed around and the engagement was sealed.

Before the union could go ahead, Beatrice's family, as is tradition, checked out Azumah's family history to ensure that there were no generational curses on the family—that no madness ran in the family—and there was no miserly behaviour in the family or any members who would tarnish their name.

Azumah and Beatrice had to wait anxiously while these checks were carried out, but approval was given. Next, Azumah had to go through the Knocking Ceremony, an event that Beatrice was not allowed to attend. As the groom-to-be, he had to go to Beatrice's house and knock on the door to ask her parents for their daughter's hand in marriage. He was then given a list of items to supply to show his worth. Traditionally, the value of items on this list varies by the level of education the girl has received and her prospects in life. Beatrice's parents were reasonable people and were well aware of how determined she was to marry Azumah. Although Azumah had limited income, their requests were reasonable, as they did not want another fight with their strong-willed daughter. They just wanted her to be happy and to continue her education.

When their big day came, Azumah arrived with his family and sat on the opposite side of the yard from Beatrice's family. The gifts he had bought Beatrice were presented. The groom's family then put forward a gift, and though traditionally the bride's family should act hesitant in accepting it, on this occasion, their gift was graciously accepted. As soon as the gifts were accepted as adequate, the union was given the blessing of both families and the celebrations began. "After everything, they liked me now, and her dad said, 'Go ahead, you are my son.' I was very happy," Azumah remembers.

These were exciting times for the young Azumah, who had just turned professional and was now entering this new era of his life with the love of his life alongside him. "Her family grew to like me by then, and they were happy when I became world champion. They knew then that their daughter did not make a mistake. She knew what she was doing."

To make their start to married life a little easier, and because of Azumah's status, the government arranged accommodation for the couple. "The government gave me an apartment in Cantonement, and I stayed there with Beatrice. I also stayed at the Paramount Hotel, which was owned by my manager," he recalls.

According to the then-sports minister, Nii Amakai Amarteifio, "He was put in one of the hotel chalets at the Star Hotel in a very nice neighbourhood—very serene atmosphere, very calm. It was a place fit for a king. The government gave him a place to live, gave him a car, gave him every facility to enable him to concentrate, not only on winning, but on keeping the title as long as he could. This was a deliberate national policy. This was a deliberate intervention by the government of the time to make sure he annexed the title and brought it home.

"This was a country that was badly in need of good news. We had bad news in this country for a long time, and it was important we had good news for a change. Azumah was good news and we paid for it. We did whatever we could to help to support him. We even went to the United States—I did—to recruit a nutritionist, people who would examine everything that went into his body, and we paid the nutritionist."

As he had been as a child, Azumah was a very focused young man, and he knew that he had to be dedicated to succeed. Azumah was still boxing under the watchful eye of his coach Attuquaye Clottey, yet Azumah was still convinced that he often saw things before his coach.

"When I am training, I catch the idea as to what I have to do very quickly," he says. "I may have to alter the way I box, and I learn the new style very quickly. This is the only thing I learn very quickly. I can't learn anything as quickly as I can how to box against another opponent. With boxing, I just see it and I know how to do it. It is my talent. I believe that before the creation of this world, God made me a boxer—all I needed was someone to polish it."

As a former featherweight who had fought twice for the world title in Ghana, Floyd Klutei Robertson was deemed the best there was. Robertson was friends with the late John Zwennes, which led to Azumah training at the Zwennes-owned Volunteer Force Gym, now known as Seconds Out and run by John's son Peter.

"Our dad was a national athlete. He ran the mile for Ghana," Peter remembers. "He was very keen on sports and was a serious football fan. My dad was a fanatical Hearts of Oak supporter, but his passion was for boxing. When they were kids, they lived in the Palladium area, in the heart of Accra. Growing up, they had all these local champions in the vicinity—Roy Ankrah, Attuquaye Clottey, Vincent 'London Kid' Okine, Sugar Ray Akwei, Razor Akwei Addo—and he told us how his father used to run a gym in Sekondi when they were all kids, so it was in the blood.

"Floyd Klutei was his classmate at school and bosom friend. When my dad was doing athletics, Floyd was playing football and then switched to boxing. My dad also had a friend who we called Uncle Henry, Henry Kofi Worglo, who was very passionate about boxing, and he, too, was an old classmate. The three of them were very involved in boxing. We [Peter and his brother Jacob] had followed Azumah's exploits as an amateur and as a young pro. But the first time we met him was courtesy of Uncle Henry. Azumah lived in Mamprobi with his dad, and Uncle Henry also lived in Mamprobi—and he had a joint called The Hawk, a drinking spot. Uncle Henry lived there, and all the attention on boxing was focused there at The Hawk. All the promoters, fighters, and managers would meet there and discuss boxing. So by the time we met Azumah, he had already linked up with Uncle Henry, who introduced him as a potential world champion."

These were interesting times for Ghana, as just prior to Azumah turning professional in June of 1979, the ruling Supreme Military Council was overthrown by junior officers and men of the Ghanaian Armed Forces in a mass revolt that came to be known as the June 4 Movement. An Armed Forces Revolutionary Council (AFRC) was set up under the chairmanship of Flight Lieutenant J. J. Rawlings to run the country.

The AFRC set about restoring a sense of moral responsibility and the principles of accountability and probity in public life. The AFRC sent out the message that politicians and government employees dealing with the public had an "obligation to put the good of the community above personal objective." They held office for only three months, as a motion had been set in place prior to the uprising that allowed general elections to be held, and they believed it was important to honour this motion. The elections were held in September, and Doctor Hilla Limann was handed power as leader of the People's National Party, which had won the elections. Ghana's Third Republic began.

Ghana's economy was still in a very poor state, with inflation estimated to be at 70 per cent for the first fiscal year of the new government's tenure in power. The Trade Union Congress claimed its workers were no longer earning enough to pay for food, let alone anything else. Strikes resulted, productivity was lowered, and so, too, was the national income. Ghana needed not only strong economic leadership, but also a hero—someone who came from the streets and had pushed through all of the problems the majority faced on a daily basis, someone to give them hope.

The start of Azumah's professional career could not have come at a more important time. Although, there was no way he could have realised how important his career would be in terms of lifting the nation. On December 1, 1979, Azumah climbed into the ring for his first professional fight. It was to be an eight-round bout against fellow Ghanaian Billy Kwame. Kwame tended to fight as a welterweight, and may well have been chosen as an opponent for Azumah to give him a stern test in his first professional fight. The fight went the distance, with the debutant given the decision on points.

Obi remembers the fight. "It was a terrible fight. The guy was a strong fighter. I can remember it, but the important thing was that Azumah finished the fight with him."

Azumah, not surprisingly, also remembers the bout with Kwame. "When you turn pro, you usually start off with a four-round fight, then six rounds, eight rounds, and build up to ten rounds. When you get to fight ten rounds, you can then fight twelve and fight for a title. My first fight was ten rounds and not eight, as the records show. It was definitely ten rounds. I won on points, and people were shocked that I won, saying, 'No, no! It is not supposed to be like that.' They had said to me before the fight, 'He is strong and experienced, and he will beat you. He is too strong for you to have as a first fight.' I listened and I said to them, 'Come to the fight and watch.' That was all I said. I did not talk too much in those days.

"I do not think it was brave to fight him first up. My belief is that I know boxing better than my opponent. Every time I enter the ring, I see them as middle school level, and I am at the university level. You will see the difference. I know that he cannot beat me, so why would I be scared?"

Just two months later, he climbed through the ropes again, this time to face another Ghanaian, Nii Nuer. "I knocked him out in the third round. He was a strong boxer, too, but once again, I was at the university level and he wasn't," he recalls with a smile before adding, "but I was not yet a professor." This is the only recorded professional fight of Nuer's career, so one wonders if he felt the schooling was a little harder than he had anticipated.

"After I fought a couple fights in Ghana, my manager, Samir Captan, chairman of professional boxing in Ghana today, decided to send me to England. He had a contact in the UK, Charlie Atkinson Senior, so he decided to send me there to train. I said okay, and we went there and started training, sparring. He is a very good coach and I learned a lot from him. I appreciate all that he and his family did for me. I did not stay with them in Liverpool. I stayed in a house that Samir set up for me, and every day I took a bus and a train to the gym."

Wondering what a young man fresh out of Ghana would make of a strong Liverpool accent and how the two communicated, Azumah explains, "I tell you, boxing is not about the accent or the place; it's about action, the science. Even if I don't understand what they are saying, I can see the science of what they are telling me. When I am with them for a couple of weeks, I start to understand them, so it was not a problem."

During the Second World War, Atkinson had served in a bomb dis-
posal unit and as an underwater demolition specialist, for which he was
awarded the British Empire Medal in 1940. He started coaching amateurs
at St Teresa's in Liverpool and produced the city's first Amateur Boxing
Association champion, Frank Hope. He moved to Kirkby and was invited
to form the Kirkby Amateur Boxing Club. He was credited as the man
who discovered and nurtured world champions John Conteh and Joey
Singleton. So he knew how to spot a talented boxer and tried to sign the
young Azumah Nelson.

"I believe they would have liked to sign me, but I had a contract
already," Azumah recalls. "If you are a coach or a manager, and you know
boxing and you see someone like me, with talent, then you would want
to sign me and try to. Charlie Atkinson was important, but not as important as Attuquaye Clottey—I liked him a lot, but he has passed away now.
We lost contact, so I am not sure where the son is now. I hope we can
meet again one day."

After training in Liverpool, Azumah returned to Ghana, where incredibly in only his third professional bout, he fought for Ghana's featherweight (126 pounds) title against Henry Saddler. This fight had an added
importance to Azumah. "One day when I was still an amateur, I was
watching a TV show and they are showing boxing. It was Henry Saddler
on the TV and he was fighting. I was watching and I said, 'One day, I will
beat him.' One of my uncles heard it, and he was very annoyed. 'Who do
you think you are, saying that? You are cocky! Get out, you stupid boy!
You think you know what you are saying.'

"I felt so much pain. I am a boxer and I say I can beat them because I
believe I can beat them. You have to. I know you have to train hard so you
can get there, but my uncle did not encourage me. I was upset, but it
made me very determined to prove him wrong. I stood up and said to
him, 'I will prove you wrong.' He was angry and left. When he was gone,
I told the tailor that one day I would prove my uncle wrong. 'I will be a
champion—you wait and see that I am right.'"

Henry Saddler had won the Ghanaian title in May of 1979 when he
defeated Abdul Rahman Optoki. (This fighter is often confused or listed

as Henry Optoki, which is believed to be his fighting name.) Saddler had gone on to fight for the Commonwealth title against the undefeated Nigerian Eddie Ndukwu, but had lost on a TKO in the eighth round. Following a six-month layoff, he would defend his national title in a twelve-round fight in Accra.

It was not to be for Saddler, who was knocked out in round nine. Just three months into his professional career, Azumah had won his first title and was the national featherweight champion. "I did fight Saddler for the Ghana title, and my same uncle was there. 'Super Rago' was his nickname, which translated means 'Black Jesus.' I knocked Saddler out in round nine. I told him he would not go ten rounds. He could not continue in round nine and they stopped it. At that time, I used to tell them the round I will finish the fight. At the end of that fight, my uncle came to the ring and carried me high." Azumah had proved one doubter wrong.

Azumah was training at the gym now called Seconds Out, but in those days it belonged to the army and the navy and that is why it was called the Volunteer Force Gym. Many former champions would train there, including D. K. Poison, as well as quite a number of prominent up-and-coming boxers. John Zwennes, at that time, owned an old rickety white Ford with the licence plate AZ 37, and with his boys, Peter and Jacob, he would leave Mataheko in the afternoon and drive to Mamprobi, where Azumah and Uncle Henry would be waiting. They would all squeeze into the rickety old Ford, the windows down and the dust blowing in, and drive to the gym. Azumah would then train. After each training session leading up to a fight, he would have to weigh himself to make sure he was on the limit. The trouble was the scales had to be accurate. But the only truly accurate scales in the area were at the Accra Racecourse, so they would all clamber back into the car and head to the racecourse and weigh Azumah before driving him home.

"I was in a hurry to be the champion of the world, and my trainer and my manager knew that I was good and that I could beat a lot of the other boxers," Azumah remembers. "But my manager was scared for me. He thought I was going too fast. I told him, 'You keep bringing them in, and I will keep knocking them out or beating them. Line them up, and we will keep going forward because I will be the world champion.'"

To prove he was a man in a hurry, Azumah's next fight came only one month after his title bout with Saddler, making it his third fight in three months. On this occasion, he was to fight another local fighter, Abdul Rahman Optoki. This was a memorable fight for young Jacob and Peter Zwennes, as it was the first time they had ever seen a live fight, with Uncle Henry buying them tickets.

Obi, too, remembers the fight, but for different reasons. He recalls how desperate Optoki was to put the young Azumah in his place. "He was another strong fighter. Optoki knocked out most of the men he fought. He was a fearsome man. He was from Labardi in Accra; they called him the Lion of Labardi. I remember that all of the bosses came from Labardi for the fight, as he was the pride of the Labardi people. They were sure that he would win the fight.

"During the build up, Azumah sent a message to Optoki to say that it would rain on the day of the fight. He said that it would rain from dawn until evening, and if it rained, Azumah would stop Optoki. If it does not rain, he will go the distance, but beat him on points. On the day of the fight, it rained all day, so it was all over. Azumah would win. He messed with Optoki's head and knocked him out in round eight."

Azumah had fought four fights in seven months, winning three by knockout and already picking up a title. He was proving he was a man in a hurry, but standing at just five feet five inches, many were surprised at the ferocity of his punch. Not surprisingly, Azumah wasn't. He recalls, "I believed when I fought these guys that I can knock them out, and I tried to knock them out. A lot of them I knocked out because I can punch hard, and that was thanks to my trainer, who taught me how to defend myself and how to punch harder. He taught me where you take the punch from so that you can be strong and hit hard. Today, the boxers just throw their hands. They do not know how to get the power. You have to take it from your legs and use your whole body. That is why I was knocking them out because I was taught well by Attuquaye Clottey.

"Attuquaye Clottey was one of the greatest boxing coaches that Ghana has produced. Early in a boxer's schooling, he teaches him how to align his body so that he is balanced. Next comes how to move, and only once these skills have been perfected did he show you how to punch. Anyone can throw a punch, but in boxing the key is being in the right position when you throw that punch so that it has maximum impact. Attuquaye Clottey was the master at teaching young Ghanaians that skill." With the power that Azumah possessed from the work he had done growing up, learning how and when to throw a punch was a lesson that would hold him in good stead throughout his long and successful career.

Azumah was back in the ring in July 1980 when he fought American David Capo, who travelled to Ghana for the bout. In the first fight of his professional career, Capo had taken on Juan Laporte and lost to the future world champion on points. He lost a rematch also on points two years later, just three months before he faced Azumah. His career record was far from impressive, with two wins, three losses, and one draw, yet in every fight he had lasted the distance. He did so again against Azumah, and in the process, he gave the young Ghanaian a good test following his earlier quick victories.

To round off what had been a very fruitful first year as a professional boxer, Azumah faced another tough fight in December. This time, he would climb into the ring with Nigerian Joe Skipper. The rivalry between Nigeria and Ghana is immense. It is similar to New Zealand vs. Australia in rugby, or Germany vs. Holland in football, or Celtic vs. Rangers, and Arsenal vs. Spurs. Neither nation can bear a loss to the other.

Six months earlier, Skipper had faced D. K. Poison in Benin and lost; now he was facing another Ghanaian and was talking up the fight. Obi, who was in Azumah's corner for this fight, remembers the press conference prior to the bout. "They interviewed us, and Azumah's manager was at that time Samir Captan, chairman of the Ghana Boxing Authority, and Skipper was there with his people. He was saying he was going to beat Azumah, but Azumah let him talk and then said, 'I will stop Joe Skipper.' He did. He knocked him down in the tenth round and won by a TKO."

As Azumah was making his way along the road to becoming a world champion, his country was headed down a very different path. In February of 1981, with the country still in relative turmoil and the government of Hilla Limmann on very shaky ground due to a worsening national debt and strikes throughout the country, Azumah headed out of Ghana for the first time in his professional career. He went to neighbouring Togo to meet Aziza Bossou, a fighter who fought much of his career as a lightweight rather than a featherweight. He was at the time the African Boxing Union lightweight champion. This would be a stern test for the twenty-two-year-old in his seventh professional fight.

Once again, Obi was in his corner. "It was a terrible fight in Lome, Togo. I remember Azumah beat him on points, but this guy was a tough champion; no one had beaten him there. There were many Ghanaians in Togo, and the whole of Africa was beginning to know who Azumah was. When they heard he was going to fight, plenty of people would go and watch him."

Two months later, Azumah was back in the ring and back in Accra, facing Welshman Don George. George from Swansea was a genuine featherweight and came to Ghana with a six wins, two losses, and one draw record. Azumah was still unbeaten. He remained unbeaten, knocking out George in round five. George has always said that this was the highlight of his boxing career, even though he won the Welsh Area featherweight title after defeating Mervyn Bennett two fights later. He also still maintains to this day that "he punched me when I wasn't looking." It mattered not to Azumah, who had notched another victory. His march towards a world title was still very much on course.

In August, Azumah flew to America for his first professional fight in a market where it was crucial to impress, not only to secure future fights, but to attract television stations, which at the time gave boxing a great deal of airtime and paid big dollars for fighters who drew in the audiences. He was his usual ruthless self, knocking out Miguel Ruiz in Bakersfield, California, in round three. This fight was also supposed to be a warm-up bout for Azumah's showdown with Australian Brian Roberts for the vacant Commonwealth featherweight title. Some may have felt that the fight was over too quickly to give Azumah a reasonable warm-up for the Roberts fight, but as far as he was concerned, it was important to go in the ring and finish the job as quickly as possible.

"I had to knock them out so no one will say the fight was close or they thought the other guy had won. I could not risk a decision going to my opponent. I had to win. If I lost, it would have affected my chances of having a go at the world title. I had to keep winning, and I had to keep knocking my opponents out. I knew that if I start losing, my chance to be world champion will take a lot longer."

Thirty-nine days later, Azumah faced another key moment in his career: the opportunity to claim another title, the vacant Commonwealth featherweight crown. Patrick Ford of Guyana had vacated the title that he had won in 1980 in order to chase a world title, and then lost on a majority decision after going the distance with WBC Champion Salvador Sanchez. Five months later, he had lost by knockout to Eusebio Pedroza in round thirteen of a fifteen-round bout for the WBA featherweight title.

Azumah's opponent for the vacant title was Australian Brian Roberts, who had begun his professional career in 1972 and had fought and defeated some high-pedigree Australian boxers, including Australian hall-of-famers Paul Ferreri and Jeff Malcolm. Mick Fernandez from Erskineville, New South Wales, trained him, and while Fernandez was training the professionals, a certain Johnny Lewis was training the amateurs at the same gym.

Azumah was well aware of how important this fight was in terms of gaining him a crack at a world title. "I had to win this fight, as it was a big step towards a world title. It was the biggest fight so far. We fought here in Accra so that was good for me. I had won the national title and I had won the African title, and I knew if I won this, it would carry me forward to a world title.

"At the weigh-in, I looked at him and I knew he could not take my punches. I am too strong for him. In the fight, I knocked him out in round five. That may sound like it was easy, but every fight is difficult. It is the way you train and prepare for a fight that will determine if you win. You prepare for fifteen rounds, and if you go in and your opponent is knocked out in the first round, you store the energy that you have not used for the next fight. You can save a lot of energy this way. So if you can knock him out in round one, it is best to do so and save that energy for another time, and you can finish early and go away and rest. The quick win over Ruiz helped me save energy for Roberts."

After the fight, Mickey Fernandez said, "Brian boxed liked a true champion, but Azumah Nelson will be a great world champion one day."

His words were to prove prophetic. Brian Roberts sadly passed away in September 2010 from a heart attack at the age of just fifty-seven years.

Azumah had moved another rung up the ladder with his new title, and never one to shy away from a challenge, he was quick to defend it, first in Lagos against Nigerian Kabiru Akindele, whom he knocked out in round five, and then against Zambian Charm "Shuffle" Chiteule, against whom he won on a TKO in round ten of the scheduled fifteen.

In between these two fights, a new government took power in Ghana, the eighth in fifteen years, and the Provisional National Defence Council with J. J. Rawlings as its chairman took control. Rawlings's vision of the PNDC was not to rule as a military dictatorship, but rather to offer a stable confederation of civilians and soldiers who would help to restore prosperity to Ghana, before once again promoting multiparty democracy.

He faced the difficult task of trying to reverse staggering inflation and drastic declines in public school enrollment. He looked to the Soviet Union for help, but when that was not forthcoming, he was forced to temper his leftist leanings and solicit aid from the West. Many of the austerity measures he initiated proved unpopular, and the PNDC found itself constantly having to quell coup attempts and domestic unrest. Despite ruthless measures at times, Rawlings saw his leadership role as being a watchdog for ordinary people as he tried to stamp out incompetence, injustice, and corruption on a government level.

As a result of monetary and fiscal policies, the country found itself in a worse state than after the coup of '79. There was a shortage of food as well as a general drought, and the people found themselves having to queue for basic foodstuffs, as Jacob Zwennes recollects. "At that time, we found ourselves having to queue for basic staples such as bread and *kenkey*, the staple Ghanaian food." (*Kenkey* is similar to a sourdough dumpling and is usually made from ground maize. Making *kenkey* involves letting the maize ferment a few days before cooking. After fermentation, the *kenkey* is partially cooked, wrapped in banana leaves, corn husks, or foil, and steamed.)

He adds, "People made light of the shortages, but most had their collarbones sticking out because they were so undernourished—and so they called it a 'Rawlings chain' after the head of state. There was also the

'Rawlings biscuit.' This was made out of yellow corn, as we did not have the normal white corn for the *kenkey*. So they imported yellow corn. It flooded the market. It was cheaper, but initially no one wanted to eat it because it was used to feed the poultry. Things were so bad they started selling it and people used it for *kenkey*. Cookies were made with the corn and it was obviously a yellow biscuit and people referred to them as 'Rawlings biscuits.' Traditionally, you would buy *kenkey* when it is cooked, but in these times, people would queue and buy uncooked *kenkey* that was still waiting to be cooked. Many people couldn't risk being in the long queue and being told the *kenkey* had run out, so they would buy the uncooked *kenkey*, take it home, and cook it themselves.

"It was like the Wild West, and it needed the military and the police to keep order. The lines were very long, and I remember we had to queue for the normal staples like *garri*, sardines, mackerels, sugar, and milk. There were very long lines everywhere, especially at the GNTC [Ghana National Trading Corporation], which was one of the main retailing shops in the country. UTC Kingsway, CFAO, and SCOA all had long lines, and the military was always there. There were lines from morning to evening, and if you were lucky, you would walk away with four cans of evaporated milk, a tin of Milo, and maybe six cans of sardines and some sugar."

Brother Peter also remembers those times well. "I remember people would go to the bakery and queue while the bread was in the oven. Sometimes people even joined queues without knowing what they were queuing for. If someone stopped outside a shop, a queue would form until they realised they were not queuing for anything. Lines were everywhere, and people just joined them because they did not want to miss out."

These were very tough times for all. However, irrespective of how dire the situation was, Ghanaians live for sport. They love their football and boxing, and even in those trying times, people were still going out to watch soccer games and boxing matches.

Boxing was a big thing, and Azumah Nelson would unwittingly play his part in giving the people of Ghana hope and taking their minds off the changes taking place in their country. The hard economic times did not change what the people thought about Azumah or the expectations they had of him. Most Ghanaians were looking to get away from what they were experiencing, from the economic pressures they were all under. They needed something positive to focus on, and Azumah became that focus. He made them proud and gave them hope.

He had come out of the amateurs and was a Commonwealth gold medalist. He was a world Military Games champion. He was an icon, and he had not even fought for the world title. Yet everyone knew him. This was just as well, as despite the food shortages, the military government enforced a curfew. The curfews ran from dawn to dusk every day.

No one could go out, as there were military personnel patrolling. Police, too, were on nightly patrols. If you did venture out, you stood a good chance of being arrested and locked up. It was dangerous to go out in the early hours of the morning or at dawn, as you never knew who was patrolling or whom you might be mistaken for. One possibility was a burglar; due to the tough economic times, looting was frequent, as families were desperate and trying to survive. The government had explained that the curfew was to guard against insurgents, whom they claimed might try to destabilise the country. That was another possible label you faced if caught out at night.

As Peter Zwennes explains, the curfews even affected boxing. "We stopped having tournaments in the evenings because of the curfews. Instead, we went to having them in the afternoon because they had to be finished by six o'clock when the sun went down. So sometimes we sat under the scorching sun, watching fights at one or two o'clock in the afternoon. The curfew meant that all the sportsmen had to change their training schedules, so boxers now trained throughout the day. For Azumah, the risk was high, but he was such a well-known figure; I am sure he got away with it. I know he used to get up and run while it was still dark. Most of the military personnel knew him and the route that he used to take, and I am sure that he was safe, but for other boxers, it was tough to go out during the curfew."

Azumah confirms this. "Yes, sometimes if it was necessary and I don't have any option, I would ask if I could avoid the curfew. Sometimes I would go jogging after six o'clock in the evening. It was not dangerous, as most of the soldiers knew who I was. If they did stop me, I said, 'I am

Azumah. I have a fight.' They are all supporting me, and they didn't want me to lose so they let me go on. If I got stopped, and sometimes I did, once they saw my face, they knew who I was. If you did not know who Azumah Nelson was, you were not Ghanaian," he says with a laugh.

No matter the inconvenience of the curfew, in June, in Accra, Azumah recorded another routine TKO win over Mukaila Bukare. Soon after, the call that he had been waiting for finally came through. Two weeks before he was to fight the great Salvador Sanchez at Madison Square Garden, Canada-based Colombian Mario Miranda withdrew. Promoter Don King was desperate to find a replacement, but not many were keen to climb in the ring with such a formidable opponent.

English promoter Mickey Duff told King about the up-and-coming Azumah, but before calling Ghana, Don King called Eric Armit from the UK's *Boxing News* magazine. In an article published in 1989, Armit revealed that the WBC was worried that Azumah may be a poor replacement, similar to John Mensah Kpalongo from Togo, who was knocked out by Carlos Zarate in round three of their WBC World Bantamweight title fight three years earlier. Kpalongo had been touted as having a forty-five-win, two-loss record going into the bout. In truth, it is believed he had actually had only five professional bouts and lost four of them. Amazingly, the WBC ranked him the number-one contender, but to be fair, at that time, record-keeping in Africa was extremely poor to the point of being almost nonexistent.

Armit, who had recommended Nelson for a world rating, received the call because, as he says, he was considered their African expert. "After a few moments' hesitation, I told them I was confident Azumah would give Sanchez a good fight," he wrote. So a phone call was made to Ghana.

Azumah had never had a timeframe in which he intended to achieve his dream of becoming world champion. As he recalls, "I know I will be the champion one day, but I did not know if I would become a champion that first year, or in three years. I know it will take time, and as long as it happens, I will be happy. I just had to make sure when the time came I was ready. I know I will be good enough, and that is why I took the challenge with Salvador Sanchez. I was not ready to fight, but I knew I could prove something. I went there to win. I was not in good condition for that fight—I wasn't ready—but I know I am strong and I can fight."

Don King also remembers this fight. "Sanchez is the best I ever had; he was a gem. I figured I'd bring him to Madison Square Garden to showcase him. But I couldn't find anybody to fight him. So I called Africa. I brought him and figured here's Sanchez's time to shine. I told him before the fight, 'This guy's an easy opponent and you'll look real good.'"

Before Azumah arrived in New York, things started to go wrong. He and his team flew from Ghana to London and then on to the U.S. Floyd Robertson, his trainer, had been unable to arrange a U.S. visa before he left Ghana, and so he intended to pick one up in London. Unfortunately for him and Azumah, he was unable to organise one there, either. So as the promoter of the fight, and with Azumah's team a man down, Mickey Duff agreed to fill the void, and he worked in Azumah's corner.

Duff had chosen an opponent who would pique the interest of fight fans. Azumah, with thirteen wins in thirteen fights and eleven by knockout, was an attractive proposition on paper for the New York fans. Sanchez was expected to toy with the young African for a few rounds, and then knock him out and set up more lucrative paydays, but Azumah had not read the script.

"They cheated me in that fight," Azumah says. "I took the fight two weeks out and flew to New York and started training. Someone told Don King, 'This guy is very strong. He lacks experience, but he is very strong.' They told Sanchez, who did not know anything about this African boy. Don King was suddenly very scared because he was going to give Sanchez a chance at the lightweight title after this fight with a fight against Alexis Arguello. He did not want anything to happen to Sanchez, so he was annoyed.

"They then gave me Salvador Sanchez's sparring partner to come and spar with me. So I spar with the guy, and after he went back to Salvador Sanchez, he said, 'Don't mess with this guy. This guy is so strong that when he hits me, it's like an iron hitting me in the head. If you joke with this guy, he will knock you out.' Sanchez did not believe him, as he had not heard of the African boy. Don King then called Mickey Duff and asked, 'Why have you sent someone like this to fight Sanchez?' Mickey Duff said, 'Don't worry. I know what to do.'

"The day before the fight, my mouthpiece went missing. So I went to the store and I bought one that the amateurs wear, and I put it in hot water and then into my mouth. But it is too big. So I took a blade and I cut it, but the edge is rough. Then in the fight, in round six, Salvador Sanchez hit me with a left hook, and I got a big cut in my mouth. The blood keeps coming, but I am a warrior so I keep fighting. I keep going forward because I know I can win this fight, and I know that if it went fifteen rounds, there was no way they will give me the decision, so I have to knock him out. But I was not ready to fight fifteen rounds. I keep pushing myself to keep going. In the fifteenth round when he knocked me down, I wake up and try to carry on, and the referee, said, 'No more.' So I said, 'Okay, but I'll be back.'"

After the fight, Sanchez paid credit to Azumah and prophetically tipped him to one day be a world champion. Bobby Goodman, who was working for promoter Don King, was reported as saying at the time, "The kid had only thirteen fights or so, so we asked his manager, 'How tough can he be?' The manager just smiled and said, 'Yeah, okay.' Well, we went through with the fight, and it turned out to be one of the greatest featherweight fights ever. I thought during the fight, *Oh, my god. This is one of the toughest guys I've ever seen.* After the fight, Juan Torres Landa, Sanchez's manager, came up to me at the press conference and said, 'Bob, do me a favour. I don't want no more easy fights.'"

"I felt that when I fought Salvador Sanchez, I was so tired I could not go on, but I believe in this world nothing good comes easy, so I have to keep punching," Azumah recalls. "The referee saw I was doing my best, but I was so exhausted he stopped the fight, and I am glad he stopped it. You can fight, but you do not have to stay there until you get hurt. The referee did well."

Azumah had had only one obscure fight in the U.S. prior to meeting Sanchez, and he could so easily have gone the way of many unknown boxers with impressive records on paper who are fed to world champions to knock over. However, he had not only shown Sanchez he was competitive, but he had shown the world. He may have lost the fight, but he had won the recognition of the boxing world. In fact, when Madison Square Garden ceased hosting boxing in 1993, Bert Sugar's

Boxing Illustrated ranked Salvador Sanchez vs. Azumah Nelson as the seventh most memorable fight at the venue; his hero Jersey Joe Walcott's fight with Joe Louis was ranked third.

"If it was not for my mouthpiece that was missing, I would have won that fight," Azumah still believes to this day. Many Ghanaians believe that had Floyd Robertson been in his corner, the outcome may well have been different, as he would have steered Azumah through those final rounds. Unfortunately, Robertson passed away suddenly in 1983, and he would never witness Azumah fight for a world title again. Azumah asked for a rematch after the fight, but Sanchez and his handlers never answered his request. They knew they had just had a lucky escape, and might not be so lucky the next time around.

Two things happened after the fight that would forever link Azumah to Salvador Sanchez. The first was that he was no longer unknown outside of Ghana. As Carl King, son of Don King, recalls, "Azumah had made everyone sit up after he fought Sanchez. Had he won, the agreement was that Mickey Duff would become his promoter. I said to my dad that we had to promote Azumah, and he said I could try but he did not see how it was possible, as he had his Ghana management, Ringside Management, with John Kermeh overseeing things. Anyway, I spoke to them and Azumah and we did a deal, and we had a hell of a ride. He was one boxer I really got along with. The thing is everyone loves Azumah."

The other event occurred on August 12, 1982. Three weeks after his ninth title defence, the twenty-three-year-old Salvador Sanchez lost his life in a fatal car accident when attempting to pass a tractor with a trailer near his hometown of Santiago Tianguistenco. The boxing world mourned a man regarded by many as one of the top all-time feather-weight champions.

Life, however, goes on, and ironically the man who Azumah replaced to fight Sanchez was given the opportunity to claim his now vacant title. Mario Miranda fought Juan Laporte in September, but lost by a TKO in round ten, the first defeat of his career.

VI

ON TOP OF THE WORLD

With his name fresh on everyone's lips, it was vital that Azumah Nelson made sure that it stayed there if he was to have another crack at the world championship. Linking himself to Don King Promotions in the 1980s was a good move. Following the success of the "Rumble in the Jungle" between George Foreman and Muhammad Ali in Zaire in 1974, Don King was undoubtedly the number-one boxing promoter of the times. He was loud, brash, bombastic, and colourful. What is more, he was everywhere with his distinctive *Eraserhead*-style haircut, a style that was described by the great Ali: "Don King's body did four years in prison, but his hair got the chair."

Many thought that Azumah, ranked number three in the world by the World Boxing Council, would be thrust once more into the ring for another tilt at a world title, but his promoter and his management were in no such hurry. Azumah was, however, back in the ring three months after his bout with Sanchez, with Bobby Lewis from the Don King camp helping him in his corner in this first fight back in the U.S.

On this occasion, he fought at the Americana Great Gorge Resort in McAfee, New Jersey, on the undercard of the Leon Spinks vs. Jesse Burnett fight for the vacant North American Boxing Federation cruiserweight title. He would face a Louisiana-born southpaw based in California, a fringe contender called "Sweet" Irving Mitchell. Mitchell had won all sixteen of his fights since turning professional and eleven by knockout, and was ranked number nine in the WBC rankings. The fight against

Azumah was to be his first defeat, with the referee, Larry Hazard, stepping in to stop the fight in round five, much to Mitchell's frustration.

In February of 1983, Azumah climbed through the ropes again, this time in Don King's hometown of Cleveland, Ohio, where he faced off against Ricky Wallace from Las Vegas. Wallace had started off impressively in the professional ranks with a record of twelve wins, zero losses, and two draws, but was coming off two defeats in his last two fights. He was to lose again with a unanimous points decision going in favour of Azumah. Six months later, Azumah was to have his first fight in Las Vegas, the boxing capital of the world. On this occasion, he would come up against a man who really was not in the same class. Alvin Fowler from Missouri had an impressive amateur record of ninety-one wins and four losses, but had struggled as a professional and had lost ten of his last twelve fights, lasting the distance in only five of them.

The talk in Vegas was that Azumah Nelson was a name that would be around for a while. Fowler took an eight-count after being knocked down in the first round and was duly dispatched by Azumah in round two. A powerful left hook sent Fowler to the canvas, and as he hit the ground, his mouthguard spewed into the air. He gamely got to his feet, but within seconds was back on the floor, and referee Richard Steele stopped the fight after forty-one seconds.

After the fight, Azumah told the viewers on the Don King Sports and Entertainment Network, "Right now, I am mad; I am angry. When I came back this time [to America], I promised my people I would bring a title home, and if I didn't bring the title home, I was not coming back home." Having hardly been tested, Azumah was back in the ring just twenty-seven days later, this time at the Richfield Coliseum in Ohio, where he would face the Pittsburgh-based Puerto Rican Alberto Collazo, who a year earlier had faced the newly crowned featherweight champion, Juan Laporte, and lost by a TKO in the fifth.

Collazo was taking incredible punishment in round two, but with no standing eight-count in the state of Ohio at the time and by staying on his feet, he allowed Azumah to pick him off at will. The fight was thankfully stopped after one minute and twenty seconds of the round by referee Pete Rademacher, who also refereed the Tim Witherspoon vs. James Tillis fight for the vacant NABF heavyweight title on the same bill. It was to prove an easy day at the office for the third man in the ring, as that bout never made it to round two!

In the buildup to these last two fights, Azumah began his training in Accra under the watchful eye of F. A. Moses and then flew to the Don King training camp in Orwell, Ohio, a month before the fight date.

"In the era that Don grew up, when you came into money, the first thing that you did was you bought a country house, just like the Kennedys had, their place in Cape Cod," recalls his son and Azumah's manager, Carl King. "Don bought this land in Orwell, Ohio, and is the longest, biggest land owner in that county with thousands of acres. He had his city house in Cleveland and his country house in Orwell. Just like the Kennedys' house, it had a compound, which had a swimming pool shaped like a fist. He built up the house for his children, Eric, Debbie, and myself, and we all lived on the compound. The compound was for your family just as it was for the Kennedys.

"Down the road, he established the Don King training camp. It was rustic and very basic. It was entirely built out of wood. It was spartan, and sleeping at the camp was in a dormitory style. Even if you didn't like it there, there was not much point sneaking out because there was not much in Orwell, except for a Dairy Queen. It was like being in prison, and that is why it was good for the boxers because it meant that all they had to focus on was their boxing.

"I remember Azumah's management did not like the camp. It was too cold. Azumah would train in the winter snows and he never complained. They were fun times. Although, winter was tough for Azumah, as winter in Ohio is very different from winter in Accra, but I never once heard him complain."

It was during his first stay at the camp that Azumah met a man with whom he would have a long and enjoyable relationship, his trainer Jose "Buffalo" Martin. Carl King remembers it well. "In 1977, when he was training Alfredo Evangelista, was when I first met him—when Evangelista, who was from Uruguay, fought Ali in Maryland. Jose was big like a buffalo, and I think that is where he got his nickname. He did a great job when he came and worked with my dad soon after."

Buffalo was a gentleman to be around. He didn't speak much English initially, but there was never any misunderstanding between him and Azumah. "He had an ability to communicate as a trainer and that was what mattered," recalls King Jr. "From the day they met, Azumah and Buffalo formed a special bond. Language differences and cultural differences never seemed to be an issue between the two of them. They had a special psychic bond, whereby they could communicate without having to speak each other's language. In the heat of the moment in a fight, the two of them always seemed to totally understand each other. It was a unique relationship. I think the two of them were very fond of each other."

Azumah remembers why Buffalo became part of his team and that first meeting. "I met him in Ohio and he was a very funny guy. He said something and he made me laugh. I want to be around people who make me laugh, so I wanted him beside me. When I went to train, I said, 'Let's go,' and he followed me, and he became one of my trainers. He was so happy. He always wanted to help me. He said he would do anything for me. He always made me laugh and would tell me funny stories and do crazy things. He was a great friend, but he was always sleeping—sometimes he would put a cigar in his mouth and he would fall asleep. It would fall out of his mouth and onto his stomach and start to burn him, and he would wake up and brush it away. We would be sitting there in Ghana—me, my wife, my uncle—and he would be smoking a cigar and he would fall asleep. We would laugh at how one day he will burn his house down. The cigar would fall out of his mouth, and when he woke and he realised that we are all looking at him, he would start abusing us, waving his arms and going, 'You stupid people.'"

Azumah established friendships with other fighters at the King training camp. One, in particular, was Tim Witherspoon. "I liked him a lot. He was a good guy," Azumah remembers. "He came to me once and asked me for some advice on his next fight, and I was happy to help him. He won that fight."

After building up his experience and his profile in the U.S., Azumah headed home to Ghana after beating Collazo. He returned because he was due to defend his Commonwealth featherweight title against Nigerian challenger Kabiru Akindele in November in Lagos. It was the second time that Azumah was to defend his title against the Nigerian, having beaten him by a TKO in round six in Sierra Leone just three months after winning the vacant title. This time, the result would be the same, but it would take him until round nine. This would be Akindele's last recorded professional fight.

With his Commonwealth title still safely in his grasp, Azumah crossed the Atlantic again to continue his journey towards the one title he was so desperate to hold: the WBC featherweight champion of the world. In March 1984, he would meet the Los Angeles-based Ecuadorian Hector Cortez at the Las Vegas Convention Center. The fight was to be on the undercard of the WBC world heavyweight title fight between his friend Tim Witherspoon and Greg Page for Larry Holmes's relinquished title. Holmes had opted not to defend his title against Greg Page and had accepted the newly formed IBF title in its place. Page turned up overweight and was outpointed in a close, unspectacular fight. Azumah's fight earlier in the evening also went the distance, and the decision went unanimously his way.

Despite his success, it was hard for Azumah to get another crack at the world title. Former Ghanaian sports minister, Nii Amakai Amarteifio, believes he knows the reasons why it was so hard to get that fight and he and Azumah's management had to make changes. "He [Azumah] was bad news. Not many people had heard of African boxers winning world titles," recalls Amarteifio. "It was not good for business, and that was why he was to be avoided. It took a lot of lobbying and contacts for him to be made the mandatory challenger. This was achieved after the 'civil war' between Gomez and Laporte."

While Azumah had slowly been increasing his stock as a boxer, much had been happening in the featherweight division since the early passing away of Salvador Sanchez. Juan Laporte had defeated Mario Miranda, whom Azumah had replaced in his bout with Sanchez, and Laporte was the new world champion. However, in March of 1984, despite a great deal of controversy surrounding their coming together, Laporte lost his title to Puerto Rican Wilfredo Gomez by unanimous decision in a bout billed as a "civil war" by the promoters.

Gomez was a remarkable boxer. After a draw in his first professional bout as a bantamweight, he had reeled off a streak of thirty-two knockout wins in a row. These thirty-two wins made him the world champion with the longest knockout streak in history.

WBC super bantamweight champion, Dong Kyun Yum of South Korea, who had been watching Gomez climb through the ranks, opted to travel to San Juan, Puerto Rico, to defend his crown against Gomez in May 1977. Yum started promisingly, dropping Gomez just thirty seconds into the fight, but Gomez picked himself up and went on to win the title with a twelfth-round knockout.

In his knockout streak, Gomez defeated some outstanding boxers, including a round-five defeat of world bantamweight champion Carlos Zarate, who was 55-0 with fifty-four knockout wins leading into the bout. After his thirty-second knockout, Gomez moved up a weight to face the world featherweight champion Salvador Sanchez, to whom he lost in round eight by a TKO.

Gomez had been desperate for a rematch with Sanchez, and when news of the champion's tragic accident reached him, Gomez, who was training to defend his title against Mexican Roberto Rubaldino only five days later, took a flight to Mexico to offer his condolences and returned to Puerto Rico the same afternoon.

Gomez left the junior featherweight division to pursue his dream of the featherweight title, but before leaving, he had established a division record of seventeen defences and a world record of the most defences in a row won by knockout. All his title defences had finished before the established distance limit. In March 1984, he squared off against fellow Puerto Rican, Juan Laporte, at Roberto Clemente Coliseum in San Juan, Puerto Rico. He achieved his dream, winning by a twelve-round unanimous decision.

Azumah was far from happy during this period. "I was annoyed because I wanted to fight Laporte," he recalls. "Gomez wanted the fight, too, because he knew he could beat Laporte; he was slow, and he could hit him and move. Laporte was strong and I thought he would win, but the way I looked at it, he wanted to make some money before he lost the title to me. By promoting the fight in Puerto Rico, both of them were going to make money. I knew that when my chance came, I would knock Gomez out. If I do not knock him out, I will not win, not with the fight in Puerto Rico. I was very frustrated. I knew the fight would happen, as I was the number-one contender and there was no way he could run. He had run so much, but he could no longer hide. I was just patiently waiting for him, preparing to fight him. I wanted to beat him so bad, but because they wanted the fight in Puerto Rico, I knew that they had all the chances to rob me. I knew I would win and I would knock him out.

"I knew when I fought Hector Cortez that he was the champion, and he knew he had to fight me, but he found a way to fight Laporte before me. So I waited for a year and then I know I am the number-one contender, and he has to have a mandatory defence with me. If not, he has to relinquish the title, and I will fight the number-two-ranked boxer. The press asked me how the fight would go, and I said, 'Listen, tell him to prepare very well. He is not going to keep the title.' This is my time. I will be the champion and nothing will change it.

"For this fight, I prepared the longest I had ever prepared for a fight. I went to America and spent two to three months at Don King's camp in Ohio. I was so focused. I told everyone, 'Tell him to get ready, 'cos I will knock him out.' I trained like crazy, climbing hills, chopping wood—it was like a *Rocky* movie. I worked so hard. I trained for six months for this fight, three in Ghana and three in America. I never trained harder. I was confident for this fight and knew I would knock him out."

As the number-one contender, Azumah was the first opponent against whom Wilfredo Gomez would have to defend his world title. The fight was scheduled for December 8, 1984, and it would take place at the Hiram Bithorn Stadium in San Juan, Puerto Rico. Azumah was once again the underdog, with many experts believing the South American would be too strong for the African.

In an interview with *Inside Boxing* magazine, Azumah had no doubt as to who was going to win. "I don't care who I fight," he said. "I'll knock anyone out. I'm not going to be knocked out. Anytime I got the chance, I'll prove it. I'll prove to the world that I'm the best featherweight. My record is eighteen-one with fifteen knockouts."

Being given a second chance to win the title and having come so close against Sanchez, Azumah was determined to make sure he had no regrets when it came to this fight. He had locked himself away at the Don King camp, leaving his family back in Ghana. "I was not happy being there for so long with my family back at home because I did not know how they were. There were no cell phones or Internet in those times. I did not know what was happening at home—if they did not have money or food. My wife was there with my baby son, and as head of the family, it was my job to take care of them, and I worried about them. But I knew that if I won the title, I would get money and would be able to make my family happy. That was all I thought about."

Despite never saying anything publicly at the time, all these years later, Azumah is still annoyed that it took so long for him to get a second chance at winning a world title. "Two years was too long. After Sanchez in one year, I have to get a title shot," he says. "Gomez was hiding—he did not want to fight me because he knew I was too strong. That was why we had the fight in Puerto Rico, because he knew if he could stay on his feet after twelve rounds, he would win. I was twenty-five; I knew I would be champion, but the year and the date I did not know. I knew that if you become champion earlier, you can hold it longer before you get old. So I was ready.

"We went to Puerto Rico about ten days before the fight. The press was there every day when I was training and asking questions: 'How do you feel? What do you think? What do you think of Gomez?' I told them I am going to knock him out. I have come to take the title and I am going to take the title to Africa."

Azumah's mood was not helped prior to the fight at a press conference held in San Juan. "At the press conference, he [Gomez] said that he knew Africans where I come from are hungry, and after the fight, I will be more hungry. I was with our sports minister, and he looked at my face and asked if I heard what he said. I said, 'Yes, but he will pay for it.' On the night of the fight when the time came and we went to the auditorium, they put us in some air-conditioned room for the warm-up. It was very cold, and I think there were people fighting with Carl [King] over this. I did not concentrate on all that was going on as Carl complained. I was so focused on the fight."

When Azumah climbed through the ropes in his red trunks with white trim, he had very few supporters in the stadium willing him on, but back in Ghana, the fight was being telecast for those lucky enough to own a television. Wherever there was a television, there were people crowded around, listening, watching, and craning for a view of the screen, all hoping a Ghanaian could conquer the world.

The first round saw Azumah dominate the centre of the ring, but neither boxer dominated and few punches were thrown. A series of left jabs at the start of the second had the champion off-balance as Azumah started to go on the attack. In this round, both fighters were happy to stand toe-to-toe and try and pick the other off, each landing some good punches in what was again a very even round.

Gomez went on the attack in round three, but a strong defence by Azumah meant that 90 per cent of his punches missed their target, and when he came in close, he was peppered with fast punches that found both his body and his head. In round four, Gomez was told to keep his punches up, but was caught by a powerful right hook that rocked him and had the crowd on their feet. For the rest of the round, he was hanging on and took another powerful right hook to the head.

"I told him to be ready and he prepared very well," Azumah recalls. "Some of the punches I threw were very hard, and he took some of them and stayed standing. It was then that I knew he was a good champion—no question about that, a very good champion—and he had a good right hand, too."

Azumah came out showboating at the start of the fifth and danced his way around the ring out of the reach of the champion, and when Gomez did try and move in, he soon found himself moving backwards. Despite landing his jab, it was not enough to stop Azumah from pushing forward and landing some powerful punches from angles that Gomez failed to see coming.

"I know even if we went twelve rounds, I will knock him out. I had planned everything about how to fight him. From one to four, from four to eight, eight to twelve—this is where he has to be stopped, from round ten to twelve. I have planned how to fight him and we go in there and box, and in the second to third, I am putting pressure on him. In four, as well, I keep up the pressure. After round four, I blocked his punches. If you learn to block, you can rest, but also the more you block, he cannot score, so you are putting pressure on him. When he was tired, I pushed him away; I worked my legs," Azumah recalls.

Gomez was slow to come out at the start of round six, but caught Azumah with a big left that had the crowd on its feet and lifted the noise level in the stadium twofold. Despite him landing more scoring shots, Azumah continued to push forward and force the champion to fight an uncustomary style, moving backwards and counterpunching. At the start of the seventh, Azumah backed the champion against the ropes and landed some thunderous rights to the head, yet Gomez managed to fight his way out and return some heavy blows of his own. Azumah was hit on more than one occasion by a low blow, yet the referee only warned the champion and never deducted a point. At the end of the round, as both fighters stood facing each other, Azumah said something that caused the champion to lash out after the bell. Luckily, Mexican referee, Octavio Meyran, quickly came between the two.

Despite more low blows and no point deduction, it was Azumah who dictated terms, thrusting his jab into Gomez's face and forcing him back. "He became very tired, and his legs were gone in round eight," Azumah remembers. "I said to him at the end of the round, 'C'mon, I told you to be ready.' I knew I had it after round eight. I knew I would win. I kept applying pressure."

Halfway through round nine, the weary-looking Gomez was caught by a bludgeoning right from Azumah that rocked him all the way to his boots. Somehow, he managed to stay on his feet, and like a true champion, even stunned the challenger with a straight left. When the bell sounded, both fighters were toe-to-toe pummeling each other, and again the referee had to step in and separate them. With his mouth open, Gomez was clearly fatigued. In round ten, his attacks were sporadic while Azumah's were constant. With less than a minute to go in the round, a big right hand from Azumah caught Gomez flush on the chin, and he again did well to stay on his feet and last until the bell.

Within the first minute of the eleventh round, Azumah crashed a right hand through Gomez's defence, and the champion stumbled forward and hung on to Azumah, who desperately tried to shake him free like a piece of paper stuck to his shoe. When he did, he clubbed Gomez with two more right hands, and the champion hung on. Gomez backed onto the ropes after breaking from the clinch, and with his defence virtually nonexistent, Azumah picked him off with right hands at will. Again, the champion held on, and the referee moved both fighters to the centre of the ring. A sneaky punch on the break by Gomez showed just how desperate he had become to hang on to his title.

The stadium erupted with everyone chanting his name as one, willing him to stay on his feet, yet sensing the inevitable, the unbelievable. An uppercut from Azumah shook the soon-to-be-deposed champion again, and blood started to spill from his mouth. Azumah stalked him around the ring and lined up right hand after right hand past a defence that had disintegrated. The tape on Gomez's left-hand glove had come loose and offered him the chance of some respite, but the referee chose to ignore it. With thirty seconds left in the round, Azumah allowed Gomez to move off the ropes, making space to crash a left hook into the side of the champion's head; Gomez lurched forward, and Azumah stepped aside and hit him with a right hook as he went past. Gomez stumbled across the ring and down onto the canvas.

He was on his feet at the count of four and took the mandatory eight-count before the third man in the ring waved the two fighters together. A left hook followed by a straight right and then Gomez's legs looked to buckle under him. As he slumped to the ground, another left hook sealed his fate. Bravely, he tried to climb to his feet again, but where the mind was willing, the body definitely was not, and he flopped to the canvas with the referee supporting him. His championship crown had been knocked convincingly from his head.

Pandemonium reigned in the ring. Azumah's corner hoisted the new champion high into the air while the deposed champion lay where he fell, eventually managing to walk groggily back to his corner past the flag of Ghana, which was being waved behind the head of the new WBC featherweight champion of the world, Azumah Nelson.

Azumah was always a compassionate boxer, and even with the passing of time, he believes the fight should have ended sooner than it did. "When I knocked him down in round eleven, he was dazed. The referee had to stop the fight, but the referee tried to help him and let him carry on. I came in and I feigned him and then threw a straight right, and he fell to the ground. He was not supposed to take that punch, and he wouldn't have had to if the referee stopped it when he should have."

Despite the adrenaline still coursing through his veins, Azumah's celebrations were relatively muted. Here was a man who had finally achieved his goal in life. He had climbed to the top of the tree. From the humblest of beginnings in a corner of Africa few people had heard of, he could now call himself the champion of the world. Yet as usual, Azumah's celebrations were kept in check.

"When I threw that punch, I am not surprised that I have won and I am the world champion because I knew I would win," he recalls. "I am not thinking I am the champion in the ring. I was thanking God for making it all possible, for showing me that I would do it one day and that now I had. He makes me cry because he loves me so much, and I don't know why. I am very lucky."

With local fans far from happy that their man had been knocked out and lost his title, Azumah and his team had to find a way back to the dressing room as quickly as possible. His entourage made a human shield around the newly crowned champ, and they moved as quickly as possible down the aisle.

Carl King, who made up part of that human wall, remembers that night well. "He had a great fight that night with Gomez, who was a very solid fighter, but Azumah was determined he was going to win the world title. He went to Puerto Rico and took the title from Gomez in his hometown. We had death threats after the fight, telling us we would not leave the country, and as we were leaving the ring, I was stabbed in my leg. I say stabbed but it was a slash of a razor that went through my pants and cut my leg. The cut was so smooth in all the jostling; I did not feel it until we were safe. My leg was wet and I thought it was just a drink that had been thrown at us. Then I realised that it was my own blood. I had to have it treated once in the dressing room. It was very scary and a night I will never forget, as I have the scar to remind me!"

In Ghana, there was a very different mood. The euphoria that greeted the victory was too incredible for words. Even though it was the middle of the night, people poured out onto the streets in celebration. Peter Zwennes, who was at university, recalls, "The Ghanaian government had bought the television rights so that the whole country could watch the fight, as long as they could get near a television. But at the start of the fight, there were problems with the satellite feed and we could not see the pictures. We could only hear the voices, and then we lost that. It was only by round six that it came back with a picture. So in between, we were scrambling around, trying to find a radio to hear the commentary, but we could not find it on any of the airwaves. We were glued to our sets and we were getting apprehensive, as we could see Azumah was clearly winning the fight, but the ringside commentators kept saying how Gomez was leading, and we knew he would need a knockout to win, and that is precisely what he did, in round eleven.

"At that time, the whole of Ghana cut loose. It was about two a.m., and people just ran out into the streets. If you had a car, you were in it, hooting your horn. At the university campus where I was, all the students came out of the campuses and there was a big procession to Accra. It was something you can never forget."

Back in Puerto Rico when the fight concluded, the commentators hailed Azumah as the sixth African to become champion of the world, yet there are question marks around this statement. Willie Smith, a bantamweight from South Africa, is credited as being the first champion to come out of Africa. He was considered world champion, having won the Olympic gold medal in 1924. Following him was Vic Toweel, another South African bantamweight, in 1950.

Nigerian Hogan "Kid" Bassey, whose real name was Okun Asuguo Bassey, became the next champion from the continent when he won the world crown, defeating the French Algerian Cherif Hamia in Paris, France, in 1957. Another bantamweight from South Africa, Arnold Taylor, claimed a world title in 1973, and two years later, David Kotei, aka D. K. Poison, for whom Azumah had been a sparring partner, claimed the WBC featherweight title when he defeated Mexican Ruben Olivares. Peter Mathebula from South Africa won the WBA flyweight title in

1980, and fellow South African Gerrie Coetzee won the WBA heavyweight title in 1983 when he knocked out Michael Dokes with a punch that hurt Coetzee even more than Dokes: His right hand was broken and required surgery five days after the fight.

This would mean that Azumah was the eighth world champion to come out of Africa; however, even that boast can be questioned, as several fighters were forced to leave Africa to gain a crack at a world title and fought under the flags of their adopted colonial homelands. Battling Siki from Senegal would be one of the most famous fights. Having moved to France and served in the military, in 1922, he faced the popular Georges Carpentier for the world light heavyweight title. The fight took place in Paris on September 24. Siki claimed that prior to the fight, he had agreed to take a dive, but when Carpentier dropped him, the outraged African decided to get up and fight. In the sixth round, Siki hit Carpentier with a powerful right uppercut that knocked the champion down and out for the count. The referee, remarkably, claimed that Siki had tripped Carpentier, and awarded the bout to the unconscious champion on a foul. With the crowd in a riotous mood, the three ringside judges overruled the referee and eventually declared Siki the champion. Then there was Victor Perez from Tunisia, who won the International Boxing Union's flyweight title in 1931; he also fought under the French colonial flag. In 1962, Dick Tiger from Nigeria, who fought out of Britain and the U.S., won the WBC and WBA middleweight titles when he defeated Joey Giardello, and then won the WBC and WBA light heavyweight title in 1966 after defeating Jose Torres.

Ugandan Ayub Kalule, who won the WBA light middleweight crown in 1979, fought out of Denmark and is often forgotten as having been an African boxer and one of the best. Cornelius Boza-Edwards, who became a good friend of Azumah's and was another Ugandan who migrated to England, won the WBC super featherweight title in 1981.

In truth, it mattered not how many African champions had come before him; all that mattered was that Azumah Nelson was now a world champion, just as he had told everyone he would be. When he returned to Ghana, his reception was unprecedented. A nation poured out its affection, and for a few days forgot about the hardships it was experiencing, as it had something very special to celebrate. For Jacob Zwennes, it was a day he will never forget. "For me, the day of his arrival when he came back with the title was indescribable," Zwennes recalls.

"We had the enviable task of picking up Beatrice and the champ's eldest son, David—in the same rickety Ford we used to pick him up to take him to the gym—and take them to the airport. We left home in the early morning, around four a.m., and got to Mamprobi and The Hawk, where we picked up Uncle Harry's wife, Aunty Sarah. Then we went to the Palladium area where Beatrice lived. Then we drove to the airport where the festivities started. He landed at about six-fifteen or six-thirty in the morning, and day was just about breaking. The moon was hanging out there, waiting to leave, and the sun was rising when the flight came in with the headlamps very bright.

"When he came off the plane, there were two groups of fans waiting for him. There were the guys from Mamprobi, where he and his dad lived, and the folks from Adenkpo around the Palladium area, where his mum and his family lived. So there were two groups and they were taking turns to sing and drum. It was so colourful, and the atmosphere was so charged when the plane landed. It will live with me forever.

"I remember Beatrice because she was so calm. She was waving a white cloth and smiling. She was very laid back and very calm. She was excited, but was hiding it. When he landed, she rushed towards him with his son.

"Not everyone was allowed into the VIP lounge or onto the tarmac, and we were very lucky that we had access to the tarmac because we were with Beatrice. When we came out of the main building, there were literally tens of thousands of people outside waiting to welcome him home and hail him as the champion. It took us a good eight hours to get back to Mamprobi. There was a procession through the streets, and the traffic was jam-packed. There was a detour to The Castle [the seat of government in Ghana] to be welcomed home by President J. J. Rawlings. People skipped work and school, and the celebrations went on for a week. At that point, Azumah announced he had arrived on the world stage."

Such a public outpouring of emotion by the people touched Azumah deeply, and the memory of it and the feeling it gave him still brings a smile to his face today. "Beatrice had stayed in Accra for the Gomez fight, but she was very happy—very, very happy—when she met me at the airport. But that win, it did not change anything, she was so sensible. When I arrived at the airport, the VIPs were waiting for me when I came in. I was so happy to be home with my family. When we walked outside of the airport building, there were so many people waiting. It was incredible. When I saw all the people, it made me so happy because I always want to make my people happy. It was so special that because of me, the nation was happy. I remember then I wished I could win all the time so that they could be this happy forever.

"I always did my best in every fight because the people helped me so much. 'Azumah, you are my hero. I can't sleep when you are fighting!' one shouted. Another said, 'I am a student and my parents woke me up to watch you fight even though there was school the next day.' People would say all these things to me and it made me happy. I put happiness on people's faces, and that is the best thing anyone can do. I thank God for passing through me to make this possible.

"It was tough at that time in Ghana. We had yellow cones where you had to queue for food to eat—it was not easy. So it was special to put a smile on people's faces when the country needed it. Every fight I fought, I felt it was important not just for my nation, but also for Africa. It was important at that time to prove to the Africans that a black man could rule the world, and to prove that whatever you are doing, you have to do it well."

Another person who was extremely proud of his achievement was the one person who had never really wanted him to box: his mother. "When he became world champion, I was standing on my feet. I was very proud. We went to the stadium and J. J. [President J. J. Rawlings]— he knows me very well—said, 'You are the one who gave the power to Azumah.' He was a very nice man. My father was very strong, so I think my boy had his strength. He was very important to Ghana, Azumah. He respects everyone, so everyone likes him. He didn't start to talk roughly to people. He is kind and he is beautiful. I am proud of him. Some of the boxers did not do what Azumah was doing. They did not respect people. I am so proud of my son."

VII

TITLE DEFENCE

Having reached the top of the world is sadly often when the problems start for many athletes, and Azumah was no different. As his mother, Madam Comfort, explains, "Ever since he was a small boy, he has tried his best for me, not for our family, but for me. When we are at Timber Market and he has become world champion, some of our family do not like me. They are jealous of my son. They make my life very hard. So he took me from there and bought my house in Dansoman."

She believes such responsibilities should not have fallen to her eldest son. "I am the one who gave birth to him, and he has tried for everyone to make Ghana proud. But the people don't look after the parents who gave him to Ghana. Charm Chituele was champion, and in Zambia they did. Azumah bought my house, but the government have done nothing. He is the one who went and fought, and the money is his. I am lucky he is responsible to take care of his mother."

Azumah was never likely to forget where he came from or his friends, and in the coming years he would try and give all of them work. He started a transportation business with a truck operating in West Africa, but after every trip, the truck would come back needing something replaced. Either the spare tyre had been "stolen" or the radio had broken. Always something happened.

"Whenever I got money, I gave it to my friends so that they could buy clothes for their children or themselves and their wives could get dresses," he explains. "I bought a truck for a transportation business, but they were using it to move marijuana, ghetto blasters, lots of things, and whenever it came back from a trip, all the money we should have made on the shipments was spent on repairs. All these boys did bad things—they were stealing from me when I was trying to help them. I knew that they had done wrong, but I still could not forget about them. There were seven or eight of us from the time we were hustlers, and we were close. I have helped others from the areas where I grew up. I bought the coffin for one who died recently. I have done bad things, but God has forgiven me. So I should forgive them, as they do not know God.

"I had a factory making pots to cook with for four or five years, but they stole from me there, taking money, and I had to close it down. I also had an alcohol shop for two years, but stopped that business, as they and young boys were drinking the alcohol without paying for it. They could not understand that this was stealing and that someone had to pay for what they were drinking."

Obi is one friend who has stayed true to Azumah over all these years, and he has no doubt that becoming the champion of the world did not change him at all. He explains why. "Why does everyone love him? He is a character; he is so humble. He knows how to speak with common people. He is kind to everyone. He is funny and kind.

"One day, we are in the ghetto and we are sitting at a place where they are gambling, and there is a lady carrying *foo-foo* that she is going to sell. Some schoolchildren were playing and they ran and hit her, and all the food fell down into the dirt. She started crying and then the children started crying. Azumah saw them and he got up and went over and asked her how much the food was worth. Then he gave her the money and asked her to stop crying. He also gave some money to the children. Everybody was just looking. Some people can have a million dollars in their pocket, but they will not give anything. 'It is only money,' he says. He is someone who will give every last bit of money to give someone food. He is a very good man."

On another occasion, when driving through Bukom, Azumah spotted someone he had known when he was a boy. "The old lady who had been buying bottles when I was a child saw me. I was now a champion. I told the driver to stop and I went to her. 'My son, how are you?' she said to me. 'My mum, I am good,' I replied. 'These days you don't bring bottles to me. I don't see you.' So I left her and I came back with a bundle of money. She did not know I was a champion. She held the money and looked at it. She stood there crying. 'See you again,' she said. I gave my money because I like to share it and help people."

Another time, Azumah was visiting the Attuquaye Clottey academy, and on seeing him, the lady there shouted, "Thief, thief!"

"I said, 'No, no,' and we both laughed about it. The reason she shouted this at me that time was because the man I hit when he caught me holding the rubber was there. He had moved to Germany, and when he was back, he asked who Azumah Nelson was. I was now the champion, and they told him it was the boy who hit him. He laughed and said he was not surprised. He said, 'You are a bad boy,' and I said, 'No. I am a champion.' We both laughed about that time when I was a boy."

Having achieved his goal of winning a world title, Azumah was determined that he was not going to give up his hard-earned status easily. There were rumours that Gomez wanted a rematch and the chance to win back his title, but Azumah was not so sure. "They said Gomez wanted a rematch, but I was the champion. I took the title, so it is was my decision. I said to him, 'Maybe you were not ready. I will give you a rematch; it is not a problem. Just name it and you get it.' But I don't think he really wanted it. I think he watched the fight afterwards when he was relaxed, and when he did, I think he realised, as it says in the Bible in Ecclesiastes, chapter three, verse one, 'There is a time for everything.'"

There are some who say Gomez was waiting to see who came through with an offer first, junior lightweight world champion Rocky Lockridge or Azumah Nelson. Whatever the truth, he ended up fighting Lockridge and won a closely scored unanimous decision over fifteen rounds in San Juan. Azumah would not defend his title for nine months, which allowed him time to relax with Beatrice and his children and take a holiday.

Though many thought he was simply taking time out, the truth was very different, as Nii Amakai Amarteifio explains. "After Gomez and with the euphoria, the reception, the celebration, the hero worship—and Ghanaians are prone to going to extremes—it had an effect on him, a psychological effect. He was supposed to defend the title in Miami, and there were opponents lined up, but for a champion after he has won the title, you do not give him another hard fight. You give him a soft option.

"He had a psychological problem getting into the ring again for the next fight: 'What would happen if I lost? Look at what my country's people did for me. Goodness me.' You know, you really have to clear these things in your mind, and it took a long time. His next fight was a long time after the Gomez fight for this reason. He had to be really, really carefully prepared for the next fight, which he was. Once he overcame that fear of not succeeding, of letting the people down, I knew he would be a great champion."

It was September of 1985 that saw him return to the ring to make a mandatory defence of his title against Chilean Juvenal Ordenes. The fight would take place at the Tamiami Fairgrounds Auditorium in Miami, Florida. Ordenes was ranked number three by the WBC and the WBA going into this fight, and had lost just two of his previous thirty-seven bouts: one to Hector Cortez on a split-decision and one against Angel Mayor nine months earlier by unanimous decision in their fight for the WBC Continental Americas featherweight title.

Azumah, in trunks the colours of the Ghanaian flag, controlled the centre of the ring in the opening round. Both boxers sized each other up, sportingly touching gloves as they returned to their respective corners. Round two saw them both use the jab to try and find a way through the other's defence; Azumah snapped his jabs out, and they landed with more regularity than his opponent's.

In rounds three and four, Azumah held his gloves high in front of his face in a peek-a-boo style, and as Ordenes looked to fire out his jab to the head and then the body, Azumah deflected many away with his gloves and his elbows. When he went on the attack, the angles from which he threw his punches caught Ordenes by surprise, and the ferocity of the blows forced the Chilean backwards.

In round five, it was all over. Azumah went on the attack. The punch that did the damage was a right uppercut that caught Ordenes flush on the jaw; a right hook followed this as Ordenes's arms dropped, and then a left as his legs gave way and he slumped to the canvas. Bravely, he beat the count, lifting himself back to his feet with the help of the ropes.

Referee Steve Crossan brushed off his gloves and called the two to box on. Azumah came running out of the neutral corner and rained punches into the body and the head of Ordenes, who tried in vain to deflect them. Within thirty seconds, Ordenes slumped down against the corner post. He tried to rise at the count of seven, but was unable to beat the count. Azumah's first world title defence had been emphatic, and he was hoisted high in the ring by trainer Jose Martin, a broad grin sweeping across his face.

Incredibly, within six weeks, Azumah was back in the ring defending his title again, something that would be unheard of today. This time, he would head to England to meet Pat Cowdell, a fellow Commonwealth gold medal winner and an Olympic bronze medal winner from the 1976 Montreal games.

Cowdell had turned professional in 1977 and had also fought the late Salvador Sanchez; like Azumah, he had taken him fifteen rounds and had also been put on the canvas in the last round. But unlike Azumah, he had managed to last until the final bell only to lose by a split-decision. It looked to be a strong match up and was eagerly anticipated by British fight fans, who rated their man's chances of taking the world title.

Cowdell was the European junior lightweight champion; although, he had won his Commonwealth and Olympic medals as a bantamweight. With both fighters remembered for their bouts against Sanchez, the fight was appealing to American television audiences, which was good news for promoters Don King and Frank Warren. It would also be the second world featherweight title bout hosted by Great Britain that year. Irishman Barry McGuigan had recently outpointed Eusebio Pedroza at Loftus Road, the home of the Queens Park Rangers Football Club, to win the WBA version.

In fact, so excited were the British about the fight and Cowdell's chances that there had been a huge debate at the BBC, which planned to broadcast the fight, over whether it should drop its regular news bulletin for the live coverage of the fight. The news department won out, the BBC deciding that nothing must get in the way of traditional programming. It was a decision that it would regret.

Prior to the fight, there was an argument over the bandaging of the boxers' hands, with Azumah's team not happy with Cowdell's team using more than the regulated length of bandages. But once this was settled, it was time for both boxers to enter the ring. Azumah had predicted a swift victory, but few could have anticipated what would happen. The fight was over before the news on the BBC had even finished. In fact, it lasted just two minutes and twenty-four seconds.

Cowdell's tactics surprised many. He abandoned his usual style, which had been described as "cagey and elusive," and decided to take the fight to the champion. There was only ever one likely outcome. Cowdell fired off a left jab and left his arm outstretched between Nelson's gloves; a right to the body enabled him to make space to back off the champion, and as he looked to throw a left hook, Azumah unleashed a swinging left hook-cum-uppercut that landed flush on his jaw. Cowdell fell straight back like a tree being felled.

He lay on the canvas with his arms out in a crucifix position and his head under the ropes. He momentarily raised his head at the count of eight, but if his mind was willing, his body most definitely was not. He had been knocked out before he hit the canvas and remained there for several worrying minutes.

Azumah, not surprisingly, remembers this fight very clearly. "He is ready to fight me. He is fit, but he made a big mistake: He is overconfident," he recalls. "Too much of anything is bad, and he was too confident. He is a tall guy and he needs to jab and move, but when the bell went, he just came to me straight on. I have prepared to chase him and put pressure on him, and when he got tired, knock him out. But when the bell sounded, he came running straight at me, throwing punches—boom, boom, boom. I started going back and I said to myself, *No, no, no. This guy is making a big mistake. You do not have to fight like that.* I went boom and he went down, and he did not wake up.

"He just came out punching. You do not have to fight like that. No one can fight me like that, even those who are strong, so how can he hope to beat me? He is not a fighter, so he needs to box to beat me. He needed to jab and move, and then he has a chance. I think his corner did not advise him well because his corner should have watched me fight so they can tell him how to stand against Azumah Nelson. He needed to move and jab and see how things were. When I hit him, he had not warmed up enough, and that is why he went down. His body was not ready to take that punch. I think he was excited to fight for a world title. He had fought Sanchez and went the distance, so maybe he thought because of this he was going to take me out. But he was wrong—you cannot beat Azumah Nelson that way."

Sadly for Azumah, he then had to endure racist abuse from a small section of the crowd, with some even trying to get into the ring to attack him. The small group of fans supporting the champion was not so lucky: They were attacked, as was American heavyweight Sam Scaff, who was pushed over and kicked by these mindless thugs. Sam had been defeated earlier in the evening by Azumah's friend, Tim Witherspoon, who had by now won and lost the WBC heavyweight title.

Azumah brushes aside claims that the abuse had racist overtones, saying it was more to do with the speed in which he dispatched his opponent. "I told everyone if they want to see the fight to come early because we are going to finish this fight early," he says. "But they did not listen to me, and when I knocked him out in the first round, some people had not come in yet. They were annoyed they had paid all that money and the fight was over. They were mad: How come we finished the fight so quickly? So they started fighting with our people because they lost their money, and they blamed them because I was their fighter. I felt bad, as they needed to understand it is was a game, and I did tell them to be there early!"

Cowdell, when he eventually came around, wept in his manager Paddy Lynch's arms. "It was my dream to be world champion, but it wasn't meant to be. It was a terrific punch—I never saw it," he said.

Azumah's knockout blow also brought talk of a dream million-pound title unification bout for Cowdell with Barry McGuigan, the WBA champion, to an end. It did, however, start talk of a unification bout between Azumah and McGuigan, and open up debate among fans and media alike as to who was the best featherweight champion.

Azumah's extended absence from the ring before his return fight against Ordenes, which was not televised nationally in the U.S., meant he had slipped from people's minds. McGuigan, meanwhile, had defeated

Eusebio Pedroza, who at the time was boxing's longest reigning champion in any weight division, and had defended his title against a highly rated Bernard Taylor.

Following his victory over Cowdell, Azumah made his intentions clear: "I want to prove that I am the best in the world. Now I want McGuigan. I will knock him out, too. I'll fight him anytime, anywhere. He could not go four rounds with me. I'm too strong," he said.

Carl King, Azumah's manager, was also on the front foot, throwing down a challenge to the Irish champion. "We want to take this opportunity to challenge Barry McGuigan," he said. "We know that Azumah Nelson is the best featherweight in the world, and unless Barry McGuigan is a coward, which I know he's not, the Republic of Ireland won't let him turn down this open public challenge that we are now making."

It was definitely the fight everyone wanted to see. Don King, who held a promotional contract with Azumah, offered both fighters a $1.5 million purse for a unification bout. British promoter Frank Warren also made a substantial offer to promote the fight, but McGuigan's manager, Barney Eastwood, turned down both offers. "Barry will take on this guy on our conditions. We don't need him, but he needs Barry. To my mind, Barry is the true world champion," Eastwood was quoted as saying.

This caused Carl King to respond. "I think McGuigan's people are afraid of us," he replied. "I feel I've got the best featherweight in the world, and I certainly don't have any problems about fighting him. I'm just afraid that someone is going to soften McGuigan up before Nelson can get to him, and I wouldn't want that to happen. I'd like for Nelson to be the one to take him out there."

While the war of words raged and the management of the two fighters tried to sort out a deal, Azumah was back in training, preparing for another defence of his WBC title. Azumah may have dreamt of winning the world title, but unlike many boxers, he was not worried about putting it on the line and fighting all the top contenders. "I was not worried, as I believe that God was with me," he explains. "It was his plan to make me a world champion, and he was with me, win or lose. If I lose, people may say, 'Why did God let you lose?' If that happened, I believed that it was meant to be, and he is going to open a new path to me. I was never worried about losing my title, and I loved to fight."

Four months after his victory over Pat Cowdell, he was at the Inglewood Forum in Los Angeles to meet Mexican Marcos Villasana. "Marcos Villasana was a very good boxer, very aggressive, a very strong boy," Azumah recalls. "He was slim but tough. He could take all the punches I threw at him, and he kept coming forward, throwing punches. It is good to fight people like Villasana, tough people, strong boxers who can take punches and throw them. It is good to fight them because it lets you know your standard of boxing. It tests you and makes you be at your best. Every fight is your biggest challenge. Boxing is boxing; the unexpected can happen. Boom and you find yourself on the floor. Even a boxer who you think will give you no trouble can hit you with one punch and catch you by surprise. A boxer you know you can knock out in the first or second round can close his eyes and throw a punch and catch you on the jaw and knock you out. You always have to be careful. That is why boxing is so tough; you must concentrate. Against Villasana, I knew I had to concentrate.

"When I entered the ring and I saw the flag, I saw Ghana. I saw the people who were cheering me. It made me stronger, as I had to put a smile on their faces. Mexicans are strong and they can knock you out. You cannot show them that you are feeling the punches, or that will give them the strength to knock you out. He hit me with some very hard punches, but I was strong and I was still looking to try and knock him out. We were both very tired and we had to finish hard. Some people fight one way and put their hands up and try and stay in the final rounds and throw a few punches, but you have to give your opponent the chance to see a fault so that he will come in and try and knock you out. Sometimes you need to change your style to beat your opponent, to suck him in and knock him out. The promoter called this fight "the fight for life" because he knew Villasana was a tough guy and he knew I was a tough guy, so whoever won, his life would be changed."

It was a bruising encounter. Despite Villasana pushing forward throughout, Azumah continued to score. In the final round, he was up on his toes, Muhammad Ali-style, firing out quick-fire jabs into the face of Villasana. When the bell sounded for the end of round twelve, the two boxers embraced, showing mutual respect for each other. Villasana's face showed just how many of Azumah's punches had found their mark, while the champion's face was virtually unblemished.

At the end of the twelve rounds and with both men still standing, it came down to the judges as to who was the victor. While the California State Boxing Commission collected the cards from the three judges and added up the scores, Villasana's corner hoisted him high in the air, and the local Mexican support hailed the man they believed was the new champion.

The scores were handed to the ring announcer, Jimmy Lennon Sr., who announced first that American judge James Jen-Kin scored it a draw, 114–114. Lennon kept the drama going when he announced that Rudy Ortega scored it 113–116 and Lou Filippo scored it 112–116, before confirming that Azumah had retained his world title.

Needless to say, the Mexicans inside the Inglewood Forum were far from happy, believing that their man had won. "I was not surprised," Azumah says. "Mexicans are huge boxing fans—they love boxing and they want their man to win every time he climbs in the ring. So I was not surprised that they said he won. I said to him after the fight, 'Okay, I will give you another chance,' which I did."

The two did meet again sixteen months later at the Olympic Auditorium in Los Angeles, California. Neither boxer, though, had been idle during that time. Villasana had fought three times for two wins and a technical draw against Puerto Rican Aristides Acevedo, following a cut on his left eyebrow by an unintentional head butt; at the same venue, he was to meet Azumah.

Azumah, too, had fought three times. He had dispatched Mexican Mauro Gutierrez by knockout in round six in Nevada five months earlier in another title defence fight. Prior to that, he had climbed into the ring on a rare occasion in his homeland of Ghana to defeat fellow countryman Aaron Duribe, also by knockout in round six. This fight had come about at the last minute when a scheduled bout at the Alexandra Palace in London for the third of December against Ramon Flores fell through. The fight in Ghana was supposed to be an exhibition bout, but the champion still had to show his class by disposing of his opponent and not allowing him to last the distance.

It was, however, his fight on June 22, 1986, against the Dominican Republic's Danilo Cabrera in San Juan that would have a major impact on his career. The following day, WBA champion Barry McGuigan was to defend his title in Las Vegas against American Steve Cruz, a late replacement for Fernando Sosa of Argentina. With both fighters being claimed the best in their division, comparisons were inevitable, and victory to both would almost certainly lead to more demand for a unification bout.

McGuigan's previous title defence had been against Cabrera, who, as he was against Nelson, had been drafted in as a late replacement. Azumah had been due to meet Juan LaPorte, but the former champion was forced to withdraw due to a rib injury suffered during sparring. McGuigan had knocked Cabrera out in a controversial fashion in the fourteenth round. Cabrera had bent over to pick up his mouthguard, which had fallen out—a practice allowed in many countries but not in Ireland. The challenger was not aware of this, and the fight was stopped.

"Having been a late replacement when I fought Salvador Sanchez, I knew that Cabrera would have nothing to lose fighting me, and he had a chance to upset me," Azumah recalls. "I had been preparing for LaPorte, who was a different fighter than Cabrera—he was taller—so I had to change my style to suit the opponent. I predicted that I would knock him out in round seven because I wanted to show McGuigan that I was better than him."

In round five, Cabrera was about to go down when the bell sounded. Azumah was on top throughout this fight, showboating and dancing in front of his opponent with his hands by his side. One thing he would have enjoyed was the television commentator comparing him to his childhood idol, Jersey Joe Walcott, as he walked across the ring with his arms by his side, stalking Cabrera.

He did not put him away in the seventh. He rocked him in the eighth, and he had him hanging on with his mouthguard knocked out in the ninth. But when the end came in round ten, it was emphatic. With his corner screaming for the referee, Jesus Torres, to stop the fight and prevent Cabrera from taking unnecessary punishment, Azumah landed a right hook to the jaw. Cabrera's knees buckled, and as he slumped, he was clipped by a ferocious left hook that saw him pitch face-first into the canvas.

The following day, Barry McGuigan, despite leading going into the last round, found that the heat of Las Vegas had caught up with him, and he was knocked down twice. He hung on until the final bell sounded, but that last round cost him his world title. The much talked about unification bout was now very much on hold.

"I regret that we did not fight, not because we did not fight to see who was the best, but it seemed like his people did not understand the game. He or his manager thought he was going to lose. This is our chance to make big money. Why are you a boxer all this time if, when the time comes to make big money, you pull out? Are you crazy? That was why I was disappointed," Azumah says, looking back.

When Azumah fought Marcos Villasana the second time, many felt that the Mexican would be victorious, but as would become a pattern throughout Azumah's career, his challenger would regret requesting a rematch. "He took two good beatings from me," remembers Azumah, smiling that irrepressible smile of his that takes one back to his cheeky street-hustling days. "It was a very tough fight and he was a very tough guy. He didn't care how many punches he took. He just kept moving forwards, and he kept throwing punches as he came at you. He was a very strong boxer and very brave."

On this occasion, the three judges were unanimous, with Azumah winning on each of their scorecards. He had retained his WBC featherweight title for the sixth and last time. The partisan crowd was far from happy, as referee from the undercard Dr. Lou Moret recalls. "I worked the undercard that night, and I was watching the fight and it was an easy victory. The place was the old Olympic auditorium and it seated seventy-five hundred people, and it was packed to the gills with Mexican fans. They didn't have much to cheer about because Azumah was winning easily.

"Well, we from Los Angeles knew that kind of crowd, and as soon as the fight ended, all the referees who were not working ran to the tunnel—it had little tunnels leading to the dressing rooms—because we knew that beer, cups, and debris would come flying into the ring and land on everybody. So then I was standing in the tunnel and Azumah came in—they barely raised his arm and he was out of the ring—and they were covering him with towels. I remember him vividly saying, 'Why are they doing that? I won every round. What would they have done if it was close?' He was a gentleman and a great fighter and barely breathing hard; he was in such great shape. A fun memory of seeing a real craftsman at work."

Former sports minister, Amarkai Armateifio, remembers the second bout. "In this fight, he had a very good strategy of soaking up the pressure and then fighting back. Both fights were tough fights."

"After the fight, I told Villasana he was a great fighter," Azumah remembers. "I said to him, 'I will leave this division for you, as I can see you will be the champion.' I wanted to move up to take the next title and wanted to take the next two titles, but I maybe left it too late, as I became a champion later than I had hoped. Villasana did become champion—he lost to Jeff Fenech and then beat Hodkinson from England. I am not sure how long he held the title, but I am glad he became a world champion.

"I decided to give up the title because I wanted to move up a weight. As I was getting older, I struggled with the weight as a featherweight. But I never went on the scales before a fight over the weight because I am a professional. If you know your work, you should never be over the weight. It is only a lazy boxer who is overweight at the weigh-in and then has to go and shed it off. As a professional, you know you are going to fight. You know you are training and have to weigh nine stone. Most boxers know when they have reached that weight. You know you are under weight; your body tells you.

"After the weigh-in, most boxers have heavy food, but because the stomach is tight, you need something hot like tea before you eat. Wait for a while, maybe thirty minutes to one hour, and then you eat heavy food. In my country, we eat corn or *foo-foo*. You eat and then you sit down for a while, maybe one or two hours, and then you go to bed and sleep for three to four hours. It is usually a deep sleep, and then when you wake up, you can't sleep again because now you are thinking about the fight. You are thinking about the plan that you are going to take when you enter the ring—what you are going to do in the first round. This guy can punch, so what are you going to do in the first round to get through it and avoid his punches? You have to be focused from before you get to the ring and be thinking about the fight from that moment until the start.

"Every fight, I had the same routine. You only change the strategies for different opponents. It is very important to have the same preparation because if you are boxing someone who is faster, like when I fought Calvin Grove, you have to box him. He will run away a lot, so you have to use a strategy to put pressure on him. You make him run and then hit his stomach. That way, you make him get tired quicker, and then when he comes in, you throw fast punches and move. In that fight when his legs went and he was tired, he found it hard to take my punches. You have to have a strategy for every boxer."

What about the matter of sex before a fight? Many boxers and trainers believe that women make a fighter lose focus and weaken his stamina. Some boxers have gone so far as to put an elastic band around their scrotums when they sleep to avoid the possibility of a "wet dream," believing that even that could have an impact on their stamina.

"Sometimes you do not even think about your woman when in training," Azumah explains. "You are concentrating and focusing on putting your future plans together. If you can think and also know that these plans will go well after you win your fight, and that you can have anything you want, and you know the woman is there for you, it is not hard. It is about looking to the future and making sacrifices now for the future.

"Sometimes there is temptation, and sometimes you will think, *Oh, I feel a bit ...* you know, but you have to realise that in this world, there is good and bad. The Bible says there is time for everything—a time for love, a time to smile, to cry, to work, for rest, for business, and fun. So when you are training, there is no time for fun. It's time for focus. When the time comes, you can then focus on the sex! After the fight, well, after the fight, there is plenty of time for your woman."

VIII

WORLD CLASS

Mirroring Azumah's rise on the world stage was Ghana's economic recovery. The country that had once been down on the canvas and had only just managed to make the count had hung in there, and was now in a position few could credit.

The rate of inflation had dropped to 20 per cent, and between 1983 and 1987, the economy was reported to have grown by 6 per cent per year. The government of the day, the PNDC, managed to make a payment of $500 million in loan arrears dating back to before 1966. As a result, international agencies pledged more than $575 million to the country's future programs.

It was not, however, all good news. Unemployment remained extremely high, and there were concerns that the belt-tightening policies of the government and the absence of employment or redeployment policies for those who had lost jobs would in fact derail the government. Student organisations and opposition groups in self-imposed exile started to question the military government's legitimacy and its promise to return the country to constitutional rule. President Rawlings was walking a tightrope, trying to redress a situation that was not of his making. He had to try and secure the financial future of the country he loved and cared passionately about, as well as ensure that his government remained in power. These were still very difficult times. To ease the tension, he announced elections would be held for new district assemblies.

Against this backdrop, Azumah Nelson offered an escape for the nation. His success from such humble beginnings proved that Ghana and Ghanaians could make it in the world. He gave the people not only hope, but also pride. He was aware of what his success meant to the country, and more importantly, its people, and he continued to work hard to never disappoint them.

"I loved training—that is where you put in the hard work," he says. "You have to work hard when you train, as this is where if you put in the work, you win the fight. Some boxers do not work hard enough when they train and then struggle in the fight when they should win easily. If you train hard, if the fight is tough, you can still keep going and it can make the difference.

"I believe I trained better than a lot of my opponents. I loved training. Often my coach would say, 'That is enough. Time for a rest,' but he did not know that I was in the gym, hitting the bag. He would see me in the gym, hitting the bag for fifteen rounds, but sometimes I was in there hitting it for twenty or twenty-five rounds. You can't believe the power that I was hitting the bag with from round one to round twenty-five. I am hungry. I am hungry to get the title. I am hungry to make money. I am hungry to live well. This was the time I have to go all out to do what I wanted, to get all of these things. I did my best. When I became champion, for ten to eleven years, no one beat me. No one took my title. It was only as I started growing older the power started coming down, and I realised that I had to stop.

"I would wake up in the morning and go jogging. When I was young, when I started boxing, I would bandage my hands before I left the house and then I would go for a run. I did this because I wanted people to see me, to recognise me. I would wait until daybreak when people were going to work and then start my run, and when they were sitting in their cars, they would see me and know I was a boxer. If people stopped, I would stop and shadowbox. I would show them what I could do. I wanted them to know: This is a boxer. I was happy. I enjoyed it. No one knew who this small boy was then. They just saw me standing there, firing off punches. They did not really look at me, but gradually as I became famous, they recognised me and they would beep their horns and shout, 'Hey, Azumah Nelson! Hey!' and wave at me. So after that, I stopped training at six a.m.

and started at three a.m., before daybreak, so no one saw me. One day, I am in traffic driving, and they started shouting because the people loved me so much. Then before you know it, bang! Someone hit my car. I parked, got out, and the driver apologised and said they would fix it for me. I had to talk to them, and then they asked me for money to fix their car!

"Usually I would run from three a.m. to five a.m., and then when I arrived home, I take a bath and have a small drink of tea. If I have a fight soon, after I come back from my jog, I went straight to the gym at my house. When I did not have a gym at my house, I would take my punching gloves and leave them where I trained. I would run to the gym and then I would get on the bag and start hitting it, boom, boom, until six a.m. I would work for one hour, and then I would go home. I would jog for one-and-a-half hours and then hit the bag for one hour. Then I take my bath and get something to eat. I then relaxed and trained again in the afternoon. Midday, I would start again. I went to the gym and warmed up with skipping. Then I hit the heavy bag and do exercises for the stomach, and then I go back again at five p.m. for a warm-up and to do some sparring. It was always the same routine—spar, skip, shadowbox.

"Sometimes when I was going to the gym, I would chop trees first. I would chop trees to give me strength. My people would take the car and cut down trees and then bring them to my house. I would take the axe and I would chop them. It gave me power in my shoulders. Chopping wood gives you power from head to toe and makes you very tired. Chopping wood is tiring. I chopped wood for fifteen to twenty minutes nonstop, and then I would go straight to the gym, bandage my hands, and start sparring. Because I am tired, it was hard to spar. But it was like in a fight. You will be tired in a fight, so this was good training, to keep you going when you were get tired. I would then train ten to fifteen rounds of sparring."

Every boxer has different ways to prepare for a fight. Most find themselves slotting into a familiar routine, and Azumah was no different. Prior to most fights, he would pace slowly in his dressing room, wearing a tracksuit and training shoes with no socks. He would weigh himself to see how much weight he had added since the official weigh-in; the amount would usually be around four or five pounds.

He would then sit down and put on one pair of socks, followed by another pair on top of those, and then his boxing boots. Focused so heavily on his preparation for the fight, he would meticulously fold down the tops of the second pair of socks to make sure that they were even with the first pair. His face was always expressionless, his thoughts his own. He would lace his boots and put on a pair of sweatpants and then quietly shadowbox, alone in his world, while the dressing room was awash with noise and people. To Ghanaians, people and noise are a comfort; they are what they are used to.

Loosened up, he would then allow his corner to start taping his hands. His corner man would issue one-word commands—open, close—and the champion would obey, his face remaining impassive. The commissioner watched the taping of his hands closely, and when satisfied, initialed the wraps. Azumah then would turn his back on the rest of the room, and after gulping down some water, produce the customary pre-fight urine sample. He would then sign his name on the lid of the jar.

At five minutes until fight time, his expression would change. A steely look would come to his dark, deep-set eyes, while his facial expression would remain deadpan. His eyes transformed his whole being. All in his presence could feel his aura. It was showtime. He would climb into his protector and slip on his shorts. He would then hold out his hands, and his corner man would push his gloves over his hands and lace them up, first the left and then the right.

Waiting to the side would be "Buffalo" Martin, who would have slipped his hands into the pads. Azumah would beat his fists together and then, after the commissioner signed the tape covering the laces, step to one side and start banging away ferociously at the pads. When he stopped, Eddie Mafuz would spread Vaseline across his shoulders and chest and over his washboard stomach. Then he would return to the pads, hammering in right and left hooks. The sweat would start to appear on his brow. If there was time, he would jump a little rope before slipping his arms into the sleeves of his robe and preparing for the long walk to the ring. It is those repetitive routines—the perfect preparations—that make champions.

Having taken on most of the best featherweights and finding it harder to make the weight, Azumah moved up to the super featherweight division in 1988. The maximum weight for a boxer in this division is 130 pounds, or fifty-nine kilograms. His preparation would remain the same, the preparation that had served him so well to date.

There was an interesting coincidence in his move to the super featherweight division: This division was established by the New York Walker Law in 1920, the state law that at that time regulated boxing, but the first English champion was "Battling Kid" Nelson in 1914, who lost his title to Benny Berger in 1915. Maybe this was an omen for the Ghanaian Azumah Nelson.

Just four months after defeating Marcos Villasana, Azumah was back at the Forum in Inglewood, California, to fight Mexican Mario Martinez for the vacant WBC super featherweight world title. Martinez had fought for the title in 1984 when, with a record of thirty-seven fights with thirty-four wins, just one loss, and two draws, he met a fellow countryman, the undefeated Julio Cesar Chavez, and lost by TKO in the sixth. Martinez had gone into that bout as the favourite with the bookmakers and so was desperate to make amends for that defeat.

Chavez had defended the title on nine occasions in three years before opting to vacate the title and chase a world lightweight title. Leading up to the fight, Azumah let people know where his focus was when he was reported in the press as saying, "I am not looking past this fight, but I'm ready to show Julio Cesar Chavez [the WBA lightweight champion] and the rest of the world who the best fighter is. That would make my day. I'm a very hungry fighter and would like nothing better than to fight Chavez. I'm ready to fight anybody in the world."

It was reported in the press that Azumah did not like Chavez, but as is often the case, the truth was very different. "There was no ill feeling," he recalls. "No ill feeling at all. He is one of the boxers I love so much—anytime he was going to fight, I prayed for him. I loved him and Marvelous Marvin Hagler. When I heard he was not well, you have no idea how that made me feel. With Chavez, it was all about trying to promote a possible fight."

Mario "Azabache" Martinez was a ferocious fighter, strong, with fists like iron. The fight went the distance, so it was down to the judges. When announcer Jimmy Lennon Jr. grabbed the microphone, he told the waiting fighters and crowd that there was a split-decision. British-born judge Terry Smith saw it as a close contest, scoring it 115–113 in favour of Azumah. Groans accompanied the announcement. Those groans turned into cheers when they heard that Judge Marty Sammon scored it 114–113 in favour of the Mexican. Martinez was already waving his arms in victory and riding high on the shoulders of his handlers. Lennon then read the scores of the final judge, Rudy Ortega, who scored the fight 115–113 in favour of Azumah. At that point, not only did the reign of Azumah Nelson as super featherweight champion begin, but so, too, did the rain of beer on the judges seated ringside. The mostly Mexican crowd was not happy with the decision and howled their disapproval.

History shows that on February 29, 1988, Azumah climbed off the canvas to claim his second world title. He had been knocked down in the tenth round, the only knockdown of the night, but was up at the count of four. He banged his gloves together in disgust and then walked forward, looking to make his opponent pay for putting him on his backside. Martinez failed to follow up this blow effectively, and Azumah took control with jabs and fast counterattacks in the final two rounds. This flurry of activity may well have swayed the judges his way.

Azumah was criticised following this fight for his lack of urgency. He had fought in spurts, and at the end of each round, would reach out and tap gloves with his opponent. After a jarring right in the first thirty seconds of the fight, Martinez was also cautious, making sure not to get caught by Azumah's famed counterattacking punches. With the crowd on his back, he was stung again in round nine when he tried to lift the pace of the fight. Azumah landed a brutal combination of a left uppercut and a right, and Martinez's left eye swelled almost instantly.

"This was a tough way to lose," Martinez said after the fight. "But what makes up for it was the way the fans got behind me and stayed behind me. The judges scored the fight the way they saw it, but the public—the fans here tonight—know who the winner was."

Azumah rates Martinez the hardest puncher he ever faced. "He hit like iron," he recalls. "I fought him twice, but in the first fight in the first round, he threw a punch and I blocked it with my arm, and my arm went down. I lost feeling—my arm was dead. So straightaway, I was thinking, 'If this guy hits my jaw, how can I stand?' He made me think the whole fight. I had to think fast, and when you have to think so much, you get tired because you have to be careful and make sure that you do not take a punch that you do not see coming. The first fight, I won on points, but it was a tough fight. After the fight, they said to me, 'No, no, no. He won.' So I said, 'Okay, that is fine. I will give you a rematch,' and I did, and I knocked him out in the twelfth round, the last round.

"After the fight, my hands were all swollen and his face was swollen and badly bruised, and they ended up pushing both of us on beds to the hospital. My people were pushing me, and his people were behind us, pushing him. It was a brutal fight. He was the hardest puncher I ever fought and a very tough man."

To many, the first fight was disappointing and the champion had looked sluggish; some felt he should never have received the decision. Yet few knew what was happening outside the ring and inside the champion's head.

The day before the fight, Azumah received a phone call from Beatrice in London. It was not good news. He rubbed his face with his hand, the phone shaking in the other. His shoulders shook, first slightly and then uncontrollably, as tears flowed from his eyes. Beatrice had been diagnosed with cancer. His first instinct was to be by her side, to hold her in his arms and try and make it all right. But there was an ocean between them, and the next day, he had to fight for a world title, a fight that could ultimately pay for a better life for them and their children. At that time, all he could think about was how success the next day could help him find a cure for her, or at least the best treatment money could buy.

"I knew she was in pain, and one day, we went to the hospital and they told us she had cancer. But we did not find it early and it had spread. We did what we could, and I took her to America and England for treatment. The doctors knew the extent of the cancer, and they determined what treatment they gave her," he recalls.

He was torn, a man in conflict. He had a job to do and people expected him to be there—people who had paid to watch him fight—yet he wanted to be elsewhere, with the love of his life in London. He had to make do with a very difficult and upsetting trans-Atlantic phone call. Therefore, was it any wonder that he wasn't as sharp as people expected in that first encounter with Martinez?

In the lead-up to that fight, Don King employee Al Braverman talked up a bout with Chavez when he said, "They have a grudge that goes back to the time Chavez made some derogatory remarks to him. Anytime Azumah sees a picture of Chavez, he starts shaking a fist at it—it's a real hate."

Braverman was doing his bit to talk up a money-spinning bout that would be exciting for fans and financially attractive to both boxers, but there was no denying that the first Martinez fight ended up being a speed bump in Azumah's career. It was seen as an easy bout on his way from featherweight to lightweight champion, and he was expected to pick up this title with ease, along with more good press, before then moving onto the lightweight division. But as often happens in sport, it did not end up that way, and no one except those in his inner circle knew the real reasons why.

In between the first and second bouts, and just four months after winning his new world title, Azumah met American Lupe Suarez at the Trump Plaza Hotel in Atlantic City. Ringside was former heavyweight champion, Pinklon Thomas, who had popped into the dressing room to wish him luck, as well as Sugar Ray Leonard and Hector "Macho" Camacho. The Angelo Dundee-trained southpaw Suarez took the first two rounds. Azumah landed two thunderous hooks in the third and several more in the fourth, but failed to maintain the momentum. Suarez started to take control of the fight and actually backed the champion up in five and six.

In his corner between rounds seven and eight, Al Braverman and Buffalo tried to inspire their fighter. "What kind of fucking champion are you? You lose this fight and you disgrace us," Braverman yelled. Azumah appeared to ignore his comments.

He did not, however, ignore the comments of Beatrice. Between bouts of treatment for her cancer in America and London, she was by her husband's side. "By then, she was okay with me boxing. She never worried.

She learned and knew boxing really well," he says.

"In the Suarez fight, I was in my corner and I was not doing what I was supposed to do. She was sitting ringside near my corner and got off her chair and came to the corner. She pulled my arm and said, 'Are you afraid of the person in the ring? Are you afraid? If not, then come on!' I was supposed to go inside, and she asked me why I was not going inside. Everyone who knows boxing knows that is what I had to do. She was still telling me what to do, but I had to go, as the bell had rung for the next round. She knew boxing and what had to be done. She was a good woman." He smiles warmly as he remembers his wife, the coach.

Back in the ring, Azumah opened the eighth with a strong combination that ended with a powerful hook that rocked his opponent. Suarez simply could not match the fury of the punches Azumah was throwing, and just after the bell, he was caught by another ferocious hook. Angelo Dundee protested to referee Tony Perez that the punch was after the bell and that he should deduct a point, but his appeals fell on deaf ears. With three more hooks at the start of round nine, the Texan hit the canvas. He rose at the count of five, but the referee waved his arms in front of Suarez's face. The fight was over.

At the time, Azumah was ahead on all three judges' scorecards. "I knew what I was doing—I knew he would punch himself out, and then it was time to attack, which I did, and I knocked him out," Azumah recalls all these years later.

This is a fight that friend Obi Oblitey remembers fondly. "When they fought, Suarez was beating Azumah from round one to nine, and his coach Buffalo told him, 'You have lost the fight. There are only three rounds left. Africa and Ghana believe in you. There are only three rounds left. They call you a fighting machine, a terrible warrior, so it is up to you to decide if you are and if you want to win. Don't let Africa down.'

"He went in and full of vigour started to trouble Suarez. They stood toe-to-toe and threw punches. Azumah used to spar with heavyweight Joe Kalala in Mamprobi, so he knew how to take hard punches. The guy fell into the trap. Azumah released all his punches—hooks, uppercuts, the lot—and the guy fell down. When he recovered, they said to him, 'You were winning from round one to nine. How did you lose the fight? He said, 'Hey, this guy is fighting like a spider. It is like he has eight arms. Blows came from all angles, and it was a terrific blow that sent me to the corner.'"

Six months later, Azumah had his only title defence fight in his home country. It was also his first fight in Accra in two years. On this occasion, he would meet Brazilian southpaw Sidnei dal Dal Rovere, the man he could have met had he fought at the Moscow Olympics. The man from Sao Paolo was no match for the champ and was knocked out in round two. It was his first defeat, and he would only climb through the ropes on two more occasions before announcing his retirement, following a second defeat to Jose Ramon Soria.

With Barry McGuigan having lost his world title, Azumah Nelson had lost out on possibly the most lucrative fight in his career. Azumah had his admirers in the U.S., but he was not earning the big dollars by being the main attraction. A unification bout for the featherweight WBA and WBC titles would have been attractive to American and British audiences. Sadly, Don King's focus on other fighters within his stable and Barney East-wood's reluctance to put his man in the ring against Azumah meant the fight never happened, and both men missed out.

However, McGuigan has few regrets. "What a fighter, an incredible fighter—in my opinion, the best African fighter of all time. At the time, when I came around, Pedrosa had been champion for seven-and-a-half years, so at that time in my mind, he was the one who had the credibility. But time sorts things out, and Azumah is now one of the greatest fighters of all time. He was a terrific box-fighter; he could box and fight. He couldn't just fight going forward. He could also fight going back. He could punch tremendously hard, and he moved relatively seamlessly through the weight divisions. He was a great fighter."

Having signed up with boxing promoter Barry Hearn, McGuigan was warming up for another crack at the world title, and it looked as if the fight to decide who was the best could be back on. He was to fight Londoner Jim McDonnell in what was to be a final eliminator for a world title bout against Azumah. The fight was set for May 31, 1989, in Manchester and was billed under the heading "Nowhere to Run."

As McGuigan said in his autobiography, *Cyclone,* "I went in thinking it was going to be a stepping stone to the next major challenge in my career. But as it turned out, it was the full stop." In round two, McDonnell, nicknamed "The Assassin," caught McGuigan with the heel of his hand and opened up a cut. It was a bad one, and in round four, referee Mickey Vann stopped the fight and the McGuigan–Nelson bout that everyone had dreamed about was gone. McGuigan would hang up his gloves following this defeat, so it would never be discussed again.

At the time, there was talk of Azumah taking on South African Brian Mitchell, who held the WBA super featherweight title, but with South African athletes in isolation and the other African nations unanimous in their stance against the apartheid regime, it was a fight that was never likely to happen.

Interestingly, here were two world champions from Africa who, in the same era, were forced to defend their world titles overseas and unable to enjoy the benefit of fighting in front of their home fans, which was tough, as Mitchell explains. "I don't think Azumah had many fights in Ghana, and I had no world title fights in South Africa. I was on the road for thirteen of my title fights. That is very tough because you are fighting against the odds—you're fighting the judges, the referee, the crowd—and you still have your opponent to fight, so it's very tough fighting away from home.

"He was a wonderful fighter. He was the WBC champion; I was the WBA champion at the same time; and there was Tony Lopez from Sacramento, the IBF champion. There was talk at one time that myself and Azumah would get it on to unify all the titles, but unfortunately, it didn't happen. I look at his record now, and I see what a big puncher he was, and I think maybe it's a good thing it didn't happen. He was a great fighter, a top fighter."

So after disposing of Martinez for a second time on the undercard of the Mike Tyson–Frank Bruno world heavyweight title bout, Azumah's next trip to defend his title was a return trip to the United Kingdom to take on the man who had finally brought down the curtain on Barry McGuigan's career, European champion Jim McDonnell. Having lost by unanimous decision in his WBA world title fight with Brian Mitchell, McDonnell had beaten McGuigan and on paper was no slouch. Yet many in British boxing circles never gave him a prayer when the fight was announced.

McDonnell had been the underdog against McGuigan and had come out on top, yet Azumah was likely to be a different prospect. British boxing fans and writers still remembered his effective demolition of Pat Cowdell in the opening round. In the press, Azumah backed up those beliefs by declaring he would win by knockout and could dispose of the challenger in any round he wished. The fight was at the Royal Albert Hall, and also on the card were the future British world champions, Lennox Lewis, a heavyweight, and Chris Eubank, a middleweight and super-middleweight.

McDonnell was known for his stamina and an ability to fight when retreating. *Boxing News* described him as "a good nuisance fighter, moving around like a mosquito and stinging when he sees an opportunity." In his preparation for the bout, McDonnell had outlasted marathon runners in his long-distance runs and had even resorted to shadowboxing under water. As is often the case, as the fight drew nearer, the British changed their tune and were talking up his chances of an upset, believing his footwork would make it hard for Azumah to find him and that his snappy jabs and hooks could build up a points lead against a champion on the wane.

Unfortunately for McDonnell, the twenty-four hours before the fight did not go according to plan. "The day before the fight, we check-weighed as the weigh-in was the day of the fight in those days, and I was perfect, or so I thought," he recalls. "I wrote it down and said to Barry Hearn, 'Nine stone four pounds. Wow! That's really light.' I had breakfast and a drink and thought I would be nine stone six. I left the place and went to the gym. I then went back to the hotel—that was a massive mistake.

"I ordered a chicken salad as I did before every fight, but the hotel said they had no chicken. So instead, I had red meat. I thought it was no big deal, but when I went to bed that night, I couldn't sleep; I worried about my weight. So I rang my brother Mark. I said, 'Can you bring your scales to the hotel?' He asked, 'Why? The weigh-in is at eleven a.m.' I went down to the Roof Gardens Hotel in Kensington and they'd moved the scales from the hotel. So Mark drove to my hotel, having diverted on his way to work, and I got on the scales. I was nine stone nine pounds. My trainer said the scales had to be wrong. I told him they were accurate and that I had used them for all my fights.

"'Then you're going to have to work,' he told me. It was raining so I ran in the hotel with all my sweat gear on for thirty minutes, and then I went to the bathroom and turned the heater on and the hot taps and skipped in the bathroom for sixty minutes. I managed to get to nine stone four, nine stone five, so I wrapped up and went for a walk and thought I should be bang on.

"We went to the weigh-in at the Albert Hall, and there were hundreds of fans there chanting my name. Azumah climbed on the scales first and he was spot on 116 kilograms—nine stone, four and three quarters. All the TV cameras were there, and I had to explain that I'd had an extra cup of tea at breakfast and that must have tipped me over. We went to a heated room and I was skipping for forty-five minutes. I managed to get down to nine stone three-and-a-half. I then drank a carbohydrate drink, which was a big mistake. Back at the hotel, I couldn't eat, and all I had was an ice cream, a knickerbocker glory.

"The day flashed by. My brother collected me at the hotel and told me to get on the scales. I always did this before a fight, and I was lighter than at the weigh-in! When we arrived at the Albert Hall, there were thousands there wishing me good luck. I was so proud, but in the dressing room before the fight, I was the loneliest bloke in the world. I felt I had been swindled. I felt let down—the negativity overpowered the positivity; it smothered it. I could hear Nelson in the room next door and all the noise. I created a monster in my own mind, and when the call came to walk to the ring, I didn't walk there with endeavor."

That night, Jim McDonnell opted to have an old pal from his days training under Terry Lawless at the Royal Oak in his corner, former WBC, European and British flyweight champion, Charlie Magri. "It takes a special kind of person to overcome everything surrounding the fight—all the pressure, the noise, the occasion. You can't get overwhelmed by it. You have to block it out. He called me and asked me to be in his corner to give him a bit of help and advice," Magri remembers. "It was great being in his corner and watching two world-class boxers. It was really special for me. Jim was technically brilliant. I was just there to make sure he did things properly and that he was careful."

The fight is now remembered for two reasons: the bravery of McDonnell and the fact that the fight wasn't stopped sooner. The start of the fight was as many predicted, with the challenger moving in and out, firing off quick jabs and sharp left hooks, and smothering Azumah at close quarters.

In round three, Azumah switched tactics, the mark of a true champion. He started walking after McDonnell with his hands held high, waiting for an opening. Halfway through the round, he unleashed a string of jabs that found McDonnell's face, followed by a big left hook that forced the challenger to hold on. This flurry of punches revealed just how much power lay in Azumah's small frame.

Azumah eased off in the fourth. In the fifth, he nailed McDonnell with another left hook. It seemed McDonnell would never beat the count of referee Joe Cortez, but somehow he did. At the count of nine, he nodded to the referee and then launched an attack on the champion that indicated he had indeed recovered.

In the sixth, Azumah stalked his opponent again, and late in the round drew blood from his nose with another stinging left hook. He then switched to a cross-armed stance similar to that favoured by Archie Moore and Ken Norton, a defence that McDonnell found hard to penetrate. Despite this, many observers gave the challenger round eight as Azumah once again eased off on his attack. This gave the partisan crowd hope that their man could pull off a surprise victory.

In round ten, Azumah let McDonnell back him into a corner and flail away at him as he deflected and blocked his punches, blood still coming from McDonnell's nose and also now his mouth. When the champion unleashed his punches, they all found the target; more importantly, they were far more telling than those thrown by his opponent. At the end of the round, McDonnell raised his arms in the air in defiance, and the crowd roared its approval.

Not long after the start of round eleven, McDonnell's right eye had closed. Referee Cortez stopped the fight and led him to the ringside doctor, Dr. Ashwin Patel, for a medical inspection. Dr. Patel allowed the fight to continue. From that moment on, McDonnell failed to see any of Azumah's left hooks coming, and they landed with sickening regularity. In between punches, Azumah spoke to Joe Cortez, pleading with him to stop the fight. He didn't.

McDonnell returned to his corner, and instead of being retired in the interests of his own safety, he was pushed back into the ring for round twelve. With a world title on the line and their boxer believed to be ahead on points, one can understand why. However, his only hope was to tie Azumah up, which he tried. Azumah pushed him away and McDonnell was soon on the canvas. The count never started and he was ordered back up to his feet.

Looking at Cortez to stop the fight, Azumah was forced to continue. He landed a left and then two rights. McDonnell tottered backwards onto the ropes. He raised his arms in what appeared to be an act of surrender, but then dug deep for one final onslaught. Azumah landed a right and he was back on the canvas. He was up at nine. The fight should definitely have been stopped. It still wasn't.

Azumah clearly was not comfortable with the situation, but did what he had to do: unleash a flurry of fast punches that saw McDonnell hit the deck once again. This time, there was no count; Cortez waved his arms over the prostrate fighter. It was all over one minute and forty seconds into the final round. McDonnell lay on the canvas for a full three minutes while doctors tended to him, but luckily recovered sufficiently to walk back to his dressing room. He was, however, admitted to hospital after the fight and stayed there for several days.

"This fight should have been stopped. No boxer wants to hurt a man. It is just a sport and we should remember that. I was pleading with the referee to stop the fight. I did not want to hurt him. He was very brave, but in the last two rounds, he could not see out of his right eye, which was very dangerous for him. I am just pleased that he did not suffer after the fight," Azumah recalls. "He was very brave, very courageous, and he was fighting in front of his people, so he did not want to give up, but his corner and the referee should have stopped the fight."

Jim McDonnell recalls the fight with a great deal of pain. As lesser British boxers have gone on to win world titles, he has the misfortune to know that he fought and lost to some of the best in the world in his era, and that has often been forgotten by the boxing fraternity in Britain.

"I was one round away from beating him, as I was ahead on the judges' scorecards," he recalls. "What was annoying was I died of fatigue in the last round. It was like I had run a marathon without any water. I had trained twice that day for two hours and then gone twelve rounds with a great fighter like Azumah Nelson, another thirty-six minutes. It was like hitting the wall when you run a marathon. I used to start fast and finish fast. I had a resting heart rate of thirty-four beats per minute. He had the power in his back pocket but I had pace, pace I could sustain. These days with a weigh-in the day before the fight, you would not have the same problems. The last twenty-four hours before that fight still haunt me today.

"I have never given Azumah the praise he deserves because he never beat the best Jim McDonnell, but he was the greatest in our era. I would never want to take anything away from him, but it pains me to this day that I came so close, and I can't call myself a world champion. I could have gone for a WBO title, but I chose to fight the greatest. I could have beaten all the others, but I came up short against Azumah. I still feel empty inside that I never won a world championship. There was no easy route to a world title back then. I am not saying I would have won, but I would have been harder to beat without the hydration problems. He was asking the ref to stop the fight, and I was saying, 'Ref, you can't stop it. It's the last round.' I think he was trying to say, 'Listen, I'm the man.' He tried it; Sugar Ray Leonard had tried it.

"He knew he was in London, a strong crowd on my side. It was a bit of gamesmanship by him. He is a good human being. I admit I did it against Steve Pollard, so we all do it. Azumah is a true great, a true gentleman. He was ring-savvy and a good puncher, a hall-of-famer and the best of the day. I fought and beat three of the top five in that era, but sadly never got to be a world champ, losing to Mitchell and Nelson. I called for a rematch—I wanted a rematch—but it never happened. Mitchell wouldn't give me one, and I always thought McGuigan avoided me. Lopez wanted one, but in Sacramento."

It is no consolation to McDonnell, but Ray Quarcoo, who has spent a lifetime involved in boxing in Ghana and who had watched Azumah develop through the amateur ranks, was ringside at this fight in London and believes to this day it was one of his hardest. "I have known Azumah Nelson since his amateur days during my tenure as the vice president of the Ghana Amateur Boxing Federation in the late 1970s to the early 1980s, and had always believed he had what it takes took to conquer the world," Quarcoo says. "I had never doubted his ability when he turned professional thereafter.

"The fight with McDonnell in London was very memorable to me, and I consider it one of the most difficult fights of his entire career because of McDonnell's tough stand, pushing the champion all the way in a bruising bout, and with the champion struggling to win. In that fight, McDonnell suffered four knockdowns, but was still on his feet before the fight was stopped by the referee in the last round."

Former world champion, Charlie Magri, who was in McDonnell's corner, recalls, "Azumah was world class. He was unbelievable. He left it until the end and turned the fight. Azumah could box with both hands and you always had to be aware of that. I thought Jim put in a fantastic performance. He boxed brilliantly that night. He was leading, but he just came up against a great fighter. Jim never mentioned the problem with the scales—that was the sort of guy he was, even though I thought he should. I thought Azumah was world class. He was the best, in my opinion—one of the all-time great super featherweights."

Azumah prior to unsanctioned fight with bare-chested Nigerian Hunter Clay centre.
Floyd Klutei Robinson is the man in the white T-shirt between Azumah and his father
Emmanuel in the white shirt and black pants.

The "Soweto" Football team
Azumah played for. Azumah is
2nd row from back and second
from left. Obi Oblitey is to his
left.

Beatrice as a little girl.

Ramos Akwei (left), Azumah (centre) and
Obi Oblitey (right)

Razor Akwei Addo the man who told Beatrice Azumah would get hurt uncomfortably posing with Azumah.

Beatrice at school with friends. Beatrice is second row on the left.

Black Bombers at the airport in Accra prior to heading to New York – Azumah is second from right.

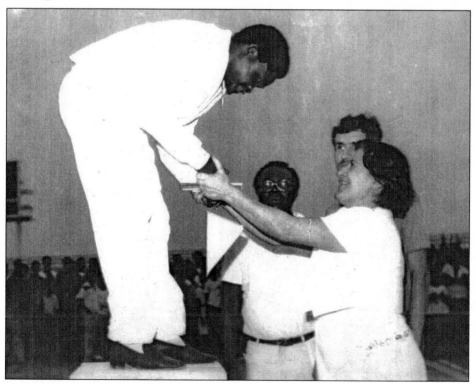

Azumah receives his gold medal at the African Games in Algeria.

Azumah (centre) at his coach Floyd Klutei Robinson's funeral.

Azumah at the Edmonton Common-
wealth Games with Welterweight Baba
Smali (left) and heavyweight Adama
Mensah (right).

Azumah signs professional forms. Front row left to right John Kermah, Seth Ansah, his managers, Azumah and his father Emmanuel. Behind Azumah standing is Razor Akwei Addo.

Where it all started at the Akotoku Academy.

Azumah's uncle "Black Jesus" who said that he would not beat Henry Saddler.

Azumah and trainer Jose "Buffalo" Martin take time out from the ring in Spain.

Azumah returns to Ghana a World Champion and the people welcome him home in their thousands.

Azumah enjoying a christening with his family.

Beatrice

Azumah with daughter Dyllis.

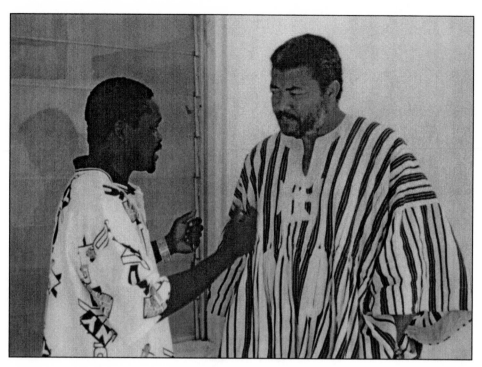

Azumah and former President JJ Rawlings.

Azuman and second wife Peggy.

Azumah's gallant effort against Salvador Sanchez comes to an end. Photo: Courtesy Ring Magazine.

Azumah and the iconic Don King who was his promoter for much of his career. Photo: Courtesy Ring Magazine

Azumah shows his true colours, proudly flying the flag for Ghana prior to his bout with Gabriel Ruelas. Photo: Courtesy Ring Magazine.

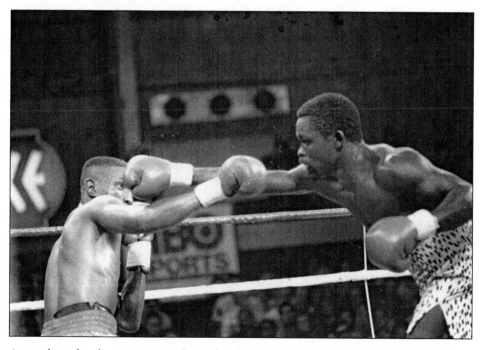

Azumah wishes he were somewhere else during his title fight with Pernell Whitaker. Photo: Courtesy Ring Magazine.

Azumah lands one on Australian Jeff Fenech in their epic bout in Las Vegas. Photographer Ken Levine, Courtesy Getty Images Sport.

Azumah goes head to head with Jesse James Leija. Photographer John Gurzinski, courtesy AFP.

The two African super featherweight champions who never met in the ring due to the apartheid regime in South Africa and who both fought outside their home countries, Brian Mitchell and Azumah Nelson. Courtesy Ashley Morrison Media.

Azumah with one of the boxers he most admired Former Middleweight champion Marvelous Marvin Hagler. Courtesy Ashley Morrison Media.

The fight that never was Part 1. Azumah with Irishman Barry McGuigan. Courtesy Ashley Morrison Media.

The fight that never was Part 2. Azumah with Mexican legend Julio Cesar Chavez. Courtesy Ashley Morrison Media.

Four fights and still friends Azumah with Jesse James Leija. Courtesy Ashley Morrison Media.

Azumah with President of the WBC Jose Suliaman. Courtesy Ashley Morrison Media.

Azumah puts one over Iron Mike Tyson. Courtesy Ashley Morrison Media.

Azumah nails Rocky. Sylvester Stallone takes it on the chin. Courtesy Ashley Morrison Media.

From fan to friend, Azumah with Dave Harper at another presentation. Courtesy Ashley Morrison Media.

Dalvin Nelson in the ring for his first public fight with his father Azumah watching from ringside. Courtesy Ashley Morrison Media.

IX

A VERY SPECIAL WOMAN

As soon as he discovered Beatrice had cancer, Azumah worked tirelessly to find a cure, and to find somewhere that could treat his wife and ease her suffering. "We went to London for the treatment, and she had radiotherapy for the cancer there. We did not have the machinery in Ghana, so I was lucky I could afford to send her to London. Everything I had I would give her to make her better," he said.

The couple had three children now: David, who was seven, Dorinda, five, and Doris, three. Azumah's cousin, Adriana Betty Nelson, who had become good friends with Beatrice, would help look after the children. She remembers this time fondly. "They were very kind to me, and I used to visit Azumah, and the children became attached to me, especially Doris, who was three at the time. When I came into Beatrice's life, it was all about God, going to church, and praying. She was very kind to all around her. I remember her telling me that when 'Champ' proposed to her, she had to go to church to pray first before she said yes.

"Champ really loved her, but he could not always have his own way with her. She was a very strong woman. I remember once when she was away, there were these drinking glasses in a showcase. They were not used; they were for decoration. So when Beatrice travelled, Champ said, 'Let's use them.' But before she came back, he was like, 'Oh, you guys, you know her. Make sure everything is back like it was,' so she would never know that he had used them. We had to make sure everything was normal before she came back. They had great respect for each other and loved each other very much.

"Azumah is a lovely man. I remember one day I told him something, and he was lying there and I did not think that he was listening, but then a few days later, he used what I had said to tease me. He was full of fun."

One thing that was apparent within the Nelson household was discipline, as Adriana attests. "I always thought that Dorinda looked like Champ, and David and Doris like Beatrice. When he was young, David knew all the movie stars, and his favourite was Chuck Norris. He knew everything about him. That was all he would talk about. I remember one day when we got together to pray, his mother asked David to pray, and he was very sensible, which surprised us. But it showed how she had instilled respect for God.

"Another time, I remember he was not doing well at school, so he was banned from swimming. We all went into the pool, and we did not know how to swim and we were splashing around. David stood by the pool, his arms folded, saying, 'Look, they do not even know how to swim.' But his mum said, 'I know, but until you do better at school, you are not allowed to swim.' She was very strong on discipline with the children. When I heard that David had gone to university, I knew it was all worth it.

"Beatrice and Azumah had respect for each other. She allowed him to be who he was, and he allowed her to be Beatrice. She was a beautiful woman who was in those days well educated, and she gave everything up to be with him because she truly, truly loved him, and he loved her, too. Champ loved her and she loved Champ."

Despite her illness, life at home was good. The two tried to find a cure for Beatrice and tried to live as normal a life as possible, but even in Azumah's chosen profession, things were not going as smoothly as expected. Being one of the best pound-for-pound fighters in the world is no guarantee of success. The smaller boxers have never been the ones to make the big money, which meant that Azumah had to keep climbing through the ropes not only for the money, but also to ensure that he remained world champion.

Azumah's hectic fighting schedule slowed dramatically as he tried to do what was best for Beatrice. In just under two years, he had just five bouts. At the beginning of 1990, the fight he had been waiting for suddenly became a reality. He would once again move up a weight to take on Pernell "Sweet Pea" Whitaker for the WBC and IBF lightweight title. It did not, however, come without its complications.

Azumah had to relinquish his super featherweight world title in order to step up a division to lightweight. Juan Laporte was lined up to fight Australian Jeff Fenech for the vacant title, with the latter looking to secure his fourth world title. Both fighters had agreed to the prefight condition that if Azumah lost to Pernell Whitaker, they would defend their title against Azumah within ninety days.

The fight that many wanted to see was Azumah Nelson vs. Jeff Fenech. *The Ring* magazine wrote, "The Australian demands confrontations, then soaks up blows while overwhelming his foes with volume punching. A title fight with Azumah Nelson will reveal whether it's been Fenech's chin or his ferocity that has made him so devastating." There was no doubt it would be a promoter's dream, with both fighters ferocious punchers and both able to take a punch.

The Laporte vs. Fenech bout was due to take place seven days after Azumah fought Whitaker, but after breaking a toe, Fenech became ill a few days before the fight and ended up on an IV drip in St. Vincent's Hospital in Sydney. The doctors put his illness down to a virus and middle ear infection; although, it was also rumoured that a doctor had incorrectly given him Rohypnol instead of antibiotics. The fight was pushed back to July. Fenech was then diagnosed with glandular fever, and the fight was eventually cancelled.

While all this was going on, Azumah was meeting Pernell Whitaker at a time when boxing was debating who was the best pound-for-pound fighter in the world, with Pernell's name being mentioned alongside the likes of Mike Tyson, Evander Holyfield, Meldrick Taylor, and Julio Cesar Chavez. A win would not only be the biggest accomplishment in his outstanding career to date, but would also set him on course for a possible showdown with Chavez.

Two titles were on the line at the Caesar's Sports Pavilion in Las Vegas: the IBF and WBC lightweight belts. Whitaker was never going to be a walkover. Having established himself as a dominant champion, he was in many people's minds the purest boxer in the fight game at that time. It was not an easy match to secure outside the ring, with archrivals Don King and Lou Duva in opposite corners. It was in fact HBO's Seth Abraham who brought the two together and helped broker the deal.

Duva's tactics were to make Azumah fight in the way that suited Whitaker. In the fight program, he was quoted as saying, "We've got to keep him at arm's length at the beginning. We'll use a lot of jabbing and a lot of body punching, but with a kid like Whitaker, you give him a game plan, but he more or less improvises as he goes along." He went on to talk about his concerns that Azumah could catch Pernell with a left hand. "When a southpaw jabs, he has a tendency to go to the right, right into the left hook. Nelson throws a wide left hook, but that may be his undoing."

In Azumah's corner, Eddie Mafuz was quoted as saying that trainer Jose Martin had managed to find Azumah some good sparring partners "to get him used to fighting southpaws." In fact, he trained with Pedro Sanchez in preparation for this fight, a boxer who had given Julio Cesar Chavez problems when he sparred with him. "Nelson's fought a few southpaws—Lupe Suarez, Mario Martinez. It's nothing new. He's been a champion five-and-a-half years now. He's a tremendous fighter," Mafuz said. He then went on to predict that his fighter would stop Whitaker in the last three rounds.

The experts were predicting that Whitaker would win by points, relying on his ability to slip Azumah's punches, as well as his natural speed to punch and move. These same experts believed Azumah had the firepower to beat Whitaker, with a punch more powerful than that of Whitaker's most recent opponents, Greg Haugen and Jose Luis Ramirez, but it was going to be crucial for him to reduce his opponent's fast-punching flurries and break up his rhythm. All agreed that Azumah had the skills to match his impressive adversary; the big question was whether the jump in weight would reduce the explosiveness and effectiveness of his punches.

What these pundits did not know was what was going on outside the ring. In his profile in the fight program, Mafuz touched on the issues when he said, "There have been a couple of fights where I think he's been distracted by being in one place while his wife is in another. She was sick for a while, too, which troubled him. Azumah doesn't need these kinds of distractions. When he's all together, he's an excellent fighter."

As usual, Azumah started his preparation in Ghana before relocating to Don King's camp in Ohio to complete his training. However, as he tried to focus on the fight ahead, Beatrice's health was deteriorating. They began to realise that there was little anyone could do to save her; the inevitable was just a matter of time. "She was in the hospital when I left for America, and President Rawlings sent people to the hospital to keep a check on her, and they would tell me so I knew how she was," Azumah recalls.

Even with these regular updates, Azumah was in a place he did not want to be, with his mind somewhere else. Normally Jose "Buffalo" Martin could be relied upon to lift his spirits and bring a smile to Azumah's face, but not even he could draw a smile from Azumah. Understandably, with his wife lying in a hospital bed thousands of miles away in Ghana, Azumah had to focus on what was potentially the biggest fight of his career, all the time knowing the doctors were not even sure that Beatrice would survive until the fight, let alone until it was over.

When asked if he had thought about pulling out of the fight, Azumah answers with a question. "Why? Why would I pull out? I was not injured. People had paid money to see me fight. I had a duty to be there and fight. I could not let people down when there was no injury." He pauses. "I thought that once I climbed through the ropes, I would be able to forget and focus on the fight, on my job, but I soon found out that I couldn't."

Back in Ghana, people once again huddled around television sets to watch the fight, Azumah having shrewdly required in all his contracts that his fights be aired in Ghana. While Beatrice was in the hospital, his family gathered at his mother's house around a small television in the courtyard that beamed the action to all who were there.

The fight took place at Caesars Palace in Las Vegas on May 19, 1990, and for the first time in six years, Azumah was the challenger. Azumah, "The Warrior," was announced to the crowd out of the red corner; wearing his leopard-print trunks and matching boots, he weighed in at 134 pounds. He looked relaxed and smiled to the fans from Ghana, who chanted his name over the applause inside the venue.

When his name was announced, Pernell Whitaker, in light blue trunks with red trim, bowed to each side of the ring. He came in one pound heavier than Azumah at 135 pounds. The referee, Mills Lane, called both boxers to the centre of the ring for their final instructions. Azumah held his head high and stared straight ahead, while Whitaker, who was only slightly taller than his challenger, bowed his head and avoided eye contact.

The bell sounded for the start of round one. The crowd chanted, "A-zum-ah! A-zum-ah!" and Azumah immediately looked to push Whitaker backwards, confident that Whitaker did not possess a punch that could hurt him. Azumah looked to go to the body, but found Whitaker hard to hit. The champion flicked out crisp jabs that Azumah walked into and then moved quickly to the side to avoid being hit. At the end of the round, the statistics showed that Whitaker had thrown sixty-seven punches and landed eighteen while Azumah had thrown forty-seven and landed only eleven. In his corner, Buffalo pleaded with Azumah to get inside and fire off combinations.

It was more of the same in round two as Azumah continued to take a lot of punches, walking into the lightening jab of Whitaker. To add to his woes, when he did move in close, Whitaker grabbed his thigh and lifted his leg off the ground to break up his rhythm and add to his frustration. He did land some solid punches in this round, but the most audacious blow came when Whitaker, with the champion's head under his arm, threw a punch behind his back to catch Azumah on the head. Understandably, Whitaker's corner was happy with the start he had made, but ever wary of Azumah's powerful punching, George Benton urged the champion to keep his arms up at all times.

When he came out for round three, Azumah had changed his defence to the peek-a-boo style of Ken Norton, with his arms across his chest and face and moving forward in a crouching style. Sitting ringside and commentating for HBO, Sugar Ray Leonard believed that this was an error against a fighter with Whitaker's speed, as it would take Azumah even longer to unload a punch. Maybe Azumah heard him, as halfway through the round he went back to an orthodox defence.

At one point, Whitaker slipped and Azumah caught him with a blow to the top of the head as he fell, but Whitaker bounced up and continued to fire off his jabs. There was no power behind them, and they were causing Azumah no pain, but they were scoring points. Not only that, they had caused a slight swelling under Azumah's right eye that needed the end-swell in between rounds. In the opposite corner, George Benton now urged Whitaker to let Azumah come at him but to sway out of the way. "When he fires, you move," he told his man.

Azumah continued to eat Whitaker's jab as he looked for a way to get inside, and when he did unload a swinging left or right, Whitaker was gone. Although he did wobble the champion halfway through the round with a right hand, it was proving a frustrating night at the office for Azumah. With four rounds gone, he had lost every round; he needed to find something special and quickly or he would have to rely on a knock-out finish as he had done against Lupe Suarez.

After another poor round, when he returned to the corner, "Buffalo" Martin sat his man down and bellowed at him: "No more rounds like this. Fight! Motherfucking fight!" Then in a slightly calmer tone, he pleaded with his man. "You don't fight now, you're going to look stupid. You waited all of your life for this time, Azumah. Don't mess up this time, Azumah, fight!" He grabbed Azumah under the chin so that he could be sure that their eyes met, but his fighter's eyes looked a long way away. "Listen to me, fight! You are the champion," he pleaded, hoping this would spark some life into Azumah—that the mention of the word would see him showcase the skills that had seen him be a champion of the world for six years. However, as his lightweight championship hopes slipped away before him, all he could think about was the life of the girl he loved slipping from her.

Despite the pleading from Buffalo, it was Whitaker who came out and landed the first telling blow of round six: a quick-fire left and right combination that caught the challenger. Azumah dropped his hands to his sides and shook his head as he bounced on his toes, as if to say, "Is that all you've got?" He then launched into an attack of his own, landing a good body shot that momentarily slowed Whitaker.

Despite having fought other southpaws, Azumah was struggling to find any rhythm and balance against his fleet-footed opponent. Yet in the seventh round, he came to life. He backed Whitaker up against the ropes in the opening minute with a good left hand. Whitaker managed to slip away and punch back. The crowd lifted at Azumah's surge of energy and intensity, and for the first time since the opening bell, his name started to ring out around the auditorium. Again in a clinch, Whitaker grabbed his thigh and lifted it off the ground, and Mills Lane stepped in and spoke to the champion. This was to be Azumah's round, as in the final minute he landed another strong right hand that rocked Whitaker. The signs were promising when the bell sounded. Azumah and his team knew that Whitaker had never knocked out an opponent after round six.

In round eight, he picked up where he left off, but the question on everyone's lips, including Buster Douglas's at ringside, was why it had taken so long for Azumah to start fighting. After the initial onslaught, Whitaker, who had dropped his hands, resorted to his jab-and-move tactics to great effect and had a strong end to the round. When the bell sounded, the two stood momentarily eye-to-eye before Whitaker tapped Azumah on the head and returned to his own corner.

There was no doubt Azumah was behind, and the pundits at HBO had him losing seven rounds to one. As the rounds kept slipping by, "Buffalo" Martin continued to try and bring out the best in his fighter. "Time for war. I don't know what's wrong with you, but unless you do something, you're gonna fuck this up. Let's go—you got three rounds to knock him out." Again, he could sense his fighter was not listening, his mind elsewhere. So his tone changed. "What's wrong with you? You are not punching." He paused. "Champ, Champ, please. What the hell happened to you? Nine minutes, that's all you have ..."

Azumah sat there expressionlessly, Buffalo's words washing over him just as the water poured over his head rolled down his body. His head was down. He wasn't listening to Buffalo, he wasn't looking at Buffalo. He was there in spirit, but his heart and his mind were elsewhere.

Nine minutes, that's all you have ... These words took on a very different meaning inside Azumah's head as the bell sounded for round nine. He raised himself from his stool, lifted his gloves in front of his face, and marched forward once again. *Nine minutes is all you have ...*

Looking back on the fight, Azumah admits, "In the ring, I just wanted to come home. I wanted to finish the fight. I am not thinking of winning or losing. I am just chasing Whitaker, throwing some punches—no calculations, no tactics, just doing what I had to do to finish the fight. Buffalo was shouting to try and take my mind off Beatrice because he knows what I am thinking, but he couldn't."

As the round started, HBO produced the statistic that Whitaker was averaging fifty jabs per round, an astonishing statistic, but the norm for this particular fighter. Once again, he fired his rapier jab into the advancing Azumah and then quickly moved to the side. Then he got in close and lifted Azumah up by grabbing his thigh. It was another round to the champion.

Desperation was the only way to describe round eleven. Azumah landed a strong right, and Whitaker grabbed again his thigh in a clinch. He landed a few more telling blows in the round, including one blow high on Whitaker's head, but the champion was still on his feet.

The bell sounded for round twelve, and Whitaker simply had to last the round to retain his world titles. Azumah had to find a knockout punch from somewhere, and more importantly, land it on the elusive Whitaker. There's no doubt that in the back of his mind, Whitaker would have thought about Meldrick Taylor's bout with Julio Cesar Chavez two months earlier, in which his good friend and Olympic Games teammate had dominated the Mexican throughout only to be stopped controversially in the dying seconds of the last round.

Azumah landed a powerful right hand early in the round and was beginning to land more and more punches. Again, Whitaker held on and grabbed his opponent's thigh; finally, he was deducted a point. Azumah landed some more solid blows as the clock ticked down, but could he pull off the impossible? Whitaker looked to hold on at every opportunity as Azumah looked to wind up his left hand and land the perfect punch, but the opening never came, and the bell sounded for the end of the fight.

The two boxers embraced. There was no bravado from Azumah, who was as expressionless as he had been since the opening bell. He knew the outcome. He went back to his corner and waited for the inevitable. When the result was announced, it was a unanimous decision: referee Harry Gibbs from England scored the bout 116–114, American Dalby Shirley had it 116–111, and Sid Nathan from England scored it 115–113, all in favour of the defending champion, Pernell Whitaker. There could be no argument. Whitaker had, according to broadcaster HBO, thrown 578 jabs and landed 286. Azumah had only landed 179 punches in total.

Following the fight, Azumah's mood did not change a great deal from what it had been inside the ring. He was a shell of his normal self. There was not even the usual disappointment that comes with a defeat, as rare as it was for him. This was only his second loss since turning pro, and both losses came in world title fights. There was no soul searching on his part. It was almost as if he was simply glad it was all over.

"That loss did not upset me. I never look at losing as a big deal," he says. "Any time I lose, I know I made a mistake. I know I have to go away and find my mistake and come back, and that is why I win all my rematch fights. I find the mistake, correct it, and I come back and win. The Whitaker fight was a mistake because I did not fight the way I should have. I don't know what I was thinking. I am not myself in the ring. But when I lose, I do not want to give excuses. So I said he should give me a rematch. I asked him, but he said, 'Only a fool will give you a rematch.'"

At the press conference, he sat next to Pernell Whitaker in a white shirt and white baseball cap, his hands calmly placed on top of each other in front of him, a cool drink in a paper cup to his left. The American press wanted to hear from Pernell, and as he regaled them with his victory speech, his opponent sat quietly, staring at nothing in particular, waiting to be told that his duties were over and he could leave. Even when Whitaker put his arm around him and praised him for the power of his punches, there was little emotion except for a weak smile that broke across his face to acknowledge the compliment.

His thoughts were back home in Ghana, and despite a nation weeping over his loss, all he wanted to do was get home to Beatrice. He hoped that he would make it before she passed away. Unfortunately for Azumah, there were no flights out of Las Vegas that night, so he would start the long journey home the next day. "There was no plane that night, so I had to leave the next day. It was the worst journey ever," he recalls.

"When I got back, I went straight to the hospital to see her. She looked nice, like she was getting better, and we talked. Before the fight, I spent a lot of time with her, but she was in good hands, so I would leave her and go home sometimes. If I had the chance to sleep at the hospital with her,

I would.

"But when I came home, I knew she was just waiting to see me before she went. When I got there, we talked some more. She was a strong woman. She did not want me to know that she was feeling pain. We talked and I left her late at night, and I went home and I slept. I was in my house asleep when she came to me in a dream. She said she is going, and I said, 'No, no, please stay. You don't have to go,' so we kept talking. She said she will wait for me there. She said she was preparing some place for me.

"It was then that my houseboy came and knocked on the door. It was five o'clock in the morning. He knocked on the door and said they called from the hospital and that I should come. I knew then that my wife was gone. I knew she had passed away as soon as he said the hospital called. So there in my room, I prayed: *God, may she rest in peace.* I then went to the hospital. When I went in, a nurse met me. She wanted me to sit down and talk to me and prepare me. I said, 'No, I know that she has passed away.' She looked at me and she asked, 'How would you know?' I asked, 'Can I see her?' I then went to her room. I pulled back the cloth and saw she looked so peaceful. I kissed her, and then I prayed with her some more.

"I didn't know she was going to die, but we were doing everything to make her live. My will is not God's will, and he does what he wants to do and he does everything perfectly. It was his will that she leave and he took her. After her passing, I had a lot of people who love me sympathise with me, who feel the pain I feel. They all came to see me—the president, the ministers. Many of the big people in the country came to sympathise."

Adriana, who was at home with the children, remembers this time vividly. "When Champ had that fight, I was home and Beatrice was in Korle-Bu Teaching Hospital. He knew she wasn't well. He knew what was going on, and he called me from the airport and said, 'I am going straight to the hospital.' He did not even come home. He went straight to the hospital to be with her. It was so unfortunate that she died so young. She was just twenty-nine."

Lifelong friend Obi Oblitey, who had seen the two fall in love and saw firsthand the influence she had on Azumah's life, remembers this time with great sadness. "She was very young when she died. It was very sad. She was always respectful and she was very beautiful. She was very strong and very kind. If she was still alive, I would be happy. He was very lucky to have her and start his life with her, and she started his life very well. She loved Azumah very much. She was very good for Azumah. She was a good girl. I liked her very much."

Beatrice was obviously a very special lady who touched the hearts of many. Thinking and talking about her still brings tears to the eyes of Azumah's brother, Mensah. "That girl was a very nice lady—very good, very, very good," he says. "She was an angel. She was an angel to everyone in the family. When you needed something, she would get it for you. She would even cry for you. She loved everyone in the family. She was too good. It was very sad. It upsets me to talk about her; she was too good. She was a strong and talented girl, very pretty. I loved her too much. It broke my heart when she died. I feel bad today when I think of her. It hurts me still."

Azumah reflects, "God gave me my wife, a woman that every man would like to marry because of who she was. She had a true love. She doesn't care if there is money or not. Today's women are terrible that way, but God blessed me with my wife. She was a very good woman. Misunderstandings are in every marriage, but I never had one with Beatrice. She was very special." Her passing left a huge hole in many lives, but none more so than Azumah's. "I lost a big thing when Beatrice died. I lost my hope."

X

JEFF FENECH

"It was very terrible when Beatrice died. The day we went to bury her, I was coming out of the church and I was crying like a baby because I was saying to myself, *What is going on? Is Beatrice there? I can't believe it.* I said to God: *Why can't you leave her with the sickness so we can be together? I will love her like that.* But he decided he wanted to take her, and he knows best," Azumah remembers, tears welling in his eyes.

Adriana Nelson, Azumah's cousin who had been looking after the children while he was away fighting Pernell Whitaker, remembers how they tried to shelter the children from their mother's death. "There were rumours that she had passed before she really had, which was terrible," she says. "I had a Christian father who lived in South Odorkor, Mr. David Hammond, who was the general secretary for the Bible Society in Ghana at the time. When he heard the first rumour that Beatrice had passed away, he said, 'Bring the children to my place.'

"When she did die, there was a family friend who took the children to their place, but it was not a comfortable place, so I told Champ about Mr. Hammond's offer. He asked who would take care of the children, and I said I would go with them and take care of them. So we were there for three weeks to one month. They did not want them around leading up to the funeral, and we kept it from them. We decided to tell them when it was closer to the funeral. We told them that their mummy had gone to heaven. But David said he knew already. We asked him how he knew, and he said that one of the boys at his school had told him. He knew and had kept it to himself.

"After a month, Champ missed them and they moved back to live with him in Achimoto. He was there for the children, who were aged seven, five, and three at the time. The two girls did not really understand, but they knew she was in heaven. David, being the eldest, knew what was going on. It was tough on these three young children, losing their mum so young. It was really tough. But they coped. After her death, there were always people offering to help, and one of Champ's sisters came to live with him and the children so they were okay. It was not long after her death that Beatrice's mum and dad died—they were heartbroken."

Azumah still has vivid memories of that time. "I was lucky. It was not so difficult because at that time I had money. If there was no money, it would have been hard, but it was easier because I had money to be able to find people to help look after the children," he recalls.

There were many who wondered if Beatrice's death would lead to him surrendering his world title and hanging up his gloves, but he says it never crossed his mind. "I did not think of retiring after Beatrice passed, but I knew it would take me some time to come back. But God is my strength, and God always gives me ways to cope. He was telling me, *This is the world I prepared for you. I gave you Beatrice to set you up, and I will give you another wife.* I do not think I am ever going to have another wife, because I am thinking, *Where am I ever going to find another one like Beatrice?* But God told me not to worry, as he had planned my life.

"I wasn't thinking about retirement, but I slowed down a little bit because a part of me had died as well. It took me a while, but when you know God, and that God does not make mistakes, and that he knows the reason that he took her, we must give thanks to God for the time we did have together and carry on."

As if he and his children were not suffering enough, Azumah then had to suffer the consequences of a rumour that started with a television station in Mexico City, claiming that he had contracted AIDS. It was both vicious and cruel in its timing. Azumah had to undergo a number of tests with nominated doctors in order to quash the allegations. The tests found that the rumours were without foundation, and he could once more focus on his profession.

Despite losing his childhood sweetheart, Azumah had little time to reflect on her passing due to the contract he had signed, forcing Juan Laporte or Jeff Fenech, whoever won his vacant super featherweight title, to defend it against him within ninety days. With Fenech's ongoing injury problems and then illness, the fight never eventuated, so Azumah stepped in to fight Laporte in Sydney in October, still as the super featherweight champion. "The reason the fight was in Sydney, I think, was because we were promoting a fight with me and Jeff Fenech or Juan Laporte and Jeff Fenech," he recalls.

"I was still struggling when this fight came. I was still thinking about Beatrice, but it looked like they wanted to take the title away from me. They said they would give me a chance to win it back, but I did not believe they would give me that chance. I had to get back in the ring and fight if I wanted to keep my title," he adds.

Laporte was a Puerto Rican who fought out of New York and had taken on Salvador Sanchez for the WBC featherweight crown and lost by unanimous decision over fifteen rounds. He had then fought for the WBA version of the title against Eusebio Pedroza, whom he also lost to, this time on a split-decision. With Sanchez's passing, the WBC gave Laporte the chance to claim the vacant title, which he did, beating Mario Miranda, the fighter Azumah had replaced when he fought Sanchez. He defended his title twice before losing to Wilfredo Gomez, the man Azumah had knocked out to claim the title.

Like Azumah, Laporte had suffered a personal tragedy in the year leading up to this fight. His son had drowned, and he had buried his world championship belt alongside him. The WBC president Jose Sulaiman, on hearing of the fighter's gesture, sent him a new world title belt to show him support and respect from the boxing community.

Laporte was never going to be an easy fight. Here was a boxer who tended to start his bouts in the fast and furious style of yesteryear, yet had never been knocked off his feet. Like Azumah, he was a popular fighter, rarely having a bad word to say about any of his opponents. To many, he was "old school," battling hard in the ring and showing his class outside it.

The fight was held at the Sydney Entertainment Centre in Australia and was aimed to whet the appetites of boxing fans in Australia, as the winner would meet the "Marrickville Mauler," as Fenech was known around his hometown. Laporte came into the fight with a record of forty-six fights, thirty-six wins, nine losses, and one draw, with nineteen of those wins coming by knockout. Laporte was desperate to prove his worth. For many years, he had fought in the shadow of Azumah.

In the lead-up to the fight, Azumah was in good spirits, training in the Sydney suburb of Glebe and toying with his sparring partners by firing off his fast jab and making them miss, a tactic he intended to employ against Laporte, who was rated as one of the hardest hitters pound-for-pound by *KO Magazine* and who also had one of the hardest chins.

Looking back, Azumah talks of Laporte with great respect. "Juan Laporte is was one of the strong boxers. He was hard-hitting, but he was very slow. I knew it would be difficult to beat him, and it was. He fought me when my first wife passed away and I was not in good condition, but he was a good fighter and he could hit hard."

In the opening round, Laporte stunned Azumah with a powerful straight right, but in his excitement to follow up, he threw his opponent to the canvas, and referee Malcolm Bulner from Melbourne, in only his second WBC world title bout, quite rightly did not count it as a knockdown. "He hit me with a good punch. I was dazed. I held him so that I could clear my head," Azumah recalls. "He should have taken his time to finish me, but he rushed to try and finish it quickly. You have to pick your punches and not rush when you knock someone down, but he was rushing and became frustrated with me holding on, and he then threw me to the ground, so I went down. As no one saw a punch, it was not a knockdown, so I took my time and cleared my head and then moved forward and settled again. He could have won the fight had he not rushed."

It was a cagey affair, with Azumah dropping his right hand to try and lure Laporte in so that he could counter with a left hook, but the Puerto Rican American had been around the fight game too long to fall for that, so the two almost negated each other. However, Azumah kept scoring with his lightening jab.

A flurry of punches found their mark for Juan Laporte in round four and had the fans on their feet, but he failed to capitalise on them, and Azumah used his ring craft to defuse the situation and finish the round on top.

"Let's go, baby! Work, Azumah," "Buffalo" Martin implored Azumah from the corner. Azumah then went into showboating mode. He leapt into the air and fired off a punch before waving both arms crisscross-style in front of him before dropping both to his side, inviting Laporte to have a free swing. When the bell sounded, Azumah offered his glove to Laporte, who, rather than touch it in acknowledgment, hammered it, showing his frustration.

His frustration continued to show in round six, but when he returned to his corner, he saw that Azumah had a small nick under his right eye, so he now had a target to try and open up. Meanwhile, Jeff Fenech ringside looked far from impressed with the work of either boxer.

In round seven, the fans started to turn against Azumah as he danced to his left and then his right, snapping out a quick jab and opting not to engage in a fistfight. So riled were they by his tactics that chants of "Fenech, Fenech!" started to ring out around the stadium. Almost on cue, Laporte landed a telling right hand that Azumah walked into as he moved to his left, and the noise from the crowd lifted. Once again, Laporte failed to find the target as he tried to follow up, and to rub salt in his wounds, Azumah dropped his hands to his side and thrust his chin forward, inviting him to have a free punch. In his corner, Bill Benton urged Laporte to get Azumah on the ropes and knock him out. One could sense that his corner could feel the fight slipping away should it go the distance. In the eighth, it was all Azumah, until with around a minute to go, as he danced on his toes, Laporte caught him with a left hand that saw him slide along the ropes. The crowd was sure that he was going to go down, but as he roared back at Laporte, he proved he had simply been caught off-balance. Back in his corner, Buffalo was far from happy with his antics and begged him to concentrate on the job in hand and not clown around. In round nine, Buffalo hammered the canvas in his corner, trying to get Azumah to fight, but still he opted to stay on his bike and pick Laporte off at distance, until midway through the round when again he was caught by a strong left that stunned him. This time with Azumah on the ropes, Laporte did follow up, and many of his combinations found their target. Azumah, however, showed all his skill to parry many of the blows with his arms, and then, when the opportunity arose, spun off the ropes to safety.

"You don't win these two rounds, you lose the fight. You don't care, nothing? You don't have a heart?" Buffalo roared during the break. "Look at me, look at me!" he yelled, and then told him at the top of his voice, "Fight! Fight, Azumah! Everything is possible in the moment." Azumah sat stone-faced, staring straight back at his trainer, giving no indication of what he was thinking.At the end of round eleven, after Azumah had given a lesson in boxing and moving and had peppered Laporte with machine-gun-fire left jabs, he put out his glove to be tapped in respect, as the two had done in every round of the fight, and again Laporte hammered it in frustration. He knew that he had just three minutes to find a knockout punch or the fight was Azumah's.

With one minute to go in the final round, Laporte went looking for the miracle punch. He landed a few telling blows, but once again, Azumah danced his way out of trouble. When the final bell sounded, the two embraced. Azumah raised his right arm into the air to claim victory, but across the ring Laporte's team hoisted him onto their shoulders to imply he was the victor.

As the judges totted up their scores, Jeff Fenech was interviewed by the Sky television channel covering the fight and was asked who he thought he would be fighting. "I think I'll be fighting Azumah, but it was a very unimpressive performance. To all the people out there who think he's going to beat me, I know plenty of my friends who'll put all of their money youse have got on me, and I can't wait to get all the blokes who've put knives in my back and put them where they are supposed to be."

Far from impressed with the fight, he continued by saying, "Azumah Nelson showed great boxing skills against someone that stood there and let him show great boxing skills. Like I said before the fight, Azumah Nelson was fighting Juan Laporte, and Juan Laporte was fighting Azumah Nelson. Neither of them has fought Jeff Fenech; neither has faced Jeff Fenech; and when they do, they'll know. They may think I am a little easy to hit, but after a couple of rounds, when I soak up what I have to soak up, they'll know. Then they'll see what it's all about. They'll see what the fight game is all about. They'll see what hungry is." When the ring announcer Ray Connelly read out the judges' scores, the first to be read out was that of Melbourne-based Australian Gus Mercurio, who scored it 116–112 in favour of Azumah. Immediately, boos rang out around the venue. Azumah smiled and kept moving around the ring. The boos continued as Connelly read out the scores from Brisbane-based Australian Eddie Francis, who had the scores 116–113, also in favour of Azumah. Additionally, Herbert Minn from Hawaii had the bout going to Azumah by 115–113. The two boxers embraced and showed genuine respect for each other as Azumah took the unanimous decision.

Azumah paid credit to his opponent. "Laporte is a great challenger," he said. "He has a lot of experience. He has been in the ring a long time; he knows what to do. I was just boxing him—I just proved to the world I am the champion. I know I can win on points. I took some punches, but he did not hurt me. He gave me a tough fight."

It was then that the Sky channel interviewer, Graham McNeice, tried to stoke the fires for the upcoming bout and draw Azumah into saying something inflammatory. Fenech, who was still ringside, watched on with interest, hanging on the champion's every word. Azumah was very measured in his response. When McNeice told Azumah that Fenech had said he would beat him, he paused and then quietly answered, "Jeff Fenech, I am waiting for the time. I am going to be ready." He then paused again before adding, "He's in trouble."

Fenech smiled, turned away from the ring, and slowly made his way out of the arena. Certainly, based on that performance, Fenech would have had every right to be confident. It was far from a memorable fight. When the lights went down and the dust had settled, there were many who questioned whether Azumah had lost the desire to fight following the death of Beatrice.

Now retired and looking back on that fight, Juan Laporte still believes he won. "I never hated him—I always respected him as a man and as a fighter," he says. "I thought I won the fight. Other people thought I won the fight, but things happen. Deep inside your heart, you know who you fought; you know how you did; and you carry that with you. If they don't recognise that glory, you have it in your heart. I live happily every day. Azumah is still a great world champion—he is definitely the best thing to come out of Ghana, and they should use him to inspire others. As a guy, he is lovely. He is one of the best human beings around. He has a good heart and does things to help his country and other people—I love him."

So the scene was set for a showdown with Australian Jeff Fenech, who in his professional career was unbeaten and had yet to be knocked down. Fenech had claimed the IBF bantamweight title in just his seventh bout, as well as the WBC super bantamweight title and the WBC featherweight title, and he now had his sights firmly set on the super featherweight title. In March 1991, Jeff Fenech signed a four-fight contract with Don King. The first part of the deal set his tilt at a fourth world title against Azumah. If he won, he would have two title defences and then move up to light-weight and meet Pernell Whitaker. The deal worth $5 million was dependent on Fenech winning all four fights.

The fight that would forever link the two fighters was scheduled for June 28, 1991, at the Mirage Hotel and Casino in Las Vegas, and would be on the undercard of the Mike Tyson vs. Donovan "Razor" Ruddock world heavyweight championship rematch, Tyson having won the first encounter by a controversial TKO in round seven.

Azumah had one warm-up non-title fight against fellow Ghanaian Daniel Mustapha. He knocked him out in round four, and following the third defeat in his first four professional fights, Mustapha decided to retire. Fenech, who was coming out of fifteen months of retirement after a flirtation with a rugby league, had a comeback fight against Canadian John Kalbhenn, whom he defeated by TKO in round four. Like Musta-pha, this proved to be the Canadian's last professional fight.

Training did not go according to plan for either fighter. Fenech opted to leave Sydney and prepare for the fight in Las Vegas. He checked in at the humble, low-key Sheffield Inn outside the city and away from the constant buzz of the casinos. For seven weeks, he acclimatised to the desert heat, doing the best he could to make sure the fate that befell Barry McGuigan did not happen to him. His sparring partner was former world junior welterweight champion Greg Haugen. Everything was going according to plan until about two weeks before the fight.

With the hot desert wind blowing, he went for a run on a circuit that he had done many times before over a few hills and on a track around a local park. Fenech spotted Mike Tyson's trainer, Richie Giachetti, with some of his fighters and decided to show them that his running was superior to theirs. When he returned to the hotel, he was sick. He had burned himself out, and admits that from that day on, he was flat in training.

"I killed myself a few weeks out from the fight, and I wish I didn't. But like I said, that's history. That's just me. I like to show people I'm the fittest, the best. It backfired on me, but I never like to use things as an excuse," he recalled.

As was the norm, Azumah started his training in Ghana with Buffalo. Three weeks out, they flew to Ohio and settled into Don King's training camp. As with Fenech, everything was going according to plan until the two found themselves in Glenbeigh Hospital in Rock Creek, nine miles from the camp.

"It was just before our time to fight. They gave me a drip, and Buffalo was also suffering from malaria, and we were in the hospital together," he remembers. "It was good that we were at Don King's camp because no one knew I was not well. I was in the hospital for twenty-four hours, and then I came out and had to shed the weight because of the fluid from the drip."

The week of the fight, Azumah moved to Las Vegas, where one of his sparring partners was Ugandan Justin Juuku, who himself would fight for the WBA and WBC world super featherweight titles, but lose to Antonio Hernandez and Floyd Mayweather Jr., respectively. He remembers his time in the ring with Azumah. "It was a huge honour, and I sparred twenty rounds with him," he says. "He was the greatest African boxer, and all African boxers try to emulate Azumah. It was an honour at that time in my career to spar with him."

Once in Vegas, the hype began, and both fighters enjoyed crowds of fans in the gyms as they tuned up for the fight. The fight was scheduled for six thirty on a very hot Friday evening, which was twelve thirty p.m. the following day in Fenech's hometown of Sydney, Australia. Around the country, sports-mad Australians found somewhere to watch the fight, all willing their man on to victory.

In the mining town of Kalgoorlie in Western Australia, the pubs were packed. One man sitting at the bar of the Star and Garter Hotel was Dave Harper, a young driller from Melbourne who was now working in the famed gold mining town. He sat there with hundreds of others with a cold beer on the bar, waiting to witness history—a moment that they would all be able to talk about for years to come. They would be able to tell their grandchildren where they were when Jeff Fenech won his fourth world title without ever losing a fight. Certainly, it was a morning Dave would never forget, but little would he know how big an impact it would have on his life.

In Ghana, even though the fight was in the middle of the night, people climbed out of their beds and made their way to find a television set to watch the fight. In some cases, fathers woke their young sons and walked for several miles in the dead of night to the nearest television set, not wanting their sons to miss out on watching a true legend go to work. No matter the distance, it was important to be there to witness the fight. It would be something they would never forget.Back in Las Vegas, it was arranged that both fighters would change in caravans in the car park of the Mirage Hotel and Casino. Few Americans knew who Jeff Fenech was, and the name on the door of his changing room—Jeff French—confirmed that. Despite Mike Tyson being the big name, Don King was billing the Nelson-Fenech bout as the main attraction, and the television commentators, Ferdie Pacheco and Steve Albert, covering the fight for Showtime, backed up his view. Sitting ringside were basketball star Michael Jordan and some celebrities of the day: Clint Eastwood, Bill Cosby, Chuck Norris, and Demi Moore with then-husband Bruce Willis. From the world of boxing, Thomas "The Hit Man" Hearns was the star attraction.

In Azumah's caravan, the mood was relaxed. "I did not have a set routine," Azumah recalls. "I did not mind who wrapped my hands—anyone could do it. When I am going to fight, I am always praying. I am praying that the other fighter would not get hurt, that I would not get hurt. Never do I pray to win, as that is God's will. So when I am getting ready to fight, we sang in the dressing room. We sang praises to God. We thanked him for this time, this opportunity. It was like a church, a party—it was nice to see this. It made me happy."

In the other dressing room, trainer Johnny Lewis was carefully wrapping Jeff Fenech's hands. These hands had troubled him throughout his career; he had to ice his hands for twenty minutes after a training session. Lewis finished encasing his hands and, as was his habit, drew a cross on the wraps to protect his fighter in the ring.

When the knock on the caravan came, Azumah finally removed the cross that he wore around his neck and handed it to Buffalo, as he always did. Then he began the long walk to the ring. Azumah had never lost a bout as a super featherweight, but on this occasion, many felt he was facing his biggest challenge yet in brawler Jeff Fenech, a fighter who could not only take a punch, but who could throw one, too, and then there was the heat.

"I had fought in Vegas before so the heat did not worry me," Azumah says about his approach to the fight. "It was not my first time. I know the terrain. I know the ring. The sun is not going to fight for me. The weather is not going to fight for me. I have to fight for myself, and what I learned is that the fighting time is like the examination. What I have learned in school, I am coming to show, and you have to show me what you have learned. You have to show me, but most of the time, I showed that I have learned better than you."

Going into the fight, Fenech believed the key to success would be his ability to cut off the ring, and with a two-and-a-half-inch reach advantage over Azumah, he had the tools to make it a tough night at the office for the champion. "I just couldn't wait to get out there and show the people what I could do, to do what I do best, which is fight," he remembers.

As the ring announcer, Jimmy Lennon Jr., introduced the two fighters to the packed crowd, both boxers' expressions were set in stone. Azumah stared straight ahead as Buffalo massaged his neck. With the announcements over, the two were called to the centre of the ring by referee Joe Cortez, and both opted to avoid eye contact with the other as they listened to his final instructions. In fact, so determined were they not to catch each other's eye, they struggled to make contact with their gloves when asked to shake hands prior to returning to their corners.

Once back in their respective corners, Buffalo issued some last-minute words of advice to Azumah, and, as was tradition, Johnny Lewis kissed Jeff Fenech. Fenech beat his gloves together, gave a quick knee bend, and when the bell sounded, sprang forward from his corner.

The opening round saw Fenech move forward straight in front of Azumah and both fighters unload. It appeared that each was trying to send a message as to just how hard they could hit; Ferdie Pacheco on Showtime described Azumah as having "howitzer hands." He went on to say that Azumah "has a great many more tricks and techniques than does Fenech, who fights on courage and raw power."

A powerful flurry of punches in the last twenty seconds of the round saw Fenech slow down, and a right and then a left looked to momentarily stop him, or as Pacheco described it, "made Fenech wave in the breeze." When the bell sounded, there was no doubt who had taken the opening round: the defending champion.

Fenech's trainer, Johnny Lewis, pushed his fighter out for round two, and he was ready and waiting when the bell sounded. Azumah punched and moved more in the second, but despite being caught by a few solid blows from Fenech, he still had the ascendancy.

Round three started with a furious flurry of punches from Azumah as he stood toe-to-toe with Fenech and unloaded, but halfway through the round, Fenech shook the champion with a straight left followed by a short left hook to the chin that had Azumah backpedaling. Another powerful left hook to the head forced Azumah into a clinch, which was broken by referee Cortez. Azumah sat on the ropes, and Fenech threw punches to the body with Azumah in defensive mode; some landed but many missed.

He then moved upstairs with the same result. Azumah weaved away from many of the blows, but some found their mark. Neither man gave an inch, both unleashing some thunderous punches and showcasing great hand speed. For over a minute, they did not move from their positions, unloading bomb after bomb to each other's body and head. Fenech was undoubtedly the aggressor, and when the bell sounded, Joe Cortez had to be quick to separate the two. Azumah had words with the referee as Fenech made his way back to his corner with blood seeping from a wound under his left eye.

In the opening thirty seconds of the next round, Azumah adopted a stick-and-move tactic before the two fighters found themselves in the same corner of the ring where they had slugged it out during the last round. Despite having the opportunity to move away from the ropes after Cortez called the two to break, Azumah opted to stay where he was. Both fighters landed some telling blows, and both showed tremendous courage as they belted each other with uppercuts and hooks to the body and head. Round five was more of the same. Referee Cortez allowed the two to slug it out, simply warning them to be careful not to clash heads. Fenech landed a telling left hook to the head, which looked to rock Azumah, but within seconds, he was forcing Fenech back with a powerful salvo of blows.

As Azumah sat on his stool back in his corner, Buffalo told him, "Let's get out of this fucking corner. Let's not stay here no more." Johnny Lewis looked across at Azumah's corner and was convinced that the champion was spent. His advice to his man was to stay out of trouble for the next two rounds.

Azumah recalls this period of the fight. "If you are fighting me and I go to the ropes, and you come to me, I have support with the rope and I sit down and I can throw more punches than you can throw," he says. "I believe that anyone I fight, if they follow me to the ropes, I can sit on the rope and they have to be careful because the uppercuts will start coming, very powerful ones, and if you watch the fight, sometimes I throw six uppercuts, bam, bam, bam, bam …

"I was fighting and throwing these punches, and Fenech was taking these punches. I ask myself, *What clay did they use to make him?* I know myself that I hit hard, and some of the punches I sat on the rope and I threw from my waist with power, but he took all these punches and I was surprised."

Both men eased up in round six, Azumah jabbing and moving and Fenech appearing to block or parry many of his far from sharp punches. At ringside, Ferdie Pacheco was convinced Azumah was trying to lull Fenech into a trap. A fast flurry from Fenech in the last minute was the only real aggression in the round.

The fight was, without doubt, a close one. In the second half of round seven, Fenech backed Azumah into his own corner, and once again both fighters found the mark with punches to the body and the head, but it appeared that Fenech was landing more. As a result, the Australian fans in the crowd found their voice and started to chant, "C'mon, Aussie! C'mon!" In pubs around Australia, including the Star and Garter in Kalgoorlie, others joined in, all willing their man on to victory. In the break between rounds, Buffalo warned Azumah that the fight was slipping away from him. When backed up into a corner, he failed to move and allowed Fenech to have a stationary target to hit. He told Azumah, "Champ, time to apply the pressure. The fight's too close; it's too fucking close."

He implored his man to punch and move and keep looking to land his uppercuts. At the start of the round, he was on his bike, popping out his jab, but when he moved in to fire off a quick volley of punches, Fenech returned fire with equal if not more scoring blows. Twice, they went to the ropes and looked to slug it out again, the second time being in the closing seconds of the round, and as the bell sounded, Azumah let fly a left hook that looked to clip a retreating Fenech. The Australian was fuming and had to be held back by Cortez as he shouted at his opponent. Back in his corner, his trainer told him not to waste energy on arguing with the referee, but to focus on the last two rounds.

If Fenech was annoyed about the late blow, he had more reason to complain at the start of round ten. The bell sounded and Azumah climbed off his stool, but his corner had failed to insert his mouthguard. Referee Cortez ordered them to find it, but it appeared that they were unable to do so. Frustrated, Azumah took a step forward and said he would fight without it, but Cortez refused to allow him. He then spoke in Spanish to "Buffalo" Martin and asked him to search his pocket. The trainer claimed he had already done so. Yet one minute after the bell had sounded, it was produced from the pocket of Buffalo!

Azumah remembers the incident and is convinced it was an honest mistake. "Buffalo was confused. He could not find it," he says. "He thought they put it in the ice bucket, and when the time came for the next round, he could not find it. He is looking around to see if it fell down, so I said, 'No, no, let me go. I will fight. It does not matter if I have a mouthpiece. Let's go!' But the referee said, 'No, you must have the mouthpiece.' Then he found it."

Azumah came out and started boxing like the Azumah everyone knew in a round that had plenty of drama. First, referee Cortez was caught by a Fenech punch, and then the two embarked on some rough stuff, with Fenech rubbing the laces of his gloves across Azumah's face. In the last minute of the round, Fenech bore into Azumah with his head, and the champion sat on the ropes once again, trading punches with Fenech. The two hurled punches at each other, with Azumah possibly shading the advantage. As the bell sounded, Azumah threw a left hook; Fenech ducked and then lifted the champion off his feet and dumped him on the canvas. As he slowly rose to his feet with the referee standing between him and Fenech, Azumah glared at his opponent.

As Ferdie Pacheco commented ringside, "Azumah could have bought some time, claiming to be injured, but being the fighter he is, he picked himself up and made his way back to his corner to prepare for the next round." The feeling was he needed a knockout to win the fight, and in round eleven, he went on the attack. But Fenech weaved away from his punches, and Azumah was frequently caught by his counter punches.

Despite the feeling of those watching on television and many at the Mirage, Buffalo believed that if Azumah could win the last round, he could win the fight. There was no panic in the corner as they urged their man to give it his all for the final three minutes. As the bell sounded for the final round, Azumah became just the fifth Fenech opponent to hear it. Azumah went searching for Fenech, looking to finish the fight, and once again, there were spells where the two stood toe-to-toe and slugged it out.

With twenty seconds left on the clock, Fenech nailed Azumah with a right hand that stunned the champion. Seconds later, he landed another powerful right hand that snapped Azumah's head back. Remarkably, he stayed on his feet, "fighting from memory," as Ferdie Pacheco said in his commentary. He managed to hold on, and as the clock ticked down, Cortez separated the two. Fenech moved in for the final kill, but the bell sounded and both men embraced in a hug of mutual respect. The crowd rose as one to applaud two great warriors.

When he finally made his way back to his corner, Azumah's face was expressionless. He raised his arm to acknowledge the applause, a gesture that some saw as indicating victory. Ferdie Pacheco announced that he had scored the fight 117–111 with Fenech a clear winner, but added, "One never knows in Las Vegas." His words proved prophetic.

When Jimmy Lennon Jr. announced, "After twelve rounds of boxing, we have a split-decision," boos rang out around the stadium. First came the score as seen by judge Jerry Roth: 115–113 in favour of Fenech. The Australian pumped the air in satisfaction. Miguel Donate scored the bout 116–112 in favour of the champion, who remained unmoved. As Lennon started reading the final judge's score, Fenech shook his head as if he knew what was coming. "Judge at ringside Dave Moretti scores the bout 114–114, a draw. The decision is even, a draw," Lennon informed a far from pleased audience. Fenech exploded, his disappointment and frustration plain for all to see.

Post-fight, when talking to Ferdie Pacheco, Azumah still wasn't celebrating. He said, "I want to give him one more chance because I want to prove that I am the best."

Promoter Don King, standing alongside Jeff Fenech after he had been consoled by WBC president Jose Sulaiman, said, "This is too good a fight—there is no loser. This fight has to have a return match. Jeff Fenech is a class act."

Choking back tears, Fenech offered to go through another twelve rounds right then and there before begging for a rematch. "I'll come back and fight him here in two months. As long as I am the main event here and I fight here, no problems," he said.

Fight promoter Bob Arum was quoted in *Boxing News* as saying the decision was "so disgraceful it made me think about getting out of boxing altogether." Yet in the same publication, legendary trainer Eddie Futch said, "I definitely had Fenech ahead, but it was close because Nelson was throwing real good counters on the inside." It was a trend that would continue in the days that followed the fight, but most fans felt that Fenech had won.

Back in Kalgoorlie and around Australia, voices were raised, items were thrown at television screens, and people vowed never to watch boxing again. "It was incredible. Everyone was in the pubs to watch their working-class hero, Jeff Fenech, teach Azumah Nelson a lesson, and he did,"

Dave Harper remembers. "Except the judges didn't see it that way. Everyone knew that Fenech had won, and I still believe that today. People just could not believe that he could be robbed in that way. The mood was far from happy, and all I can say is it was lucky the fight was in America. The whole nation was annoyed and felt ripped off."

Respected referee Joe Cortez recalls this fight as one of his most memorable. "That first fight made history because these guys threw so many thousands and thousands of punches," he says. "It was a day to remember. It was like 115 degrees with the lights off. With the lights on, it felt like 150 degrees, and these guys came out there and wanted to knock each other's head off. When it got to the point where Jeff Fenech was able to, I don't know how he did it, Azumah threw a punch and it went over his shoulder, and he picked him up and slammed him to the ground. I thought this was a wrestling match! I said, 'Whoa, wait a minute!' I held these guys back and I thought I was in a fight. I told them, 'I did not come here to fight. I came to referee. What's the matter with you guys?' It turned out to be the fight of the year."

For Fenech, it was heartbreaking. Even with the passing of time, he is still understandably frustrated. "You've seen my reaction. I knew what was going to happen," is how he recalls the announcement of the split-decision. "If he won three rounds that night, that was three too many, as I don't believe it. Boxing's boxing and it's history; everything happens for a reason. Azumah was walking around with his arms in the air. Fighters who do that are crazy because they know they are going to get decisions. I would never do that. If that was me in that fight, I would have went and sat in my corner, congratulated him.

"In fact, I congratulated him after the fight. I was holding him in the twelfth round; he couldn't stand up. Had there been thirty seconds more, it would have been a knockdown. But that didn't happen, and all I can say is he must have the largest heart in Africa, and he is one of the toughest guys to ever have put a glove on. He's a great fighter."

Looking back on this fight Azumah, not surprisingly, has a different view from his opponent. "Had it gone fifteen rounds, would he beat me? No, I was not that tired," he recalls. "I was trying to set him up in round twelve for a right hand, but he did not let me throw it. When I threw it, he saw it and he countered back, and when he did, I was wobbling. He hit me with a good punch. I was not tired, but he made me wobble. People thought I am tired, but if we are going fifteen, I will go fifteen. If we are going twenty, I will go twenty.

"I did not feel anything when it was a split-decision. Some of the boxers, when they lose, they start shouting. I never lost and shouted. It's just a game, so give me a rematch. No, I didn't think I had lost the title, but if I lost it, I lost it. I don't give any excuses because I am sick—I am not going to give an excuse. I will always give you a rematch. Even if you do not want one, I will offer you one."

In the twenty-four hours after the fight, accusations of a fix filled the air. In Australia, a nation felt that it had been robbed. So strong was the criticism of the judges that Miguel Donate, for whom this was his twentieth world title bout, resigned from the WBC and never judged a major fight again. "I am a religious, honest man with a lot of friends in boxing. I will miss them, but it is not worth the controversy, hassles, and accusations that have come from this fight. Nelson won the fight because he was the more accurate, stronger puncher, not like the windmill-type action of Fenech," he declared.

This decision has linked Azumah Nelson and Jeff Fenech for life, and in the challenger's opinion, changed his life forever. "When he done what I done after the fight and sat down and watched the fight, I reckon he thought, *Shit, what do I do?* These guys don't get up every morning and go for a run. They don't die. They don't starve. They don't go through fights with broken hands, and they don't get needles. I done all that and one guy was able to ruin my career. I would have been the first fighter ever to win four world titles undefeated."

The fight resulted in polarised opinions, many feeling Azumah was lucky to hang on to his title, but even all these years later, he is adamant he won the fight. "Everybody says he won the first fight. I am in the ring. I know if he won. I know if I lost. I know that because the guy is punching, and he threw a lot of punches. People counted all the punches, but a lot did not land. That is was why I offered him a rematch anywhere in the world," he says.

No one can change what happened, but Azumah's supporters may be tempted to refer back to a pamphlet published in 1933 by Nat Fleischer, founder of *The Ring* magazine, entitled "How to Judge and How to Referee a Fight." In it, he warns judges and referees not to be misled by "the man whose aggressiveness consists simply of boring in, of forcing the battle by keeping on top of his opponent, but fails to land effective blows." He goes on to say, "Defence, good guarding, slipping, ducking, and good countering—all should be given their proper credit in the awarding of points."

Mind you, this was a long time before the ten-point scoring system. If the first bout had been one to remember, the second promised to be a massive drawcard and a big payday for both fighters.

XI

THE REMATCH

Once back in his room, Jeff Fenech put a videotape into the machine and eased back into the sofa. He then sat through the twelve rounds he had just fought. "I wanted to make sure that what I knew, I had done. I wanted to confirm it, and when I watched it, and every time I watch it, I win easier," he recalls. "I mean, anyone who says I didn't is crazy, and even in the first round when he hit me, he didn't. It hit my glove and I was a bit off-balance. I think the commentators were so used to seeing the great Azumah Nelson, they hadn't really seen me. They didn't know what to expect, what they would get, or even what to call me. It's all part and parcel of boxing.

"As I say to people, if you can't write, you are not going to be a book writer. If you can't cook, you aren't going to be a great chef. But in boxing, you can make a lot of bad decisions and still be a judge."

While Fenech was feeling the injustice of the judges' decision, Azumah had to live with the fact that many of his loyal fans felt that he had been lucky to get a decision that meant he was still world champion. "I thought I won because he did not care where he was throwing the punches, whether I was blocking or dodging them, but the judges could see," Azumah explains. "He got me in the last round because I was so tired and weak, and I think that is why he thinks he won the fight. Don King is not the referee, not the judge—you see it as you want.

"Everyone I fight thinks they have won if they last twelve rounds with me. I don't blame them—they believe if they can finish the fight with me,

185

they have to be called the winner. I am too good. If they finish the twelve rounds with Azumah, they put something in their minds to say they have won: *He is so experienced. If I finish the fight with him* ... Some run away until the end of the fight and still claim they won, which is what Jim McDonnell did until I knocked him out. If he finishes the fight, he wins the fight, and he did everything to finish the fight. If I come to your home, I have to knock you out. Most of my fights were in the opponent's home, so I did my best to knock them out. I tried to knock Fenech out, but he was very strong."

Fenech was quoted in *KO Magazine* as saying, "I thought maybe I hit him harder than I actually did," on hearing Azumah was convinced he won the first encounter. He went on to say, "He's a proud bloke, and that's what happens when someone stays on too long. I can show him in the rematch that I won the fight."

There was no doubt that both men had good reason to accept a rematch, as both had a point to prove. There was one thing for sure: Come the rematch, there would be no lack of pride or commitment in the ring from either boxer. Azumah claims he agreed to a rematch as soon as the first fight was over. "I could see he was upset in the ring and that is when I said to him, 'I will give you a rematch. Wherever you want the fight to take place, I will be there. If you want the fight to take place in Australia, I will be there. Your mother can be the referee; your father can be the judge; and your friends can be the supporters. I will knock you out.'"

However, in boxing, nothing is that simple. Fenech's camp believed that the draw had brought an end to their contract with Don King, as Fenech had failed to secure the obligatory win. King, however, sensing what a bonanza the rematch promised to be and with Azumah signed up to his camp, warned them that the fight would never happen if they walked away. However, with the contract written under Australian law and not under American jurisdiction, King did not have a leg to stand on, and instead tabled a new offer to Fenech.

WBC president Jose Sulaiman was keen for a rematch and was concerned that Fenech would opt to take on WBA champion Hector Lopez, as they had installed him as their number-one contender. Eventually, an agreement was reached. Fenech signed a new contract with Don King for one fight only; the Australian would receive a percentage of the television rights and $2 million. Azumah would receive the same pay prior to paying expenses to his management support staff. The fight was scheduled for March 1, 1992, and would be staged in Melbourne. The rematch was good news for Azumah, as it finally guaranteed him a substantial payday to match his glittering career. He had only suffered one defeat in the past nine years, and that was to Pernell Whitaker on the eve of his wife's passing away.

Fenech decided to have a warm-up bout against twelfth-ranked WBC challenger, Miguel Francia of Argentina, in Melbourne in September. He was expected to put him away easily, but ended up winning by unanimous decision over ten rounds. By his own admission, his preparation for this fight was not good. "In preparation, where I had never been hurt before in my life, for that fight I started to feel punches. My sparring partner would punch, and shit, it hurt, but I kept saying, *Get back in the office and it'll be all right.* In boxing, when you start getting hurt, maybe it is a sign. But it was a sign I didn't want to believe," Fenech explains.

Azumah, meanwhile, had headed to Spain for an operation on his elbow, which had troubled him in the first fight. He had the operation in Zaragoza and based himself there for his recuperation and training with Buffalo before heading to Melbourne.

On November 21, the "Tooheys Big Blue" was confirmed for Princes Park, the home of the Carlton Australian Rules Football Club. It would have a capacity of forty-two thousand with fifteen thousand seated on the grass around the ring. The ring would be covered so the fight could go forward, rain or shine. At the announcement, Fenech was quoted in *Fist* magazine as saying, "I've really lived for this moment, when I can get Nelson into the ring again. Now that we've signed and got a date and a venue, I'm a very relieved and happy man. There have been some great sporting events in Australia, and this will be as big as any." He went on to "guarantee" there would be no draw in the rematch. Probably his most shocking statement was when he was quoted in the media as saying, "The only way they're going to take him home to Ghana is in a body bag."

Azumah's reported response was, "Tell Fenech he is playing with fire, and it will burn him." Azumah, having broken with tradition, was focused and training brilliantly with Buffalo in Spain; things in Australia were not, however, going as planned.

"Rightfully so, we would have thought the real winner would come from that next fight, and we were so sure it was going to be us," was the view of Fenech's trainer, Johnny Lewis. "We were so sure that we were going to go out and do a job on him in Melbourne. In preparation for that fight, I was never really, really comfortable with what Jeff was giving us. Mind you, I think in the first fight, I don't think Jeff was … he was about 80 per cent of the real Jeff Fenech in that fight. So the next fight, going through gym sparring sessions and everything, I just noticed that Jeff certainly wasn't the same Jeff Fenech prior to the first Azumah Nelson fight."

Fenech and Lewis have long since fallen out. Fenech today bristles at the fact that his trainer did not believe he was putting in the required work, but admits that he was also at fault. "After the first Azumah fight, something was taken out of me—I lost something. Maybe it was the time in boxing, and I'd had enough," he recalls. "I trained hard, but sparring was not the same. I did not feel the same. Suddenly, these guys who I was sparring with, who had never hurt me—wow, I started to feel their punches. Maybe if he [Lewis] was more responsible being my promoter and my manager, who took 25 per cent of my purse, we would have won the fight."

In fact, in his authorised biography by Paul Kent, it is claimed that Lewis did call promoter, Bill Mordey, suggesting that they call off the fight. Mordey, knowing that this was probably the biggest world championship fight in Australia since Jack Johnson vs. Tommy Burns in 1908, was never going to do that.

The Fenech team visited Princes Park a couple days before the big event. The ring was up and standing in the centre of the oval. Lewis looked at the position of the sun and asked which corner was Nelson's. When he was shown the red corner, he enquired as to where the sun would set at the time of the fight. He wanted the champion looking into the sun. The ring was taken down and erected again with the red corner facing the direction of the setting sun.

On the Friday before the fight, the rules meeting was held, and everyone was there except for Azumah. Buffalo represented him. The Fenech camp raised again their displeasure over the scoring of the first bout. Both camps were then warned by WBC representative, Gabe Penagaricano, that they would face the risk of disqualification if they misplaced a mouthpiece or used any other delaying tactics to buy their fighter time. "You're about nine months too late," Fenech told Penagaricano. Buffalo and Fenech then engaged in a war of words before the meeting closed.

Outside the meeting, Carl King faced accusations from the Australian media that his father had conspired to rob Fenech of victory in Las Vegas. He smiled and parried their questions with, "I'm flattered that everyone thinks my family has so much power."

Everything was calm at the Saturday weigh-in, with both fighters on the scales at 129 pounds. However, very few paid any credence to the comments of local lightweight Scott Brouwer, who had worked with Nelson as a sparring partner in the lead-up to the fight. "I've sparred with both of them. Azumah is stronger and he hits harder. Jeff will have to be 100 per cent to beat Nelson. Anything less and he will lose."

Finally, the day of the most anticipated sporting event in Australia arrived. The fight was to take place on a Sunday to tie in with television in the U.S. On the undercard that night was another boxer with a bright future from the Johnny Lewis stable making his professional debut, Kostya Tszyu, who knocked out Australian Darrell Hiles in just seventy seconds.

The rain started to fall in Melbourne, which reduced the crowd from an expected sell-out to close to thirty-seven thousand. However, many Australian highfliers were ringside, including media tycoon Kerry Packer, Olympian Dawn Fraser, iconic Aussie actor Paul Hogan, and former WBC featherweight world champion Johnny Famechon, who arrived in a wheelchair after having been hit by a car while jogging outside Sydney's Warwick Farm racecourse the previous year.

Fenech, a picture of concentration, made his way to the ring as the partisan crowd hailed his arrival by chanting his name. He walked, head bowed, with his gloves on Lewis's shoulders, trusting his trainer to lead him to the ring. He climbed through the ropes and bounced with nervous energy, trying to stay loose in his black robe with white piping. He acknowledged the crowd and everything appeared normal, but Lewis noticed something. Fenech had forgotten to cross himself. It was a ritual that he did every time he entered the ring, as much of a habit as putting in his mouthguard, but on this occasion he had forgotten to do it.

Azumah, smiling and looking extremely relaxed, made his way to the ring to the strains of the Ghanaian song, "asem be re ba ooo," meaning "something is about to happen," wearing a white silk robe and a black velvet crown with gold stars on it. Though this type of hat was commonplace at most markets in Accra, in Australia it reminded everyone who the reigning world champion was. Because of the weather, Azumah had no sun to contend with, so the rebuilding of the ring to try and gain an advantage had been for nothing.

As the introductions were made, the rain cascaded down, and three openings appeared in the canopy over the ring. They did not distract either fighter. This was Azumah's seventeenth world title fight in almost ten years. He was thirty-three years of age; he had fought in seven different countries; and he had been a world champion for eight years. Yet few gave him any chance of victory against a younger fighter in his own backyard.

In fact, before the fight went ahead, Azumah had received a call from the president of Ghana, J. J. Rawlings. "He said to me, 'People are saying that you are going because of the money,' and he had been my manager when I was an amateur. I said to him, 'Mr. President, you know me. When I say something, I have to do it.' He then said to me, 'I believe in you, Azumah, but I am afraid.' I said to him, 'Don't get scared. I am going to knock him out,' and I went and knocked him out."

Azumah was incredibly confident going into this rematch and, as he had done previously, had ensured that the fight would be aired live on television back home in Ghana. Knowing that there would be plenty of excitement back home, he contacted his good friend, Obi Oblitey. Obi recalls, "He sent a message to me and one of our friends, who has now died, as he knew the Ghana Broadcasting Corporation would come and interview us. He said they will ask us how we see the fight and told us to tell them he would stop Fenech in round seven. So we did."

In his corner, Azumah had his brother, and he had told him to tell him when round six had finished so that he could be true to that prediction. As in the first fight, both fighters avoided eye contact as they received their instructions from referee, Arthur Mercante, in his ninety-seventh world championship bout.

It took Azumah one minute and forty-five seconds of the first round to have Fenech on the canvas. "Before the fight, I hear his coach telling him—he is a good coach—he is telling him, 'Be careful. Azumah's left hook is dangerous. Watch out.' So from the first round, the guy was watching my left hook. All of a sudden in the first round, I just jab, one, two, three, four, and then boom—I landed a right and he went down. The left hook didn't come because I knew he was looking for the left hook. I changed the style and I put him down. I knocked him down again in the second and almost in the third," Azumah remembers with a trademark smile.

There was no doubt that the first round was Azumah's, as he landed the most punches and looked the sharper of the two fighters. Round two saw Fenech come back well from the knockdown, but Azumah was still the aggressor and benefitted when what appeared to be a slip by Fenech was ruled a knockdown by Mercante. This was a very different fight from the one in Las Vegas. Azumah looked stronger, fitter, and much sharper than his opponent, and went forward more often than he had in the first encounter. Round three saw the two toe-to-toe, as they had been in Las Vegas, and Fenech landed some telling blows. The bell sounded and Mercante struggled to separate the two, and words were exchanged. Azumah, despite his prediction, failed to knock out Fenech in round seven, and he explains why this was the case. "I told my brother, 'Listen, I will knock this guy out in the seventh round. I will set him up, and after the sixth round I will knock him out in the seventh, so when we get to the sixth round let me know.' But in between the rounds, my brother was enjoying watching the fight so much and he was so happy. At the seventh round, he came to me and said, 'Brother, sorry I forgot to tell you it was the sixth round. It's the seventh round.' I said, 'I told you to tell me the sixth round, so I could knock him out in the seventh. Now I cannot knock him out in the seventh. I will have to do it in the eighth and set him up this round.' The bell went for the seventh round, and I start setting him up. At the end of the round, I looked at my brother, and I said to him, 'Now I am going to knock him out this round'—and I did.

"In the seventh and eighth rounds, I give myself to him and he just starts punching. When I set him up, I went to the corner. He is throwing the punches and I am blocking, but I slow my punches down, so I am just touching him. I am hardly hitting him, just touching him. Then he realises the punches are slow and there is no power. He could lose himself and start throwing punches, trying to knock me out. As soon as he did that, his guard came down and I went boom, boom, and landed the punches and he went down."

If you watch the replay of the fight, it is exactly as Azumah remembers. Fenech started to unload and left the right side of his head exposed. Azumah landed one left hook flush on the side of his head, and two more blows soon followed before a right landed and Fenech crumpled to the canvas.

Ever the warrior, Fenech quickly leapt to his feet, but that could have been his mistake. His trainer, Johnny Lewis, climbed the steps to the ring, towel in hand, desperately trying to see how his fighter was, but Mercante, who waved the fight on, obstructed his view. Azumah turned Fenech back onto the ropes and fired off six unanswered blows to the head before Mercante stepped in and stopped the fight at the same moment that Lewis's towel hit the canvas behind him.

Two minutes and twenty seconds into round eight, Jeff Fenech had lost his first professional fight, and Azumah had recorded a victory that was named the "Upset of the Year for 1992" by *The Ring* magazine. The disappointed Australian crowd that had booed Azumah when his name was announced at the start of the bout showed great sportsmanship at the end of the bout, acknowledging a great champion. Many realised that they had just witnessed two great champions go head-to-head in their own backyard. It was just as well that Azumah knocked Fenech out, as incredibly two of the judges had had the fight even when the knockdown came, while the other, Britain's Harry Gibbs, had it 68–65 in favour of Azumah.

Carl King, despite the animosity between the Fenech camp and his father's organisation, praised Fenech post-fight. "These people shouldn't be disappointed in Fenech. He fought his heart out, but simply lost to a great champion. I only hope that people will finally give Azumah the credit that he deserves. He was magnificent," he said.

All these years later, Carl King Jr. admits that this victory was the sweetest of them all. "In Vegas, I knew Azumah was sick and we kept it quiet. When he knocked Fenech out in Melbourne, that was one of my most cherished moments in boxing. I'll never forget that after the fight, Fenech said to me, 'Do you feel better now?' He was disrespectful to America and I did not like that, so I wanted Azumah to knock him out for America. And he did."

If it was sweet for Carl King, it was even more enjoyable for the boxing fans back home in Ghana. "It was important for us in Ghana. Fighting Fenech was a case of fighting injustice. Fighting Fenech was about getting revenge," former sports minister, Nii Amakai Amarteifio, says. "Fighting Fenech in Australia was very important because of George Barnes and Attuquaye Clottey. For him to defeat Fenech was very symbolic and very important for this country, as well as for me. As a young man from Accra, his mentor, Attuquaye Clottey, the man who taught him how to box, had fought in Australia two times and was robbed both times in favour of a chap called George Barnes. They fought for the Commonwealth welter-weight title. So beating Fenech was justice for his mentor and revenge—sweet revenge."

Attuquaye Clottey had fought George Barnes in 1955 and 1957; both occasions were in Sydney with Vic Patrick as the referee. Attuquaye would never hold a title outside his native Ghana, despite an impressive record of thirty-seven wins, twelve losses, and two draws in a career that saw him box in Cote d'Ivoire, Australia, France, Germany, Italy, and Britain. He would, however, become one of the greatest, if not the greatest, boxing coaches Ghana has ever produced. Barnes, on the other hand, was the first son of a national boxing champion to emulate his father. He was also the first Australian to win the British Empire welterweight title. Despite what many in Ghana may have felt, he is regarded in Australia as one of the greats. His career spanned sixty-seven professional bouts and forty-two wins over fifteen years, with many against world-rated opponents.

It was after this fight with Jeff Fenech that Azumah went from being

"The Terrible Warrior" in the ring to being known as "The Professor," a moniker that certainly suited his age far better. There has been conjecture over who gave the champ his new ring name, but it would appear that it was in fact Azumah himself. At the press conference after the fight, where both fighters complimented each other, Azumah said, "I am a professor of boxing. Fenech is a great fighter, but today I proved that I'm better." The media around the world appeared to love the description, as the title "Professor" was linked to his name by more than one media outlet in their post-fight write-ups. Ultimately, the origin matters not, but from that day forward Azumah Nelson became known as "The Professor."

This time, there was no way Jeff Fenech was going to head to his hotel room and watch a replay of this fight, as he had in Vegas. He had been comprehensively beaten, and to his credit, he has always acknowledged the fact. "The great thing is he was able to go home, and when everybody thought he couldn't, he came back and he won. Did he beat the same Jeff Fenech? Did he beat Jeff Fenech at his best? No doubt in my mind he didn't, but I have never made any excuses. All he can do is beat what is in front of him, and he done that. But I know that wasn't me," Fenech says.

Not surprisingly, having lost his unbeaten record and the chance of a fourth world title, the pain of the decision in Las Vegas lives on. "The WBC knows who won the fight. The world knows who won the fight," Fenech adds. "The sad thing is, and Azumah is a great fighter, but anyone who goes around putting their hands in the air at the end of a fight, that's a no-no. You see it in boxing today. It's a slur on boxing. You know in a fight when there's two people, you know who punches you more in the head than the other person. You know by someone's demeanour at the end of the fight who's won the fight. At the end of the fight, the guy could hardly walk. Yet he still had the energy while Carl King held his hand up, saying he won. That is an embarrassment. If they done that to me, I would throw my hand away and throw them out of the ring. I want to conduct myself and respect this sport, and this is why boxing today is no longer where it was.

"A few years ago, I was in a hotel in Vegas and I walked out of my room. A guy in the room opposite mine coincidentally happened to open his door at the same time as me, and he said, 'Excuse me, are you Jeff

Fenech?' I said, 'Yes, I am.' He then said, 'I just want you to know something, son. I have never watched another boxing match since that robbery in Las Vegas—never watched boxing since. I go to UFC [Ultimate Fighting Championship] now.'"

Many speculated that it was the hurt from that first encounter that saw Fenech invite Azumah to climb back into the ring with him in 2008, ten years after Azumah had hung up his gloves and twelve since Fenech had. This fight, for all the recriminations, also saw a unique coming together, and a friendship formed. Dave Harper, the young driller who had watched the first fight in Kalgoorlie, had come a long way in the years that followed and was now based in Ghana, running his own drilling company, Geodrill.

Having always been a boxing fan, it was at a function in Accra that he was introduced to Ray Quarcoo, the then-president of the Ghana Amateur Boxing Federation. "We started talking about boxing, and I told Ray that I had watched the first Fenech fight, and I was sure that Fenech had won. It was then he told me that they were having a rematch for charity," Harper recalls. "I told him I would be interested in coming on board as a possible sponsor, and the next day, I was sitting in my office with Ray and Azumah Nelson. I was too late to come on board in a sponsorship capacity, but Azumah invited me to go as part of his entourage.

"I went and thoroughly enjoyed the experience, and from that point started a very special friendship. We have become very good friends, and I help him in his business dealings wherever I can. But that is secondary. I do that because he is a mate. He has become a dear friend—dare I say, one of my best friends. He is an incredible individual." The post-retirement fight in Melbourne saw Jeff Fenech awarded a majority decision after both boxers completed ten rounds. All three judges were from Melbourne, and Andrew Campbell and Aneeka Williams both scored the bout 94–96, while Ignatius Missailidis scored it a draw at 95–95. Sadly, a fight that should have been a coming together of two great champions ended up being the fight that soured the relationship between them.

Azumah recalls how the fight came about and what transpired. "I love farming and I was on my mango farm. Jeff Fenech, he never called me after the fight. Then all of a sudden, he called me. I was surprised. I asked

him if he had a problem, and he said no. I then said, 'Can I help you?'
and he said no. Then he said, 'Listen, I want us to fight so that we can
raise some money for your foundation.' When he said this, he made me
so happy. I thought, *Oh, this guy is a good guy.* So I said, 'Okay, listen, I
cannot fight right now. I'm too big. Give me three months to shed some
weight off.' He said, 'No, no, the Olympic Games are coming, and we
have to fight before the Olympics.' The Olympic Games were in six
weeks' time, so I had to train and shed the weight and then go and fight,
all in six weeks. Anyway, I said, 'Okay, I will do my best.' After all, it was
for my foundation.

"Before he went, he said, 'Listen, the press is going to call right now,
so tell them you are going to knock me out.' I said okay. As soon as he
finished talking, my phone rang, and it was the Australian press: 'Hey,
Azumah, we hear you are going to fight Jeff Fenech?' I said, 'Yeah, yeah,
that's right. I'm going to fight Jeff Fenech, and I am going to knock him
out in the seventh round.' How stupid am I?

"Anyway, I went home and I told my wife, Peggy, that I was going to
fight Jeff Fenech, and she started laughing. 'Look at you! How can you
fight Jeff Fenech?' she said. 'How can you shed all that weight and fight
Jeff Fenech in six weeks?' I told her it was not a fight—a real fight. It was
an exhibition to make some money for the foundation. She then asked,
'Jeff Fenech said that?' And I said, 'Yes, he is a good man.'

"So I started training and then I came down to Australia and he
[Fenech] said, 'Hey, Azumah, listen, the money that we are going to
make, we are going to share fifty-fifty, okay?' I told him that was good.

"Then we had the fight, and after the fight, he said he won the fight. I
said, 'Okay, if that makes you happy.' I think he wanted this because after
I knocked him out, I hear everyone was always telling him, 'Hey, Azumah
knocked you out,' and he was not happy about that. So he wanted to
retaliate.

"When we are fighting, I don't even want to hit him because I feel
good in my heart for him; he wanted to help my foundation. It would
not be right to knock him out. I could not come and knock him out after
all he was going to do for me. But he had a different plan. So after the
fight, he said he won and I said, 'That's fine, if it makes you happy. Now

where's the money?' He told me that someone very bad had taken the money after the fight. I said, 'What are you talking about?' So I handed it to my accountant to look at everything, and he told me how much I was owed, and I said we would fight to get that money." Azumah has since received some money, but not all that he believes he was entitled to, and that has soured the relationship between the two, which is sad—especially when the two are frequently seated next to each other at boxing reunions. It creates a very awkward situation, with neither talking to the other and both avoiding eye contact, just as they had done in the ring. Jeff Fenech's account of events is a little different from how Azumah remembers them. "I was in Thailand. I was supposed to fight Samart Payakaroon. We made a deal. I was going to take a team and have a holiday with some Aussies, but he pulled out at the last moment, so a friend of mine called Azumah Nelson. He got in contact, and he said he would take the fight. I did speak to him after my friend, Dean Bourke, called. I did tell him there was an opportunity to make money. I think he got more than he got for 90 per cent of his fights. I do know he got more than me.

"Max Markson [the promoter] was saying we could earn a $1 million. He tried to sell tables for thirty to forty thousand dollars, but they couldn't sell one—I'm a liar; they sold one table for a deal with a newspaper, so it was given away and they gave us all the publicity. If Mick Gatto hadn't come on board, we wouldn't have earned a hundred and fifty thousand, because Mick helped me sell all these tables at ten thousand a table. So I would have loved, like Max was saying, to have earned $1 million, but we didn't. I never had that thought; I never believed it. As I say, I wish we had earned $1 million. I wish I earned four hundred thousand, but it didn't happen. The thing is, it had nothing to do with me. I didn't collect one dollar from ticket money. I did not pay Azumah; I got paid from the same people who paid Azumah.

"The result was no closure to me. It was great to be able to lose that weight and compete, but that was not Azumah Nelson or Jeff Fenech. That was us two having a dance. I don't say I beat Azumah Nelson, no chance—I beat him in the first fight. I love the guy and if the money was his problem, he could have had my share. It destroys me because I love the guy. To me, what we earned was amazing."

Azumah, despite their differences, still acknowledges the fighter that was Jeff Fenech. "Yes, I respect him as a fighter. When it comes to boxing, I give him 20 per cent, but as a fighter I give him 95 per cent. He just comes and fights. When you fight someone like that, you need to know how to box, and that is why I beat him."

XII

ROAD WARRIOR

"I am a road warrior—when I come to your place, you are in trouble," Azumah says. Victory over Jeff Fenech garnered "The Professor" newfound respect. Very few had given him a chance against a fearsome fighter such as Fenech, but he had answered those critics emphatically. Azumah was undoubtedly the biggest drawcard in the super featherweight division. Yet as is so often the case, the boxers in the lower weight divisions do not attract the big paydays.

The late boxing aficionado and writer, Bert Sugar, thought he understood why this was when a few years later in 1995, he said, "Bottom line: As the heavyweight division goes, so goes boxing. This goes back to John L. Sullivan, and it has something to do with being American. Americans are always obsessed with big things—cars, houses, breasts, fighters. We could have ten Roy Joneses or ten Pernell Whitakers, but we'd still be waiting for the heavyweight division to come back."

It was for that reason that many speculated that Azumah would once again look to step up to lightweight. A rematch with Pernell Whitaker was out of the question, as he was looking to take on Julio Cesar Chavez for the WBC light welterweight title. Some boxing scribes even believed that if Azumah did step up, many genuine lightweights would be loath to take him on because he would be too strong.

Azumah was even tempted to consider taking on WBA light welterweight champion, Edwin Rosario. "I thought if I win that title before Whitaker, it will force him to give me a rematch, and as everyone knows,

I always win the rematch. I think that is why he would not fight me," he recalls.

Nothing eventuated with Azumah moving up a weight, so eight months later, he defended his title against American Calvin Grove. From Pennsylvania, Grove had turned professional in 1982 and had won the IBF featherweight title in 1988, with a TKO over Puerto Rican Jose Antonio Rivera. He had defended his title just once before losing on points to Mexican Jorge Paez.

The fight was at altitude in Lake Tahoe, Nevada—six thousand three hundred feet above sea level—and both fighters arrived in town early to let their bodies acclimatise. Grove, at thirty, was confident his time had come. Going into the fight, he said, "What it took for me to win a world title was a lot of hard work, a lot of dedication, and a lot of sacrifice. To get the title now is even harder than it was then, so I have to double what I did before to get this other title. As long as I don't slug with him, then Calvin Grove is gonna be successful. I'll box him, make him box me, the way I know I can, and I will come out that night world champion."

He was convinced that the fights with Fenech would have taken their toll on the champion. "Azumah Nelson, I think has had too many wars, and the two fights with Fenech, he has come off two hard fights. He's not the same fighter anymore. You can't be on top forever—someone else has to come up—and I'm the guy who's coming up to win the title."

Azumah seemed to have been reborn after the Fenech fight. That old cockiness was back, and a smile came across his face more readily. It was like he had come to terms with the loss of Beatrice and was enjoying boxing again; in fact, he said after the Fenech fight, "I did not want the fight to end. I was having such a good time." As for Calvin Grove's comments, he parried them with a smile. "You want to move, fine. You want to fight me pound-for-pound, make my day! Anything you say, anything you do, I know better. In my weight division, no one can beat me—not in the featherweight, not in the super featherweight."

Grove climbed through the ropes at Caesars in Lake Tahoe in a black sequined robe, oozing showmanship. Azumah was all business as he made his way to the ring surrounded by singing supporters, waving the Ghanaian flag. He was robeless and stripped, ready for action. Unlike Grove, who acknowledged the presence of promoter Don King the moment he climbed into the ring, Azumah, focused, simply danced from one side of the ring to the other, trying to keep his body loose before the opening round.

Azumah was four years older than Grove, but as he had showed against Fenech, age would be no problem. The areas of concern for the defending champion were Grove's three-inch height advantage and his superior reach: seventy-one inches (180.3 centimetres) to Azumah's sixty-four inches (162.6 centimetres). The two fighters could not have been more different as the national anthems were played. Azumah looked expressionlessly at the flag of Ghana, knowing how once again a nation few had heard of before he won the world title was expecting him to deliver. Grove, with his right glove over his heart, sang along with Bobby Dickerson.

In the opening round, a left hand drove Grove to the canvas. It did not hurt him and he was up quickly, but the sheer power of Azumah knocked him off his feet. Grove was caught again late in the round by a powerful left, and it looked like it was going to be one-way traffic. Yet in rounds two and three, Grove came out and jabbed, moved, and kept Azumah at bay. Slowly, Grove's jab started to snap, and he began following through with a right hand that started to land. Yet Azumah kept moving forward with his hands in a crossover defence, which restricted the speed of his punch.

By round five, Azumah started to cut off the space in the small, seventeen-foot ring, trying to force Grove to fight his style of fight. In his corner, Buffalo urged him to keep applying pressure on the challenger and not wait for the perfect punch to finish the fight. Halfway through round six, Azumah started to jab; suddenly, the spring went from Grove, and more of Azumah's punches found their mark.

Grove started to stand in front of Azumah, and with his hands held low, Azumah had no trouble landing punches, his jabs popping out with more regularity. Yet it was still close, as Buffalo was only too well aware when he pushed his fighter out for the eighth with the words, "It's rumble time." After landing a few solid early round blows, Grove stood in front of Azumah, showboating and waving him forward. The Professor smiled and thought to himself, *I'll come when I am ready, and you will know about it.*

Ringside commentator, Ferdie Pacheco, described Groves's actions as "whistling in the cemetery." In the latter half of the round, Azumah went into a crouching position, coiled and ready to unleash a killer blow. He stalked Grove, who looked like a gazelle that had spotted a lion about to spring into attack … a gazelle facing an inevitable end.In round nine, Azumah went on the attack in a fashion rarely seen in the ring before. Still in a crouching position, his body leaning forward from the waist and his head well forward of his body, he took long, fast strides towards his opponent and let fly with swinging left and rights that found their mark. "It looks like something out of a Tarzan movie," was the comment made by Pacheco before noting that Grove now had fear in his eyes. Despite having no defence at all, Grove seemed mesmerised as Azumah started to showboat, pulling out the bolo punch.

Azumah was totally dominant. Grove tried to fight back in the eleventh, but as much as his flurries of punches had the crowd cheering, few landed. In the twelfth, Grove opted to showboat again when he needed to fight, while Azumah kept pressing forward. The minute the bell sounded, Grove raised his arms in the air before climbing up onto the ropes and saluting the fans, somehow believing that he had deposed the champion, when quite simply he had not landed enough punches.

Waiting for the judges' scores, Azumah's corner was calm. Across the ring, Grove's seconds were hoisting him in the air and shouting, "You did it!" Maybe they were celebrating the fact that he had lasted the distance. Then before anyone knew it, he slumped on his stool from exhaustion.

Jimmy Lennon Jr., the ring announcer, read out the judges' scores after declaring a unanimous decision: judge Dave Brown 115–112, judge Doug Tucker 116–111, and judge Keith Macdonald 114–113. He then announced that Azumah had retained his world super featherweight title, much to the disbelief of Grove's corner, where Grove himself was heard to comment that it was "highway robbery" before asking into a camera, "What do I have to do?" Yet another fighter who had gone the distance believed he had won. However, on this occasion, there was little doubt that Azumah was the winner.

Unfortunately, it did not end there. As Azumah was about to be interviewed on Showtime, Grove came into the shot and said, "I won. You know I won. Good fight, man," but then realising the cameras were rolling, he embraced the champion.

"I'll give you a rematch," Azumah offered.

"A rematch, baby, sure, anytime," was Grove's response.

After having fought so bravely and having done his reputation in the ring a world of good, it was disappointing that he had to react in such a way. "He was a good boxer, moving around all the time, so you had to be patient and take your time and put pressure on him, and when he got tired, you got on top," Azumah recalls. "Before the fight, I did not think it would go the distance, but when he started running, I decided I would settle for a win on points and just keep putting him under pressure. I can change my style at any second, and I did that in this fight. That is why I am called The Professor."

If Grove's reaction soured Azumah's mood in any way, it must have been curdled when Ferdie Pacheco turned to interview the WBC's number-one challenger, Mexican Gabriel Ruelas, who had been ringside watching the bout. The rumour was that a fight between Azumah and Ruelas had fallen through because Azumah was demanding a $2 million purse, so Ruelas was far from happy and was looking to force the issue.

"My time is going to come, and I know he is not going to hide as he did this time," Ruelas told Pacheco while facing Azumah in the ring. "It should have been me in here, and I would have stopped him."

A wry smile spread across Azumah's face as he took in all that Ruelas was saying. "I been hearing about him all this time, and I want to beg Don King to make the fight before December. I will prove to him that I will clear the super featherweight and move up to lightweight. I wish I could fight Ruelas tomorrow and then move up to lightweight," Azumah said to Pacheco as a smiling Ruelas stood there, shaking his head. Azumah then called out to Don King in the ring. "Don, I want to give this guy a rematch, but I want to finish this guy before this December," he said, putting his hand on Ruelas's shoulder. "Anytime, anywhere, any day, wherever you want us to fight, I will be there," he said, jabbing his open hand towards Ruelas.

Ruelas then leaned in to the microphone and said, "I wonder why you didn't give me the chance right here."

"Well, I'm ready. You ready right now? C'mon, go put on some gloves—let's do it," Azumah replied, appearing to be a little agitated and genuinely wanting to get it on right there and then.

Pacheco let the last word go to Ruelas, who said, "I've just got to say he's lucky, very lucky today, but you know I'm glad because I'm going to kick his ass."

Azumah put his hand on Ruelas's shoulder and turned towards the camera with a smile on his face. One thing was for sure: He would not forget that comment.

Years later, Azumah laughs about the altercation. "It didn't annoy me—that is boxing. We have to act for a fight so we can make as much money as possible. If people think we are all friends, they will not pay to watch us fight," he says. Unfortunately for both fighters, Azumah did not get his wish—a fight against Ruelas before December—but he would be the champion's next opponent. Good to his word, Azumah agreed to fight him in his own backyard, Mexico.

There are no boxing fans in the world more passionate than the Mexicans, and that passion rises when one of their favourite sons climbs through the ropes. Gabriel Ruelas was born in Yerbabuena, Jalisco, Mexico. At the age of eight, he was smuggled across the border into the U.S. with his brother Rafael by his aunt, Juanita, and uncle, Nik, and lived with his sister, Victoria, in California.

At the age of twelve, Gabriel and his brother, Rafael, found their way to Ten Goose Boxing, Joe Goossen's gym. As an amateur, Gabriel racked up an impressive record similar to Azumah's—fifty-five wins, three losses, and he won the California Golden Gloves Championship. With his dream of representing the U.S. at the 1988 Olympics dashed due to not being an American citizen, Goossen rushed him and his brother back across the border to Mexico to see if they could qualify for the land of their birth. Unfortunately, Gabriel lost the final elimination bout to Miguel Angel Gonzalez, who boarded the plane for Seoul.

Gabriel headed back to the U.S. and turned professional. He was undefeated in his first twenty-one fights and lost for the first time against

Jeff Franklin, when he was forced to quit due to an injured elbow in the seventh round. With that loss and injury went the opportunity to fight for a world title at just nineteen years of age. It was a cruel blow. His arm had been broken in two places, and it is amazing he managed to continue boxing at the highest level, especially as he could no longer straighten his right arm. Following that injury and an operation to have the bones in his arm set a second time, Ruelas won twelve consecutive bouts and established himself as the number-one contender for Azumah's super featherweight belt.

The fight was to be part of the biggest night in boxing history. It was to be held in the majestic Estadio Azteca in Mexico City, a venue that had hosted the 1968 Olympic Games, witnessing American Bob Beaman's world-record-breaking long jump, as well as the 1986 World Cup. Diego Maradona had scored his "miracle" goal against England in this very stadium, so it was used to hosting historic sporting events. Topping the bill was Mexico's favourite son, Julio Cesar Chavez, who was putting his WBC super lightweight title on the line against Greg Haugen.

That night, February 20, 1993, saw four world champions put their titles on the line in front of a world-record crowd of one hundred thirty thousand: Chavez, Michael Nunn, Terry Norris, and Azumah Nelson. Interestingly, Joe Goossen trained four of the combatants that night: Greg Haugen, Michael Nunn, Terry Norris, and Gabriel Ruelas.

The night air was cold, but it had heated up earlier when Azumah's camp rejected the idea of three Mexican judges at ringside. Korean Dae-Eun Chung and American Tom Kaczmarek replaced two, while Mexican Jose Medina Solares remained. Once again, according to many boxing pundits, the odds were stacked against Azumah. He was thirty-four years old, while Ruelas was just twenty-two. Yet with age comes experience, and Azumah had shown he had plenty of that.

The day of the fight, however, Azumah was not sure he would even make it into the ring. "I will tell you what I went through—you would not believe it," he recalls. "I was sick in my stomach, and I knew it was not just my stomach; it was something else. If Buffalo was here, he would tell you I was crying like a baby on the floor. The pain did not start on the day of the fight. It started two to three days before. It was like I had pneumonia and a cramp. When I lay down, the cramp woke me up. I wish you could feel the pain to understand what I went through. I did not know how I was going to fight.

"I prayed to God when it came time for me to go to the ring. I said, *God, I am going to stand in the ring for twelve rounds. Even when I touch my stomach with my little finger, I am in pain. How am I going to stand and take punches? You know you are my God, my strength. I will go and fight for you because you are always fighting for me. You always say to me to ask for help, as it says in Matthew, chapter seven, verse seven, 'Ask and it will be given to you. Seek and you will find. Knock and the door will be opened to you.'*

"One thing that has helped me all my life is God. He took me from nowhere and lifted me to the highest. Why he chose me, I do not know. So when I was going to the ring, I was thinking about how to protect my stomach. As soon as we got in the ring, the referee started giving instructions and I forgot about my stomach. We started fighting, and I couldn't feel anything in my stomach. It was a miracle because I had been in so much pain."

Azumah had been accused over the years of getting "hometown" decisions when he fought in America, an accusation he still laughs off all these years later. "How can that be so? I am from Ghana," he says. There was no doubt that in the Estadio Azteca, 99 per cent of the fans wanted to see a Mexican victory, and with every punch that Ruelas landed, they cheered their man on. The question was: Would the crowd influence the judges?

It certainly was not influencing fellow Mexican and referee, Jose Guadalupe Garcia, who warned Ruelas twice in the fourth for hitting on the break, and went across to his corner at the end of the round to warn him to fight clean or he would deduct a point. At the end of round seven, the referee again spoke to Ruelas in Spanish; in his frustration, Ruelas shook his head and ignored the tap of gloves at the end of the round. In the break, his corner argued with the referee, who, it appeared, was trying to force the challenger to change his style.

Azumah looked to take rounds eight and nine, but sitting in his corner, he looked far from his usual composed self between nine and ten. Commentating ringside, Ferdie Pacheco put that down to Buffalo speaking in Spanish to his fighter, but Azumah remembers it very differently.

"Mexicans are terrible ones for the spiritual things. I fought a couple of them who did these things. Gabriel Ruelas, if he tells the truth, will know what I am talking about. Somebody working for him could have done it, or maybe someone did it on his behalf and he does not know, but they tried to use spirits to beat me.

"In the ninth round, they threw something at me in the spiritual realms. They threw it at my face so that I would get a cut, so he would win. But as soon as I saw it coming, I turned my face and it hit me in the back of the head. Only spiritual people can see this. It hit my head, and I had a big cut and the blood was flowing. I swept it away with my glove. The referee saw it and stopped and wanted to look at it, and I told him it was nothing, and we finished the fight. Explain to me how a fighter can get a cut to the back of his head? Watch the fight and you will not see our heads hit each other. I am telling you, it was the spirits."

In round ten, Pacheco noted the fire in his eyes as Azumah offloaded some powerful blows that shook Ruelas down to his boots, and when the bell sounded, the Mexican looked relieved to still be on his feet.

When he came out for round twelve, Ruelas needed to take the round convincingly or knock out the champion to dethrone him. It was, however, Azumah who landed the heavy blows early in the round, and then he got up on his toes, popping out his jab into the face of Ruelas. When the final bell sounded, Ruelas raised his arms in the air to declare himself the champion. Azumah looked to tap gloves, as is customary, but Ruelas shook his head and refused the gesture. Azumah smiled a beaming smile as if to say, "You are kidding if you think you won."

Even Buffalo was smiling as he climbed through the ropes to towel off his fighter. Eventually, Ruelas and his team crossed the ring to shake hands, and the common courtesy of acknowledging one's opponent was carried out. With the television cameras in the ring, Ruelas turned and spoke into the camera, saying, "If they don't give me this fight, you know what's happening."

When Jimmy Lennon Jr. read out the first judge's score, that of Mexican Jose Medina Solares, groans rang out from the crowd: He had scored the bout a draw, 115–115. The other two cards were close: Dae-Eun Chung scored it 115–113 while Tom Kaczmarek had it 115–114. As soon as it was announced that Azumah had retained his world title, Ruelas left the ring and stormed back to his dressing room. His trainer, Joe Goossen, tried to make him observe boxing protocols, but the hotheaded young fighter would not be swayed. Despite believing he had won, he interestingly never lodged an appeal against the decision.In *Business of Pain*, Araceli Martinez-Rose's book on the life of Gabriel Ruelas, Joe Goossen is quoted as saying, "Gabriel was a young challenger, solid in boxing skills, handsome, hammering valiantly and elusively enough to avoid the typical traps of the great Professor Azumah. During twelve rounds, both of them connected, exchanged punches, weighed the power of the opponent, and waited for the moment to knock the other out. It never came."

He goes on to say, "To be honest, it was a card organised by Don King, whose name carries a lot of weight as a promoter. So when Ruelas lost by one point, in reality, it meant that he unofficially won the fight—and the conditions had been logical. It was well known that Don King used to influence his cards. When there was no knockout, he used to put pressure on a judge and that was it."

Looking back, Azumah says, "It was always going to be close because I was fighting a Mexican in Mexico. If I knock him out, then there is no argument. The referee in that fight was terrible. He kept talking to him and let him do all sorts of things. He was terrible. I am a professor; I know what I can do in the ring. He didn't have to tell me.

"I had no reservations fighting in Mexico, and I dedicated that victory to Salvador Sanchez. I am a warrior; I go everywhere to fight. The world does not belong to anyone. It belongs to God, and God is my brother, my father, my everything, so I am not afraid of going anywhere to fight."

Once again, Azumah had proved many of his doubters wrong. Age was not proving to be a great barrier for the wily champion, but maybe Ferdie Pacheco was right when, during this fight, he commented that Azumah rarely was involved in a war in the ring. It was seldom you saw him take a lot of heavy punches. Then there were the breaks he had between title defences; these undoubtedly helped prolong his career. But one thing he never did was shy away from a challenger.

One of the reasons Azumah looked to be back to his relaxed style with that twinkle in his eye was that prior to his fight with Calvin Grove, he had found love for a second time in his life, and it came when he was not really expecting it. "A couple years after Beatrice passed away, God said, *I am giving you this girl.* So I said okay. God gave me Beatrice for eighteen years, and she was there to prepare my way for me. When she left, then he gave me Peggy.

"Peggy is very different to Beatrice, and she is fourteen years younger than me. Her father and mother were boxing fans. One night in Accra, I went out with one of my friends, Tony, from America, and we saw Peggy. She came to ask me for school fees. She was about fifteen or sixteen. Tony knew her parents, so we went back to them and asked, 'Is this your daughter?' Her father said yes. I said okay and I left.

"A few years later, Tony came to Accra again, and he was chasing Peggy's sister. He asked me, 'Have you seen Peggy? She is working at Labardi Beach Hotel. She is beautiful. Let us go and see her.' We were not doing anything so I said okay. When I saw her, I asked her if she was Mr. Yoofi Booham's daughter, and I said, 'Okay, I will marry you.' She said she was too young. I said I will keep visiting. I went a few times to see her, so that the people knew that she was my girl. My word is my bond. She told her mother, who said to her, 'I know Azumah is a good guy, a humble guy, but are you sure you love him?' She said yes, and so she then said, 'Okay, you can marry him.'

"When she finished high school, I married her. She was still working at Labardi Beach when we were married, but then stopped work. She wanted to go to secretarial school, so she went on this course. We went to church together, and she then went to the pastor school. After three years' study, she can then preach. God opened her eyes, and I am so proud, so happy. I leave everything in her hands; I trust her. Whatever she wants to do, she does it, and as long as she is happy, I am happy.

"She wanted to have a restaurant, so we sold one of the houses I owned to buy the restaurant. We invested in a restaurant. The factory I owned we closed down because it went bankrupt. I have the building still, and I can sell that when I need to. The restaurant did well, and later she opened another at Osu. God gave her intelligence, and she loves to use it for a good purpose.

"After Beatrice died, people said I changed as a boxer. I didn't change as a boxer, but I was different. Two or three years later, I married again, and my second wife, Peggy, took over what my first wife was doing. She would come jogging with me and to the gym with me. She took an interest in my career. She closed that gap that was there after Beatrice died. I remember she would jog with me sometimes, even sometimes when she was pregnant. She would walk while I jogged with her stomach sticking out. It was very funny, but it was good to have her there."

XIII

"BRUJERIA"

Mexicans, like people in many African nations, believe in calling on the spirits for help in times of need. In Africa, this may be called *muti, nganga,* or *voodoo*, and in Ghana, *juju*, but in Mexico it is known as *brujeria*. Those who carry out such practices are known as *brujos* if they are men and *brujas* if they are women; *brujos* is also the plural should they be male or female.

In South America, to refer to somebody as a *brujas* or *brujos* is to label them an evildoer. So these people have adopted the term *curanderos*, meaning "healer." However, in Central America, *brujas* and *brujos* are usually far more respected and are often sought out for healing purposes. In Mexico, there are *brujas blancas*, white witches, and *brujas negras*, black witches. The white witches are the ones who do good, and the black witches are believed to cast spells for people who are deemed mean or envious. The *brujos* are understandably paid for their work.

Today, Mexican boxers have become synonymous with the red head-band worn into the ring and made famous by Julio Cesar Chavez, but few realise when or why this trend started. In November 1987, at the Hilton Hotel in Las Vegas, two giants of the sport faced off across the ring to determine who was the best lightweight in the world. The challenger was the then-WBC super featherweight champion, Julio Cesar Chavez, the pride of Mexico. Across the ring was the reigning WBA lightweight champion, Edwin "El Chapo" Rosario, fighting for the pride of Puerto Rico. The pressure on each man to win was immense.

Folklore has it Rosario turned to *brujeria* to give himself that extra edge. Rosario's mother is believed to have practiced *brujeria* where he grew up in Toa Baja, Puerto Rico. A photograph of Chavez was placed in a bucket of ice and a spell was cast on him so that on the night of the fight, he would suffer a head cold and struggle to concentrate. The man to hear about this *brujeria* was Chavez's then-assistant trainer, and ultimately Azumah's trainer, Jose "Buffalo" Martin. He reported this to the Chavez camp.

Like most Latin people, Chavez was superstitious and did not take this news lightly. His head trainer, Cristobal Rojas, suggested that Chavez see a *brujo* himself in order to counter the spell on him. The story goes that it was a man who occasionally worked Azumah's corner, Don King employee Eddie Mafuz, who advised Chavez that in order to counter the spell, he would have to wear a red band across his forehead the night of the fight. Chavez has admitted that at the time, he was embarrassed to wear it, but that there was no way he was going to take any chances. So Chavez and his entire entourage wore the red headbands to counter the effect of the "bad spirits," and as a result, the famous Mexican red headband was born. Had Chavez lost, it may never have been seen again.

Being a deeply spiritual man himself, Azumah was very wary of the spirits being conjured up by his Mexican opponents. "Like I say, they use a lot of things in boxing circles—things we call spiritual things, like witch doctors," he recalls. "I fought a couple boxers who were bad people. They used these spirits. If you use these spiritual people, one day you will have a problem.

"If you use these spirits, you have to pay them, and because they are spirits, they never die. If you don't pay them—and every year you have to pay—when you die, your children have to pay. If your children don't know about your debt, the spirits will start attacking them. They start hurting them, making them useless, unless by God's grace your children come to know God, and then they will be released."

Azumah's victory over Gabriel Ruelas was his first in a succession of fights against Mexican fighters; in fact, from his fight with Ruelas until his retirement five years later, he would fight seven fights, all against Mexican opponents. His next opponent, seven months after his world-record-breaking bout in Mexico, would be back in the U.S., but once again, it would be in his opponent's backyard. He would fight at the Alamodome in San Antonio, Texas, the home of Jesse James Leija, an American with strong Mexican roots.

The Alamodome, which opened on May 15, 1993, at a cost of $186 million, is a sixty-five-thousand-seat multipurpose facility used as an American football stadium, a basketball stadium, and a convention centre. This fight would be one of the first events to be hosted at the new stadium, and on the same bill would be Julio Cesar Chavez, who would challenge Azumah's old foe, Pernell Whitaker, for his WBC welterweight title.

With Leija fighting in his hometown, many believed that the older champion would come unstuck. Over the years, they had witnessed Azumah pace himself throughout fights and win rounds when he needed to in order to claim the decision. Certainly, knockouts were becoming far less frequent than they had been at the start of his career, but he still possessed a powerful punch. In fact, Azumah's style in recent years was probably best described by *The Ring* magazine's Nigel Collins, who wrote, "If they set Nelson's fights to music, a Beethoven symphony would be appropriate. The master craftsman usually starts slowly, teases with occasional flourish, and then finishes with a breathtaking crescendo."

Leija was an aggressive opponent who lacked a killer punch, but he had made up for that by throwing a huge volume of punches. At this point in his career, he had worn down a lot of his opponents. Unlike Ruelas, he was no young pretender: He was twenty-seven years old, having turned professional at twenty-two—the same age Azumah had already won and defended his WBC featherweight title twice. The big question was whether Azumah would be prepared to let this fight go the distance and trust the fate of his title with the judges.

Despite his age, Azumah was in peak condition, which was ironic, as in the state of Texas where this fight was held, boxers over thirty-five years of age had to undergo a physical before being granted a license to fight. Apart from age, there was little to separate the two. They were the same height, and Leija weighed one pound more than Azumah at 129 pounds, but the champion had a three-and-a-half-inch reach advantage.

As ring announcer Jimmy Lennon Jr. introduced the challenger, the roof nearly came off the Alamodome as the sixty thousand locals showed that their support was fully behind their man. Leija raised his arms in the pose of a champion to acknowledge their support. Undefeated with twenty-six wins and one draw, they believed that their man had what it took to finally dethrone Azumah. As the announcements continued, the "Pride of San Antonio" hit himself on his face and chest with his gloves and bounced up and down.

Across the ring, the blue corner was the complete opposite in terms of reception and behaviour. Azumah was booed the minute his name was announced. His face was expressionless as he paced calmly in a small circle. He looked calm, not at all fazed by the negative reaction his name provoked. After all, he had seen it all before: This was his tenth title defence.

The two fighters were called to the centre of the ring, and Leija, with his mouthguard pushed forward in his mouth and his head tilted to one side, looked almost sheepish as he stood face-to-face with Azumah. The champion, calm as ever, gave a wry smile before offering his glove to the challenger and saying, "Good luck." Neither of these actions was normal for Azumah. Maybe he was mellowing with age; maybe the Terrible Warrior was no longer as terrible. All would be revealed in the coming twelve rounds.

Leija looked to find Azumah with his jab in the opening round, while the champion looked to throw the challenger off his stride. In the opening minute, he dropped his arms by his side and windmilled his right as if setting himself up for a bolo punch, a move that was met with boos from the packed crowd. He missed with a few left hooks, but still landed some strong blows, firing off punches with more snap and purpose than Leija.

In the second round, Leija had the crowd on their feet as he backed Azumah onto the ropes and let fly with a flurry of punches, but very few found their target. Azumah then dropped his right hand as if to invite Leija to come forward and have a free punch, but when he didn't, Azumah circled his opponent and doubled up his jab, frequently finding the target. Yet it was Azumah's ability to slip and slide punches that was evident in this round, and Leija looked to raise the pace.

The third round was definitely Leija's, as Azumah seemed to sit back and allow him to come at him. Leija popped out his jab, but followed up with some effective right hands that found the target. Back in his corner, Azumah sat expressionless as Buffalo pleaded with him not to relax, knowing that this round had probably gone to the challenger. At the start of the fourth, Azumah was up off his stool before the bell, waiting for Leija. The two touched gloves before continuing where they had left off in the previous round. Leija was on the receiving end of a barrage of punches from Azumah, and was lucky that a few of the champion's wild swings failed to land, and then he fought back, landing a solid right hand of his own that had the Alamodome crowd on its feet. The pace had lifted and the round was extremely close, but it was Leija who returned to his corner with a nick over his left eye.

The fifth was another close round to score. Leija landed a strong left hand early in the round and apologised for a low blow in the last thirty seconds. One thing was for sure, Azumah was in his toughest contest since his first fight with Jeff Fenech.

Leija tagged Azumah with a right hand flush to the side of his head in the sixth. His work rate and volume of punches thrown was higher than the champion's; although as he came forward, Azumah frequently landed with blows to the ribs. At the start of the seventh, Leija again landed a strong right hand to the head. Halfway through the round, the two stood toe-to-toe, each firing off some telling blows. There was no doubt that Leija threw more punches, but, as was so often the case, Azumah managed to avoid many. In another close round, Leija's work rate probably edged it.

In the eighth, Azumah came out with a greater level of aggression and landed the more solid blows. He used his ring skills to control the direction in which Leija moved, and when Leija moved in close, The Professor outboxed him. Surprisingly, it was the younger man who appeared to be tiring, as Azumah started to find more and more punches getting past his defence. In his corner, Buffalo urged him to keep up the pressure. In the tenth, Azumah continued to be the aggressor and had the higher work rate as he started to work the body, causing Leija at one point to complain about a clash of heads. Yet there was no doubting that when the heads collided, it was purely accidental. At the halfway point in the round, the two again went toe-to-toe, but as was so often the case, Azumah showcased his defensive skills, blocking many of Leija's shots with his arms. One could sense that even the partisan San Antonio crowd knew the fight was slipping away from their man, as the volume of their vocal support dipped.

Leija's corner worked furiously on a second cut to his left eye, which was believed to be a result of the clash of heads, and told him he had to win the next round, as he had lost the previous one by not throwing enough punches. The crowd tried to get behind their man in the eleventh as chants of "Leija, Leija!" rang out around the stadium, but Azumah gave him a lesson in boxing. If he wasn't popping his jab into the face of Leija, he was finding the target when they moved in close and managing to slip the tired punches being thrown back at him.

As he walked to his corner, Leija had a look of resignation on his face. It was as if he knew that he would need a knockout in the final round to take the world championship belt off the holder. His corner tried to lift him. "You are three minutes away from being champion of the world, okay?" they called, but then added, "But the fight is close enough that if you don't win this round, you may not get it. You've got to win this round, okay?"

Across the ring, Buffalo told Azumah he wanted a round like the first, where his fighter dominated and kept Leija at arm's length. The bell sounded and the two showed their respect in a longer-than-normal embrace. Despite the pleas from Buffalo, Azumah went into exhibition mode in the final round. He dropped his hands to his side and landed swinging blows starting from his hips. He jumped into punches and still found the target. So much for Leija, the younger man, who was meant to be the one to get stronger as the fight wore on. It was Azumah who had the spring in his step, who picked off the lead-footed Leija almost at will. Some of his outrageous punches did fail to find their target and allowed Leija to land some punches of his own, but it was predominantly one-way traffic.

The final bell sounded and Leija unbelievably threw his arms in the air, proclaiming himself the winner, as was becoming a habit with most fighters who went the distance against Azumah. The champion laughed visibly at this action and raised a single arm momentarily before heading to his corner. Leija, meanwhile, ran to a neutral corner, climbed onto the ropes, and saluted the San Antonio crowd, again proclaiming himself the new world champion.

His corner hoisted him onto their shoulders and paraded him around the ring; having seen him completely outclassed, this had to be gamesmanship—stir the local crowd up into a frenzy of emotion and force a decision. That should never happen in boxing, as with each round being scored at its conclusion, the final result should be clear-cut. However, as many fans and fighters know, that is not always the case.

Leija soaked up the applause. Azumah just took in the whole spectacle in stride. He had seen it all before. Leija came across and embraced Azumah. Despite what looked like an almost heated exchange, he was heard to say, "We party no matter who wins. Hey, we're both winners."

The television commentator, Bob Sheridan, had Azumah as the winner, but they warned that the fight could go either way. After what seemed an eternity, referee Jerry McKenzie called both fighters to the centre of the ring. He grasped Leija's left arm and Azumah's right arm. The bell sounded and Jimmy Lennon Jr. announced that after twelve rounds there was a split-decision.

Boos rang out around the Alamodome. Leija gestured to someone ringside, asking who had won, but he never appeared to get an answer. Lennon declared that Belgian Daniel Van De Wiele had scored the fight 116–115 in favour of the champion. Next came Lawrence Cole's score, which was 115–113 in favour of the challenger. Leija, hand on hip, looked unmoved as the crowd cheered and his corner men pumped the air. Azumah simply smiled. "Judge at ringside Dadzie scores the bout 118–112," Lennon announced, "in favour of the winner and still champion Azumah Nelson."

Boos greeted the announcement. Azumah was hoisted into the air and waved a hand in acknowledgment of those who applauded his victory, but had no smile on his face. The television commentators were surprised at the score from Lawrence Cole, but believed that the right man had won.

Several minutes later, after Leija's fans had started to calm down, Jimmy Lennon climbed back into the ring to announce an error with the scores. On this occasion, he first read out the scores of Lawrence Cole and Keith Dadzie. Their scores remained the same. Azumah, with his hands draped over the ropes, looked sick, as if he expected the fight to be snatched away from him. Meanwhile, Jesse James Leija was on the other side of the ring in deep conversation with WBC president Jose Sulaiman. "Judge Van De Wiele's score should correctly read 115–115 even, a draw," Lennon announced. "The decision is a split-decision draw."

Azumah remained expressionless while Leija's arm was raised by one of his corner men. The fans were still far from pleased, and boos rang out once again. Within minutes, Azumah had gone from being the victor to the participant in a draw, though he still retained his world title. Yet as usual, he seemed unperturbed when interviewed in the ring by Ferdie Pacheco.

"Dr. Pacheco, I am telling you I don't care about what they do. If they give the title to him, I go, 'Okay, it's a game I lost,'" Azumah said, adding what he had said so many times throughout his career. "If they want, I'll give them a rematch anytime, even if they want to do it right now and we start again."

There was no doubt the discrepancies between the judges' scores were embarrassing, and many cynics believed the altering of the result was purely to appease Leija's hometown fans, but that was not the case. It was a mistake that quite simply should never have happened.

"Buffalo" Martin told Pacheco, "I complained before the fight about the referees because the referee was from Dallas. It's ridiculous; it should not happen to this man." He pointed to his fighter.

To add to the ridiculous situation, Lester Bradford was quoted as saying post-fight, "Let's be honest about this. We're talking about a nice guy here [Azumah], but the bottom line is, Jesse was robbed. This guy fought his heart out and they did this to him. Azumah gets more respect from the judges than he deserves. It shouldn't be that way. If you beat a guy by an inch, you should get the decision. You don't have to beat him by ten yards."

Leija was more magnanimous. "It was an honour and a privilege to be in the ring with Azumah Nelson, but I won the fight. He knows I won the fight," he said.

There were not many outside Texas who agreed with that sentiment. Bob Mee from *Boxing News* wrote, "For what it's worth, my card was 116–112 for Nelson, which I accept may have been slightly hard on Leija. Similarly, I can understand Van De Wiele's interpretation, even though I feel it was generous to Leija. The Texan press around me had Nelson winning the fight by margins big or small. However, I fail to see how Cole could vote Leija a two-point winner—and if any doubts about the competence of the judges should be raised, they should be directed at him."

Looking back on the fight, Cole remembers, "I thought James was a little quicker, outhustled him. James was a great fighter for eight rounds, and then he would tail off at the end, and that was when Azumah would usually put on the pressure. He'd then cut off the ring and work the body and come up to the head. He doesn't give away early rounds, but lets a fighter dictate the pace and then counters it, letting them run out of gas and then taking over the fight."

On the issue of the scores being added up incorrectly, Cole adds, "I don't know what happened, but I think the commission used a concentration sheet, and they had somebody who didn't have any experience with the sheet, and they added it up incorrectly. They gave the decision to Azumah and then they came back and corrected it. They retallied the scores and gave it a draw. It was an incredible fight on an incredible night. It was the undercard of Terry Norris against Joe Gatti, and then Julio Cesar Chavez Sr. fought Pernell Whitaker." That had been another fight that was marred by a controversial decision.Jesse James Leija also has a view on the fight now. "It was my first title fight, and to go against the great Azumah Nelson, you can imagine how a twenty-seven-year-old first-world-title fighter would feel," he recalls. "I was nervous all the way through. I was actually in awe of him before the fight. After all, he was the great Azumah Nelson. We knew we had our hands full, and that goes for every single fight I had with him. I have great memories—and I think that is what people are going to remember me by—fighting Azumah Nelson four times.

"I thought I had won the fight. I thought I had the early rounds, but me being the rookie and not knowing enough, I kind of coasted the last three rounds and he picked it up. I thought I had enough rounds in the bag, but that was me because I didn't know any better. But I learned a lesson, and that was to fight every round as if it's your last round, and that's what I did."

Azumah experienced something he had never experienced in a fight before, something that he put down to the spirits, yet he remains philosophical about the shambles at the end of the bout. "When I fought Leija, the same thing happened as had when I fought Ruelas," he says. "I like him—Jesse James Leija—so much that I didn't want to hurt him. That was the first time I ever felt like that. In the ring, I found I couldn't even hit him hard. I was going to throw a right hand and I could not throw it. I pulled it back and then I just touch him. There was no power in my punch. I was just playing with him. After the fight, they say I won, he won, and then it was a draw, which proves anything can happen in America!"

It was understandable that Leija would want a rematch, but there were plenty of other young guns looking for a chance to climb between the ropes and hopefully send the ageing Azumah back to Ghana once and for all, without his title.

Again, there was talk that Azumah was looking to move up a weight and take on Miguel Angel Gonzalez for the WBC lightweight title. Yet former trainer and commentator, Gil Clancy, was quoted in *The Ring* magazine as saying, "Nelson looked pretty good against Leija. He didn't really show his age. I thought he won by a comfortable two or three points. He keeps himself in excellent condition, and if he stays at 130 pounds, I think he can stay at the top for another couple years. But it would be a mistake moving up to lightweight."

The fight with Gonzalez never eventuated, but a rematch with Leija did. According to Leija, this was because it was the fight Don King wanted most at the time. "Don King wanted the rematch and that was great for me, as that was my second opportunity to fight Azumah Nelson," he says. "But I was more worried the second time because everyone knows what Azumah Nelson does to his opponents in the second fight. I mean, Martinez and Jeff Fenech, he just knocked them out. Being the kind of fighter he is, he even said, 'If I don't knock you out, I'm gonna retire.' But that made me think, *Boy, he's really going to come after me,* and

I was really worried."

The rematch did make sense from King's standpoint, as Don King Promotions managed both fighters, so he had nothing to lose. Then again, Don King Promotions also managed Gonzalez. Once again, despite Azumah reinforcing his claim to being a professor who teaches the young boxers ring craft, there were many who said he was too old. The wise ones who had followed his career knew better than to write him off.

The fight was scheduled for January 29, 1994, and was to be part of Don King's Super Grand Slam of Boxing at the MGM Grand in Las Vegas. This was to be the first fight card at the latest MGM Grand, as the hotel was formerly known as the Marina Hotel and had only opened a few weeks earlier on December 18, 1993. In a night of firsts, Julio Cesar Chavez, who fought on that card, was knocked down for the first time in his pro boxing career by Frankie Randall.

However, while all the other fights scheduled for that night happened, the one between Azumah and Jesse James did not. It was moved back to May 7, 1994, at the same venue under the "Revenge" billing. The card would see Chavez try and win back his title from Randall; Julian "The Hawk" Jackson try and win back his title from Gerald McClellan; and "Terrible" Terry Norris look to avenge his defeat at the hands of Simon Brown.

Azumah remembers this last bout clearly, as both fighters turned to him for advice prior to climbing in the ring. "Norris lost his title when he was knocked out by Simon Brown in December and wanted to regain the title in a rematch," he says. "Brown came and asked me how to retain his title, and I told him how to do it. Then Norris asked me how to win his title back, so I said you have to do this. I told both of them what they needed to do, and whoever did it best, won. On the that night, it was Terry Norris."

Norris remembers it well. "I listened to what Azumah said that night, and I went out and did what he told me and I won," he recalls.

In the entourage making its way to the ring was Azumah's son, David, who was attending his first fight with his father. As Jimmy Lennon Jr. made the announcements, he held his father's world title belt in the air. On this occasion, Jesse James Leija seemed much calmer and assured than he had been going into the first fight. Azumah, despite always being calm, seemed a little less focused than normal. His eyes wandered as the announcements were being made, and he did not seem to be in the "zone," an area he inhabited once he stepped through the ropes.

The Professor was about to defend his title for the eleventh time, and as referee Mitch Halpern gave his final instructions to the two at the centre of the ring, Leija stared directly at his opponent. Azumah, with Buffalo massaging his shoulders and neck, looked at the floor.

The bell for the opening round went, and both fighters came out with purpose and looked to force the pace. Azumah looked like he was intending on making a quick night of it as he tried to land a knockout blow. He unleashed some furious left hands, but few managed to land on the button. Leija, meanwhile, kept snapping out his jab, and towards the end of the round, landed several blows with his right. To reinforce his mood, Azumah chose not to touch gloves when the bell sounded.

The start of the second saw Leija moving backwards; he covered up well and slipped many of Azumah's punches and then did the unthinkable: He knocked the champion to the canvas. Azumah missed with a swinging right hand, and as he bobbed up, Leija nailed him with a left of his own. The champion fell forward onto his knees with just over a minute of the round gone. Mitch Halpern started the count, and Azumah rose by the time he had reached six and took the mandatory eight-count.

He looked shaken, no doubt wondering what had happened. The crowd sensed an upset, and the volume of support for Leija lifted. For the remainder of the round, it was Azumah who was the pursued as Leija looked to push home his advantage. With Azumah standing directly in front of him in the final minute, he again landed some telling blows, but the champion managed to stay on his feet.

In the third round, both corners were shouting for their fighters to jab, and Azumah was probably the more effective; although, Leija managed to parry many of his punches, and he was tagged by a swinging right late in the round. There was no doubt that Leija's defence was more compact and his punching crisper than during their first fight.

At the start of the fourth, Azumah unleashed a flurry of venomous punches that opened up a cut over Leija's left eye. He took what was thrown at him and landed some punches of his own before referee Mitch Halpern called time for the ringside doctor to inspect the cut. With the blood wiped away, he was given the all clear to continue, and at the end of the round, it was he who was on the attack and had the champion covering up.

In rounds five and six, Leija shortened the distance between the two of them, making Azumah's wild swings miss their target, sliding off his shoulders or the back of his head. "You fight, Azumah. Stay close to the man, Azumah!" Buffalo implored ringside. But Leija's rapier-like jab made it hard to stay close. There was no doubt that Leija was the more effective of the two, and late in the sixth, an uppercut jolted Azumah's head back, and the crowd started chanting Leija's name.

Azumah was fighting an uncharacteristically untidy fight, and early in the seventh, he let fly with more wild, swinging punches; some landed, but Leija managed to bob and weave out of the way and then move in and land a solid flurry of his own. Azumah continued to look for openings that never came. Buffalo continued to plead with him to lift his work rate.

The start of the ninth was delayed as the referee made sure that ice was cleared from the canvas. Then, with just over a minute to go, Mitch Halpern sent Leija to a neutral corner. Azumah stood bemused and then watched Halpern instruct the judges to deduct a point for a low blow. Azumah looked to his corner quizzically and then at Halpern, his gloves upturned, asking for an explanation. It was a bizarre call from the referee, as the blow had appeared to hit Leija on the hip, yet just thirty seconds earlier, the challenger had hit Azumah flush on the protector. As he signaled to the judges, Buffalo joined in the questioning, shouting, "Why, why, why?" with each question becoming louder. The deduction meant Azumah was going to have to lift his work rate considerably in the final three rounds to gain a decision, as Leija was now clearly ahead.

Soon after, as if to try and restore parity, Halpern moved in and warned Leija for dropping his head and told him that was his last warning. The round finished with the two boxers having to be separated in Leija's corner. As he slowly made his way across the ring to his own corner, Azumah's face revealed a flicker of frustration. His face was set in stone, but his eyes told a story of their own.

Azumah took round ten, despite a late flurry of action from Leija, and at the start of the eleventh, landed some powerful punches; Leija, to his credit, stood and took them and fired back some solid blows of his own. In this round, it appeared that Azumah had found his range, popping his jab into the face of Leija, and as the challenger tired, he took many of his counterpunches on his gloves. However, it all looked like too little too late. The question was: Could he find a late knockout punch to hold on to his world title just as he had against Gomez to win his first?

The two warriors touched gloves in the centre of the ring for the start of the twelfth round. There was no doubt that Leija had prepared better for this fight than he had for the first; he still went on the attack in the final round, and with Azumah taking risks to try and stop the fight, he managed to land some good shots on the champion. With fifteen seconds remaining and the crowd chanting Leija's name, Azumah uncharacteristically raised both arms in the air as if to say, "I am still the champion." But the question was: For how much longer?

When the final bell sounded, the two fighters embraced and simultaneously raised their arms in the air; the packed crowd rose to their feet to applaud what had been a great fight. As Leija was hoisted high by his support staff, Azumah paced in his corner. Buffalo stood expressionless. There were no smiles or hugs from either man or anyone in his corner.

With his feet back on the ground, Leija announced to the television camera following him that he was "not even tired." Jimmy Lennon Jr. took his place in the ring and read out the scores. Judge Karmel Youssef from Egypt scored the bout 113–114; the U.S.'s Jerry Roth had it 109–117; and Jose Juan Guerra from Mexico had it 110–117, all in favour of the new world champion, Jesse James Leija.

After an exchange of words, Leija showed his respect by raising Azumah's arm, acknowledging him as a true champion. Post-fight, when asked if there would be a third fight between the two, Leija dismissed the idea. "I don't think so," he said. "Azumah Nelson promised that if he didn't win, he would retire. I think he is going to retire now. Good."

Now looking back on that fight, he understandably has great pride in winning the title. "I was on my game, and I probably fought the fight of my life in beating Azumah Nelson," he says. "I beat him fairly easily the second fight. Dropped him one time in the second round—probably the only fighter to drop him since Salvador Sanchez. So I was really quite happy after that." In fact, Mario Martinez was the only other fighter to knock Azumah down.

Azumah does not take anything away from Leija and concedes that he won the fight, but once again, says things were not as they should have been inside the ropes. "The second fight—I just can't believe what happened—I was in the ring and I could not see him," he now says. "I cut him, but I did not even know I had cut him. You know I do not fight rough. They say I hit him low, but I did not even see where I hit him. I did not even see the punch that he hit me with that made me go down. It was then I knew I was fighting something else. So I said, 'Okay, enough. There is something happening.' I lost, but I said, 'Whatever you do, you pay.'"

Not only did Leija beat a fighter who had never lost in a defence of either of his world titles, but he also had another first: No fighter out of the seven who fought Azumah a second time had ever beaten him. This was a fact Leija was not aware of. "That makes me feel good. I did not know that," he says. "I didn't realise that, as I had never looked at his record fighter for fighter, but that makes me feel good knowing that now."

XIV

THE COMEBACK

After five years and three months as WBC super featherweight champion, Azumah Nelson was no longer a world title holder. If you include the three years he had held the WBC featherweight crown, it had been eight years that he had been a champion of the world. Not surprisingly, Azumah was not too upset. "It is a game. It is nice to be world champion, but you know when you climb in the ring, one of you will win and one of you will lose," he says.

The loss to Jesse James Leija brought to an end Azumah's relationship with Don King Promotions. It was one that the media had claimed to be fractious, but Azumah has a different view. "Carl King, he was my manager and his father was my promoter. We did good business together. They are good people, and I cannot take anything from them," he says. "I am okay with them. If something was wrong, it was my managers, who did not speak English well, and they did not know boxing too well. If you had not met Don King before, and you sat beside him and negotiated, he could say, 'I will take 90 per cent and your boy gets 10 per cent,' and you would say, 'Okay.' But in the middle of all this, I realised that this was not good. I negotiated with Don King myself and got a better deal.

"I knew and Don King knew I am coming to the end of my career, so it was no big deal. So towards the end, I managed myself. I am no longer with Don King, and he was not promoting me. It was no big deal to him, either. Everything is okay. I can go anywhere. I am happy with him, and he is happy with me; we are friends.

"In this world, everybody has made mistakes—we learn from our mistakes and we need to learn how to forgive. The judgment is God's, and if you believe in him, you will have to account for everything when the time comes. So whatever you are doing, do it with your mind clear. My mind was clear."

Another relationship that came to an end, but far more abruptly and tragically, was the one Azumah had with Jose "Buffalo" Martin. The Spanish trainer lost his life in a car crash, leaving behind a wife and a young child. "He was a good friend. He made me laugh, but he would never sleep at night, so he would go to town to a bar or nightclub," Azumah recalls. "Then in the daytime, he would start sleeping. He would sleep anywhere. He was a nice guy. When there was time for work he worked, but when he was free, he would party!

"I told him many times to be careful when he was driving. The way he sleeps, they said it was a sickness. I told him he should not drive because he could die. 'No, no,' he told me, but when I heard he had an accident, I asked who was driving, and they said it was him. He fell asleep.

"He was a friend. I liked having him around. I made him come to Ghana most of the time. He did not go home to Spain; he stayed with me in Ghana. He loved it so much. He wanted to marry and live in Ghana. It was very sad when he died, but it was not a surprise."

While Azumah stayed at home in Ghana with his family, Jesse James Leija was given little time to bask in the glory of being the man to strip Azumah Nelson of his world title and become the first person to win a second bout against The Professor. Just four months after his victory, he was back in the ring at the MGM Grand in Las Vegas, defending his title against the number-one contender, Gabriel Ruelas. He went the twelve rounds, but lost by unanimous decision. His reign as champion had lasted just 133 days.

Looking back, Leija says he learned some valuable lessons. "I say this, and maybe some of the young fighters can realise that you always learn something from losing, and one thing I learned from losing my title to Gabe Ruelas is that I fought so hard for seven years to make it to the top. Heck, when I beat Azumah Nelson, I wanted to relax," he said.

He adds, "Don King had this thing where I had to fight the number-one contender. Who fights the number-one contender after they win the world title? No one does, but I had to. After beating Azumah Nelson, I was so worn out mentally and physically that I took a break for two months. Well, lo and behold, I had to fight Gabe Ruelas, who was a hungry young fighter who wanted to win the world title as much as I did. I was just too far behind in training, and my weight got up too high because I had reached the mountaintop and I wanted to relax. Now I realise when you reach the mountaintop, you have to work harder to stay there, and don't take anything for granted. I lost my first title defence because I was not prepared mentally or physically to fight Ruelas."

Ruelas's victory meant he and his brother, Rafael, had created history by becoming the first brothers to win world titles in the same year. As he says in the book on his life, *Business of Pain*, "The victory had greater significance for me, since Jesse James Leija had defeated the great Azumah Nelson. For me, the fact that I had dethroned Leija after he had just defeated a legend was a praiseworthy and impressive achievement.

"My fight against Leija was the culmination of twenty years of dedication to boxing, and it fed my hunger for securing a place in the history of the sport. I was sure that a wonderful lifetime was beginning for me and my family."

In January of 1995, he defended his title against top-ten-ranked American Freddie "The Pitbull" Liberatore. The bout was stopped in round two due to an injury to Liberatore's hand. After the fight, he underwent an operation; the tendons that held down his metacarpal bones had torn, causing the bones to start to pop up. By the time he went under the knife, all his metacarpal bones needed to be fused. As a result of this boxer's injury, the challenger was forced to retire from the sport altogether.

Four months later, Ruelas climbed through the ropes again, this time at Caesars Palace in Las Vegas to defend his title against Colombian Jimmy Garcia. The challenger boasted a record of thirty-five wins and four losses. Just six months earlier, he had lost by unanimous decision against Genaro Hernandez for the WBA version of the super featherweight title.

Just like Ruelas, Leija and hundreds of other boxers, Garcia dreamed of returning to a hero's welcome in his hometown of Barranquilla with a world championship belt wrapped around his waist, his place and name never to be forgotten by the boxing fraternity. He will never be forgotten, but sadly for very different reasons.

The fight with Ruelas was a one-sided affair, and Garcia took a great deal of punishment as he struggled to protect himself. Respected referee Mitch Halpern, who was renowned for having control in the ring, asked Garcia several times in the fifth round if he was okay to continue, and the fighter said he was. His corner kept sending him back into the fray. Finally, in the eleventh round, Halpern stepped in and stopped the fight. As the Mexican contingent celebrated Ruelas's emphatic victory, pandemonium broke out in the Colombian's corner. Within seconds, he was on the canvas, unconscious. Despite the presence of four ringside physicians, one of whom was a neurosurgeon and who was operating on Garcia within thirty-five minutes of his collapse in the ring, the Colombian passed away thirteen days later. Understandably, the outcome affected all three men in the ring. Although there is no definite link to the tragedy, referee Mitch Halpern took his own life in August 2000; he was just thirty-three. For Gabriel Ruelas, the pain was made that much harder to bear, as prior to the fight he had promised to make someone pay for the weeks he had spent training to fight Garcia. Unfortunately, Garcia paid with his life. Ruelas did say in a post-fight press conference, "I regret saying that—I'm not a fighter who talks a lot. Unfortunately, what I said kind of turned out to be true."

He tried to come to terms with Garcia's death as he prepared to defend his title in another bout billed "La Revancha"—The Revenge—against former world title holder, Azumah Nelson, who was hungry to win back his crown. He was now thirty-seven years old and had not fought for nineteen months. Azumah was no Jimmy Garcia; he had been involved in twenty-one world title fights in three weight divisions and was hungry to reclaim his title.

There have, unfortunately, been other boxers who have had to live with the fact that their opponent passed away after a fight: Emile Griffith, Sugar Ramos, and Alan Minter are a few. All managed to come back after the tragedy and compete in major fights and, more importantly, come out victorious. Others, like former heavyweight champion Ezzard Charles, never fully recovered; Ezzard was said to have changed his style and seldom went all-out in the ring after the death of an opponent early in his career. However, when the bell sounds and your opponent starts hitting you, there isn't time for a debate as to whether you should continue or not; fate dictates at that time that you have to. The question was: How would Ruelas react?

Trainer Joe Goossen told *Boxing Monthly* in the lead-up to his defence against Azumah, "When a fighter is in fighting mode, that switch is turned on. All thought processes go out the window. At that point, it's all training and instinct. Gabe's given me all sorts of indicators that he's ready to roll and start boxing. He's ready to mix it up."

Once the fight was announced and a date and venue confirmed—December 1, 1995, at the Fantasy Springs Casino in Indio, California—Azumah headed back to Ghana to prepare to win back his title. Azumah had put on weight during his fifteen months away from boxing, but started preparing for this fight four months out. Most of the training was done at the purpose-built gymnasium at his house in Achimoto. He started his sparring sessions, taking on lightweights and middleweights. As the fight drew closer, he moved down in weight with the size of his sparring partners, finally working with flyweights and bantamweights to help him with his speed.

Once focused on his training regime, he did not use weights; instead, he chopped wood. He abstained from drinking and stayed away from what had become a favourite passion of his, Chinese food. He ate salads and fruit and slowly got his body back into shape. He was also looking to find a way to beat a much-improved Ruelas.

"I didn't feel rusty once I started training for the rematch," he recalls. "I was praying for God to show me how to fight this guy. I went to bed one night and was sleeping when the Holy Ghost came to me and told me to wake up and go and watch some fights. I woke up and went to the hall and took the first tape I saw. I put it in the video machine and started watching. It was a Julio Cesar Chavez fight; I forget against who. I was sitting there watching, and he hit him up top and then he hit him down on the body. I knew then that this was the way to fight him. So I went and trained for this way to fight him.

"When I got to the U.S. before the fight, at the press conference I said I would knock him out in the fifth round. People were laughing, saying, 'How can you knock him out in the fifth round?' I said, 'Okay, I will show you.'"

Once again, Azumah's chances of victory were written off by many of the boxing scribes, convinced that his loss to Leija was a sign that he was finished.

Ruelas's trainer, Joe Goossen, was not so sure, telling *Boxing Monthly*, "He's getting older, sure, but they said he was getting older three years ago! I don't assume something that isn't in evidence. I'll tell you if he's getting old after the fight. Azumah Nelson is a very strong person, and this type of experience can make for a long evening, even if you are winning. This is the type of fight where we've got to be just as smooth and as elegant in the ring as Azumah can be. We've got to put on the type of performance that Gabe put on against Jesse James Leija, where everything worked."

Most boxing journalists were already writing that this would be the night the curtain came down on Azumah's career. Few could see how he could possibly win against a man twelve years his junior, who they believed was faster and fresher, especially after nineteen months off. The betting was all on Ruelas, who was a 3–1 favourite to retain his title. Some cynics were even saying that Azumah was only fighting for the money.

The two super featherweights were top of the bill on the five-fight card promoted by Bob Arum's Top Rank, and this was the first major promotion at Fantasy Springs, a casino operated by the Cabazon Indian tribe on the outskirts of Indio, a city of about thirty-two thousand people a two-and-a-half-hour drive from Los Angeles. It would be an unforgettable night for those in attendance.

After the fight, Ruelas said that he had just wanted to get it over with as quickly as possible. Maybe that was why he fought wildly, appearing to have forgotten all that he had learned in boxing since walking into Goossen's gym at just age twelve. Azumah, wearing silk shorts in the colours of the Ghanaian national flag, held his gloves high, simply biding his time and waiting for an opening. It came sooner than he expected: in fact, just seventy-five seconds into the fight.

A powerful jab followed by a right caught Ruelas, and he hit the canvas. Azumah did not go in for the kill, well aware that he had plenty of time to take his opponent out. Although, he almost dropped him again in the final seconds of the round with a strong left hook.

In the second, Ruelas continued to fight recklessly. Azumah jabbed and parried, but it was Ruelas who did enough to win the round on two of the judges' scorecards. The noise from Azumah's supporters ringside drowned out the bell, and the two fought on. Ruelas won the third on all three judges' cards, but touched the canvas again, this time when he over-balanced following a wild left hook. The longer Azumah stayed on his feet, taking everything Ruelas had to offer, the more he sapped the champion's confidence and energy.

Despite how the judges were scoring the fight, one felt that the wily ex-champion was simply biding his time and waiting for his chance to attack. That opportunity presented itself in the fourth. Ruelas drove Azumah to the ropes, a place he was happy to go, and Azumah stepped up a gear and his hand speed defied his years. He fired a left hook to the head and followed that up by smashing a left hook into Ruelas's body. The champion crumpled to his hands and knees. A right hand clipped him on his way down, just for good measure.

Ruelas managed to beat what was a very slow count. Television replays showed that he was actually down for twelve seconds, but officially he climbed to his feet at the count of nine. With less than ten seconds left on the clock, Azumah did not have time to finish him in that round, despite unleashing six or more stunning punches. However, it was clear from that one blow the fight was over. Ruelas had caught Azumah with a few good punches, but none ever seemed to trouble The Professor, who always seemed to know what he was doing. Ruelas's attacks were frantic and wild, lacking structure and purpose, while Azumah was composed, solid, and always seemed to land the cleaner punches.

A dazed Ruelas made his way back to his corner. Trainer Jo Goossen stood over him, asking if he was okay. Ruelas mumbled something in response, and Goossen then raised his voice and told him in no uncertain terms never to let his opponent know that he was hurt. Goossen raged on and only stopped when the referee, Marty Denkin, came over and enquired as to whether Ruelas was coming out for the fifth. "Are you going to fight?" Goossen yelled at his downcast fighter, almost daring him to say no. "Want me to stop it here?" he enquired.

It should have been stopped. Ruelas was still shaky, and he was soon caught by left and right uppercuts. Azumah continued to be patient as Ruelas put up little resistance and hardly threw a punch in retaliation. Ruelas backed to the ropes and tried to duck and weave, but a thunderous left-right combination jolted his head back. Azumah continued to land punches almost at will. One minute and twenty seconds into the fifth round, referee Marty Denkin stepped in and stopped the fight. Denkin had himself shared a tragedy in boxing, having been the referee when Welshman Johnny Owen lost his life in a fight with Lupe Pintor fifteen years earlier. He was understandably keen to protect Ruelas.

In the ring after the fight, Azumah said, "I told Ghana that I would win back the title before I left. I am a man of my word. It was important to my people that I do as I said."

Despite what had happened in their last bout, Goossen was far from happy the fight had been stopped. Post-fight he said, "Azumah was throwing some very good punches, and it was up to the referee at that point. But I probably would have liked to have seen it go on." He did, however, concede, "Azumah did a great job tonight. Gabe had his mind somewhere else. I don't know whether it was due to Azumah or due to Jimmy Garcia."

At the press conference after the fight, Ruelas, whose future was now in doubt as questions were being asked about both his physical and mental state, said, "I could see Jimmy in the ring. I saw the person that I wasn't fighting. It's not an excuse, but my mind was just somewhere else. At times, I thought I was fighting Jimmy. I'm not saying that's why this happened—Azumah's a great fighter and deserves all the credit due to him—but it had something to do with it," he claimed.

Yet twenty-four hours later, he told *Los Angeles Daily News* reporter, Michael Rosenthal, that he had originally blamed his loss on the after effects of the Garcia tragedy because he did not want people accusing him of making excuses. Talking to Rosenthal, he claimed he had suffered intestinal pains and displayed flulike symptoms prior to the fight, and had spent most of the night in his hotel bathroom.

Goossen corroborated his story, saying, "I've never made excuses for any of my fighters, but Gabriel was sick."

In the book on his life, *Business of Pain*, Ruelas appears to combine the two stories when he says, "The diarrhea was so severe. I feared I would have to leave the fight and go to the bathroom. The image of Jimmy, with the mask of a frozen smile, made fun of me, blinded me. My fists were paralysed; my heart was fragmented. I no longer existed."

All of this detracted from another great emphatic Azumah victory—a victory where, once again, he had predicted in which round he would win. Post-fight, he said, "A lot of people said, 'Oh, Azumah, you are too old.' But I know myself and I knew I was not too old. I had been a champion for eight years, and my body needed some rest. I went home to rest for a while, came back, and proved to everybody that Azumah Nelson is back. I'm the best. I'm The Professor. As soon as I get in there, I know what I've got to do."

Looking back now, he remembers it well. "At the end of the first fight, he [Ruelas] says he has won and said something foolish over the decision, so I said I will give him a rematch. But I lost my title, and then he beat Jesse James Leija, but we had the rematch just the same. I told him there would be no doubt who the winner is the second time.

"The referee stopped it in the fifth—I was on top by the end of the fourth. His coach was upset the fight was stopped, and he was arguing and pushing the referees. 'Why did you stop the fight?' he was yelling, but he was beaten. I was not happy that the fight was stopped, as I was just warming up. I wanted to keep going."

To show that his heroic status had not waned with the passing of time, when he arrived back in Accra, over sixty thousand people were reported to have turned up at the airport to greet him. Now living in Achimoto, about a twenty-minute drive from the airport in normal circumstances, it took him six hours to get to his house.

Immediately after this fight, Azumah had to again suffer the indignity of being accused of something he was not guilty of: doping. It appeared that his victory over the much younger Ruelas in such comprehensive style had set tongues wagging. "They accused me of doping," he says. "The WBC wanted to end my career because I had been world champion for too long. So the question was asked: Where did I get my stamina from? My stamina in my career had never been in question, but now it was. They thought I must have taken something. So the WBC medical people took a urine sample and tested it and found nothing."

Many believed that this emphatic winning-back of his title was the ideal time for Azumah to hang up his gloves. He had other thoughts. "When I took the break before the fight, I was so restless. That was when I knew I wanted to keep going. I was strong and I was fit, so why not? When I am in peak condition, nothing scares me and I don't feel pain. Anyway, I needed money because glory is not going to feed you when you are an old man. I needed money for my family and to be able to help my people."

Since he had moved to Achimoto, people came to his house on a daily basis, asking him for help. Some were lucky to have him help with their education and return today as qualified lawyers and doctors to thank him. Outside the gates of his house stands the Blood of Jesus Church, and all around traders set up stalls each morning. It is known as Champ's Market. Knowing how hard it is to make ends meet, Azumah's household help would wander among the stalls daily, picking the best and freshest fruit and going some way to supporting these people toiling to make a living.

"They are my people. I am one of them. I know what it is like to be hungry," he says with genuine feeling. "That is why I try to help as many people as I can. A champion must remain one of the people. He must share their interests and understand their hardships. If you do not, then they will soon no longer like you." Following the Ruelas victory and the recapturing of the world title, Azumah took a rare holiday to the United Kingdom with his family—but it was not all play. Britain had a young, confident, showy featherweight from Sheffield called Naseem Hamed, and he was itching for the chance to meet Azumah Nelson. Hamed was, at the time, the WBC international super bantamweight champion and had just won the WBO featherweight title in September 1995 with a victory over Welshman Steve Robinson.

Azumah played to the gallery. "He's a showman and I like his style, his confidence, but I will knock him out," he said. The press lapped it up, and talk of a possible showdown filled the papers. However, when Azumah said, "A fight with Hamed is worth three million [sterling]," he probably scared off the promoters.

"I was not really interested because I was near the end of my career," he remembers. "If I was going to fight him, it was purely for money. It was like when somebody fights Muhammad Ali at the end of his career and he won the fight. He had it on his record he beat Muhammad Ali. I know people saw that I am coming to the end. They see that and look to take advantage of it. He was looking to have it on his record as one fighter who beat Azumah Nelson. I was never really interested in the fight or the money."

Now back as world champion, Azumah was not afforded another nineteen months off; he was to climb back between the ropes in June of 1996 to once again face Jesse James Leija. However, in the buildup to the fight, calls were still coming out of the United Kingdom for him to meet Hamed, presuming he defeated Leija, even though a rematch with Ruelas was also in the pipeline.

Hamed's promoter, Frank Warren, tabled an offer for Hamed, but Azumah rejected it. He then told *Boxing News* he would fight him for seven hundred thousand pounds. "For seven hundred thousand pounds, we can make the fight, but tell Naseem I am ready. If he is sure he will win, let the winner take all," he said. The gauntlet was thrown down, and it appeared that The Professor had spotted a flaw in the showman's technique he knew he could exploit.

Azumah was fired up for his rematch with Leija and had a point to prove. "If I lose a fight, I know the reason why," he told *Boxing News*. "There's not a boxer out there who can beat me. Watch out. This fight will be over quickly." On this occasion, Azumah paid for the fight to be aired on Ghanaian television. No longer part of Don King Promotions, it was not part of the contract negotiations, and he shelled out sixty thousand dollars so that his fellow countrymen could watch the fight. This was not the same Jesse James Leija who had taken the title from Azumah two years before. Since that victory, he had quickly lost his title to Gabriel Ruelas and had two wins over Jeff Mayweather and Rodney Garnett, but he had also been forced to retire after two rounds in his fight for the WBO light-weight title against Oscar De La Hoya.

While Azumah had found a new lease on life in the ring at thirty-seven, Leija, at thirty, appeared to be looking for an exit. In fact, it was reported that if he lost this bout, he would re-evaluate his future. One thing Leija was not worried about was being knocked out. In his last nine championship bouts in six years, Azumah had only knocked out two opponents, Jeff Fenech and Gabriel Ruelas; his fight against Daniel Mustapha had not been a championship fight.

"I've fought twenty-four rounds with Azumah and I felt his punches, and some of them were hard, but nothing that remotely shook me up at all. I always knew what was going on," he told *Boxing Monthly*.

Going into the fight, there were concerns about Leija's weight, as he had struggled to make the mandatory limit when he lost his title to Ruelas. There was no doubt that he did not want to be left having to lose vital pounds in the week coming up to the fight, as that would leave him exposed to the heavy body punching of Azumah. As was becoming the norm in any fight, there were also concerns from the Leija camp that English judge, Richard Davies, was not the right man for the job; this was his first title fight as a judge, having worked previously as a referee, a very different role. "This fight was a challenge for me, "Azumah remembers. "I had to show people I could beat this guy. Some people believed I did not know how. They doubted The Professor."

The fight was held in a makeshift outdoor arena at the Boulder Station Casino Hotel in Nevada, a twenty-five-minute ride from the Las Vegas strip. An hour before the fight was due to commence, Azumah emerged from his trailer-cum-changing-room. Joining him were his boisterous supporters banging on drums and singing loudly. It was over one hundred degrees in the parking lot where the trailers were situated. Azumah started to shadowbox. Many who witnessed him felt sure he had been confused about the start time of his fight. He kept on shadowboxing. Then he moved onto the pads, sweat pouring off his face. All the time, his supporters kept singing and banging their drums. Leija, whose trailer was no distance from Azumah's, must have sneaked a peek outside to find out what all the commotion was about. No doubt he would have looked on with disbelieving eyes as Azumah kept this up for a full forty-five minutes.

Azumah's old friend and former world champion, Cornelius Boza Edwards of Uganda, was one of those who witnessed the scene. "Azumah, you're going to leave your fight in the parking lot," he said. "He replied, 'Don't worry about it,' and just kept dancing and shadowboxing. It was almost like he was in a trance."

Leija came to the ring first, wearing a black silk robe. Then came Azumah unlike we had ever seen him before. He wore no robe. He was bare-chested. A Ghanaian song played. Smiling, he bobbed, weaved, danced, and sang along on his way to the ring. If he was in a trance before, he wasn't any longer. Never had he been more relaxed. Gone was the focused look he had worn to the ring in previous fights. He looked like he was there to enjoy himself.Azumah had predicted that he would take Leija out in the opening round, and in the opening minute following a left jab, he tagged Leija with a looping right hand and then moved in and fired off a barrage of punches. Leija withstood this salvo and started to jab the champion. In a clinch, he then unloaded four solid punches to the bicep of the champion, trying to weaken the power of his jab. In the final ten seconds of the opening round, Leija found himself on the canvas. A right hand caught him flush on the chin, his right leg buckled, and he slumped back beneath the ropes. He rocked forward quickly onto all fours, his eyes glazed, and then took a deep breath before moving onto one knee and then climbing to his feet on referee Richard Steele's count of nine. As Steele wiped his gloves, the bell sounded. Azumah had not knocked him out, but he had certainly rocked him.Between rounds, the ringside doctor went to Leija's corner to check he had recovered adequately to continue, and it was deemed he had. Leija did well to recover so quickly, and also to withstand another salvo of punches from Azumah midway through the round. Rarely had the champion begun a fight at such a furious pace. The statistics for round two from broadcaster HBO showed that Azumah had thrown 138 punches to Leija's 116, but the key factor was he had landed seventy-two to Leija's thirty.

Azumah's new trainer, Hector Perez, told him between rounds, "You find the target, and then release the power," something he had done with great effect in the opening two rounds. The question was whether he could keep this pace up as Leija worked his body at every possible opportunity.

At the start of the third, Azumah showed great glove speed, speed that defied his age, but midway through the round, he backed off Leija and let him pick him off with punches. Was he tiring? In the last thirty seconds of the round, he moved in close again and offloaded a powerful right and a good left that both found their mark.

As the bell sounded for the fourth, Leija had already proved Azumah wrong: Pre-fight, he had said it would not go beyond three. The fourth was a very close round, and at the end of it, Leija landed his best flurry of punches in the fight. Was the champion running out of gas? Many felt he had taken the first three rounds and that Leija had definitely taken the fourth; the momentum looked to be shifting Leija's way, having survived the early assault.

At the start of the fifth, Leija avoided many of Azumah's punches and then countered effectively. Leija continued to slow Azumah by working the body, and as the two stood toe-to-toe, he landed more blows than the champion, who looked happy to take some punches and weave out of the way of others. With one minute to go, Azumah landed a textbook left hook and opened up a huge cut over Leija's right eye. Seeing the blood, Azumah moved in to finish the fight.

Leija could feel the blood and tried to cover up the cut, which left his body open, and Azumah again landed some fierce rips to the body and a few powerful rights to the head, but the bell sounded and Leija had survived. Leija's cut man, Joe Souza, had his work to do; the cut was deep and long, right below the eyebrow where the skin goes over the eye socket itself. He climbed off his stool for the sixth and was immediately hit on the cut by a double left hook. Blood immediately burst forth again and ran into his eye and down his right cheek. Referee Richard Steele was paying close attention to the damage; Leija had sent a message to Steele via the press prior to the fight, saying that if he was cut, he hoped he would give him time to fight on. Azumah was landing punches almost at will, and one minute and fifty-eight seconds into the round, Richard Steele stepped between the two and waved the fight over. Azumah had avenged his loss and remained the world champion.

The fans were not happy and voiced their displeasure, but when the fight was stopped, there were no protestations from Leija. Azumah, on the fight statistics from HBO, had landed 51 per cent of the punches he threw, totaling almost twice as many punches as Leija. In addition, all three judges' cards had Azumah in front when the fight was stopped.

"I told you before the fight that no one can beat me twice," Azumah told HBO's Larry Merchant inside the ring. "This is the history I am making, and no one can beat me twice. I wanted to take him out in the first round, but I decided not to take him out in the first round. I wanted to punish him for a while and prove to people who think I am old and can't go the distance. I changed my mind and decided I wanted to knock him out in the eleventh round or twelfth round so people know the stamina that I have is unquestionable."

Merchant asked what was up next and when Azumah would be back in the ring. "I wish I could fight tomorrow or next week," was his response, before saying his new promoter, Bob Arum at Top Rank, would help decide that.

"I was the same fighter. It was just his night. The other two times were my night," was how Leija viewed the fight. He would not be drawn on whether Richard Steele had stopped the fight too soon, but finished his conversation with Merchant by saying, "Maybe he'll give me a rematch like I gave him a rematch."

Looking back, and with the passing of time, Leija says, "Don King wanted it—a third bout—but by that time, I outgrew 130 pounds and I killed myself to make 130 pounds. Azumah, being a great fighter, in the first round he knocked me out. I mean, he dropped me so bad I should've been knocked out, but I lasted six more rounds and made a fight out of it. I was cut real bad and they stopped the fight. He was on his A game and I wasn't. It's that simple."

Azumah had always had a reputation for being a nice guy, but in the lead-up to this fight, he stunned many when he said he wanted to leave Leija in a coma. Looking back on those comments, he says, "I did not want to do that, as I like the guy, but I was so focused. Each time I fought him, something happens—I could not throw my arm and I could not see. I wanted to be sure I won and knock him out quickly before anything happened."

If there was controversy over his comments prior to the fight, there was more after it. Leija's camp had protested prior to the bout about Azumah training at a gym in Las Vegas owned by referee Richard Steele. With Steele stopping the fight in some people's estimations too early, questions were raised as to how the Nevada Athletic Commission or the WBC could allow such a situation to occur. Throughout this debate, however, no one questioned whether or not Azumah was the worthy victor.

So who would Azumah fight next? There was no doubt Leija wanted a rematch, emphasising that it was one fight all with one draw, and a fourth would be the decider; it would also guarantee him another reasonable payday when, following two defeats, many were saying his career was over. What they failed to realise was that those defeats came against two of boxing's all-time greats, Azumah and Oscar De La Hoya. Leija would, of course, prove he still had plenty of fight left in him.

With Bob Arum and Top Rank acting as Azumah's promoters, the much talked about fight with Naseem Hamed was more or less a non-starter. Hamed's promoter was Frank Warren, who was linked with Don King and not archrival Arum. A unification fight with IBF champion, Arturo Gatti, was another option. Also in the mix was former WBA champion, Genaro Hernandez, and a third fight with Ruelas. The one thing that seemed to be forgotten was the idea of his retirement. Suddenly, the thirty-eight-year-old was being touted as a threat to most challengers.

The Ring magazine wrote a feature article on Azumah that October and summed up a remarkable career in several ways. Writer Nigel Collins described him as "an exotic curiosity" to American audiences "from a place they'd have trouble locating on a map, an enigma who shows up on our shores every now and then and beats up some guy we thought had a pretty good chance of beating him. The thing is, he's been doing it for so long, even folks who don't read boxing magazines are finally getting the message. This strange fighter from a strange land is something special," he wrote.

Collins went on to try and describe Azumah's fighting style, characterising it as "a strange hybrid" and going on to say, "He's best described as a cerebral slugger, and it's what goes on inside his head that is his greatest asset. He's cool, calculating, with just the right touch of fanaticism. And never, even under the most trying circumstances, does he get discouraged."

Collins also recognised a key component in Azumah's continued success at a time when many fighters of his age were retired and well past their prime, noting that, "Despite his prestige and prosperity, he's never grown soft or complacent."

"I think I am very careful," Azumah says, looking back. "I don't do a lot of things, like smoking, drinking, chasing women. I am focused on the boxing. I was so focused and I trained so hard not because I wanted to win or lose—I wanted to win—but at the same time, I have to come home without being hurt. Even if I lost, I do not want to be hurt.

"If you are not in good condition and you take some big punches, these punches can affect you when you get to forty-five or fifty. You cannot talk well or walk well, but if you are in good condition, and you know boxing well, you can come out from all of this okay. But you must not stay too long. When you realise your energy is missing or something is missing, you must listen to yourself and your body and leave boxing.

"The boxing game is I hit you, and you don't hit me. If I enter the ring with you, and I know I can stand there with you, and I realise that you cannot stand there with me, I will stand and fight you. But if I realise that your hands are heavy, I will try to move, to box and run away from you and throw punches. I will change the fight to suit me, to not make it difficult for myself.

"You need to learn boxing well. I always say thanks to God for giving me a coach like Attuquaye Clottey. Whenever we talk about boxing, I don't give glory to him because that goes to God, but God should let him rest in perfect peace and bless his family for the lessons he taught me.

"Watching the old films of Joe Louis and Jersey Joe was very, very important. This was going to be my future, so I had to focus for twenty-four hours and think about boxing all the time. Attuquaye was the one who brought the tapes and showed us the different styles and how other fighters would beat that style. If he were in this world, there would be nothing he could tell me to do I would not do. If he wanted me to carry him, even if he did not ask, I would carry him wherever he wanted to go."

When Azumah's next opponent, Genaro "Chicanito" Hernandez, was announced, there were a few raised eyebrows at the choice. The Mexican had defended the WBA version of the super featherweight title on eight occasions before relinquishing it to move up to lightweight and have a tilt at Oscar De La Hoya's title. He was unsuccessful, having walked over to the referee after the sixth round to advise him he was retiring from the fight. Many unfairly labelled him a quitter, but Hernandez later revealed he had broken his nose in twenty-one places.

Eyebrows were raised, as Hernandez obviously had a point to prove. He also had a huge height advantage over Azumah: six inches (15.2 centimetres) to be exact. He also had a four-inch (10.2 centimetres) reach advantage. Hernandez was no up-and-coming boxer; at thirty-one, he had been around for a while and was a seasoned professional. He openly admitted that he had no great love for the sport, but pursued it to give his wife and daughter a better life. He had managed to move them out of the troubled South Central neighbourhood of Los Angeles, but had still not secured his future financially.

He had plenty to gain from a fight with Azumah, whereas Azumah had it all to lose. What was more, Hernandez had been a sparring partner for Azumah in 1988 and was well aware of what he was capable of and how good his defence was. After his defeat to De La Hoya, he had dropped off the radar, but then picked up two more wins to boast thirty-four wins, one draw, and one loss in his thirty-six fights.

Azumah's preparation was not ideal as he prepared for the showdown in Ghana. He suffered a broken hand, which postponed the fight. Having recovered from that setback, the date was set for March 22, 1997, at the Memorial Coliseum at Corpus Christi on the Texas Gulf Coast.

In the lead-up to the fight, which was billed by promoter Bob Arum as "Even Money," Hernandez joked in an interview with *Boxing Monthly* magazine about how most of Azumah's devastating wins had come in rematches. "I'm hoping I can beat him so good that he won't want a rematch," he said. He went on to reveal, "One thing I've worked on for this fight is staying in the middle of the ring. The ropes are a dangerous place when you are fighting Azumah."

Having started his preparation in Ghana, Azumah arrived in Texas three weeks before the fight. Hernandez had only been knocked down once, early in his career, so it would take a special punch to knock him out. Having been a world champion, Hernandez knew that if he stood in front of Azumah, he was likely to get hit by some big shots, as Ruelas and Leija had found out the hard way.

After Azumah's two emphatic victories, there were only a few boxing pundits who favoured Hernandez this time around, most believing that Azumah's power and strength would be too much for the Mexican. One thing was certain: Azumah, after seventeen years as a professional boxer and forty-four contests, including eighteen championship victories, was not going to relinquish his title easily. Hernandez was going to have to work hard to win his title off him.

From the opening round, Hernandez's reach proved an obstacle, forcing Azumah to lunge in with his punches or duck under his taller opponent's jab and try and offload at close quarters. Hernandez's punches were a nuisance; they lacked power or real purpose, but with him landing more than Azumah, he was bound to be ahead in the judges' eyes after each round.

The size difference made for a scrappy affair, but occasionally both fighters landed telling blows, with Azumah landing a powerful left hook that shook Hernandez as he backpedalled in round two, and Hernandez later in the round replying with a good straight punch of his own.

By the end of round three, Hernandez's height and reach advantages were more than apparent. His jab had the same effect as an adult holding a child's head while the child swings his arms, desperately trying to reach the grown-up. Azumah took many of Hernandez's follow-up blows on his arms, but was simply unable to get past his jab to land any meaningful blows of his own. Between rounds, there was no doubt that Hernandez was expending far more energy than the champion, and one wondered if he had the stamina to last twelve rounds.

Rounds four and five saw Azumah become the aggressor, pushing forward with a high guard, his gloves in front of his face in order to get past the jab and in a position to land blows to Hernandez's body and head. The Mexican counterpunched well with speed but no power. He did, however, frequently manage to slip away from Azumah and make him look as if he was off-balance.

In the sixth, as he had in the previous two rounds, Azumah came out aggressively and landed a good right to the head, but after thirty seconds of aggression that pushed Hernandez backwards, he went back to boxing from behind his gloves. There was no rhythm to his fight, and the fleet-footed Hernandez frequently managed to skip his way out of trouble. But as the round came to an end, Azumah was on top and the spring looked to be fading from the challenger's step.

Hernandez started to hold on, leaning on his smaller opponent and trying to sap his energy. Azumah was still missing with a high percentage of his punches, but in the seventh, it appeared as if his body punches were taking their toll on Hernandez. The problem was he could not get in close enough to follow up.

In the last thirty seconds of the round, Hernandez looked to hold on whenever he could and hardly threw a punch. With ten seconds left on the clock, Hernandez missed with a tired right hook. Azumah pounced. He backed the challenger into his own corner and let rip with lefts and rights to the head and the body. The bell sounded as Azumah landed a left to the jaw, and as referee Lawrence Cole stepped between the two, Azumah caught Hernandez flush on the chin with another left hook. Hernandez fell to the canvas, and with one arm through the ropes, immediately rubbed his throat. His corner men were in the ring within seconds. He spat his mouthguard out and tried to get up, but his legs looked to have a mind of their own. Azumah was going to apologise, but then stopped and returned to his corner. Hernandez remained on one knee; he was obviously having problems breathing, and the doctor was soon in the ring. Thirty seconds after the bell and twenty-seven seconds since he hit the canvas, Hernandez was told by referee Cole, who had consulted with WBC President Jose Sulaiman at ringside, that he had five minutes in which to recover. After the doctor checked his throat, Hernandez complained of a pain in his jaw at the spot where the left hand had landed prior to the bell.

Lawrence Cole reflects on this moment years later. "The night before at the Roy Jones vs. Montell Griffin fight, there was a weird controversial decision that we were discussing … and we got lightning in a jug twice." In that fight, Roy Jones Jr. had hit Griffin while the fighter was on one knee and was disqualified.

He adds, "Genaro was hit literally right at the bell. It was literally a split-second after the bell, and he got hit with a left hook. He got hit on the outside of his chin when his chin wasn't down, so he ended up being hit in the throat and Genaro went down. It was after the bell. I called time and we tried to work through the situation. Part of being an official is selling the sell. Theoretically, because Genaro was hit after the bell and could not continue, Azumah would have been disqualified. But because he continued, it made it a very dramatic fight in the end, partially due to Rudi Hernandez, who was Genaro's trainer and brother. He basically pleaded with him, 'You are not going to win the title like this. You are going to get up and win it on your feet.'"

Hernandez, under WBC rules, could easily have won the bout on a foul, as Azumah's punch was after the bell. WBC President Jose Sulaiman went to him and advised him that if he could not continue, he would be crowned champion.

As Cole stepped in to separate the two fighters, he had his back to Hernandez. When asked all these years later if he had seen the punch being thrown or land, he said, "No, I'll be honest; I just faked it. I had to do what I had to do at the time, and it just appeared to me that it was after the bell. But sometimes after the bell, you can curtail when a punch is going in motion. You can kinda pull off it."

Azumah says, "I didn't hear the bell. I was on top and he was tiring. They say I hit him in the throat, but I do not think so. They gave him time to recover when I was getting on top. It changed the fight."

Hernandez sat on the floor of the ring with his corner men all around him and an ice pack on his throat while his shoulders were massaged and his head kept cool. He was talking to them, taking deep breaths, and looked to be in minimal discomfort. In the opposite corner of the ring sat Azumah Nelson on his stool, waiting for the five-minute recovery period to end. He must have been pondering how if that fist had connected just one-and-a-half seconds earlier, the fight would be over.

If Hernandez was stunned from the blow, it was quick thinking on his part to buy time. The television replays do not show the punch connecting with his throat, but they do show it smashing into his jaw. Following the events the evening before, no one was taking any risks.

The fight did continue, but well after the five-minute recovery period. The officials took far too long to clear the ring of the doctor and Hernandez's corner men. The two touched gloves and round eight commenced. The spring had definitely gone from Hernandez's step, and once again, he was happy to hold on whenever Azumah moved in close. As the round came to an end, Cole spoke to Hernandez about pushing the champion's head down. He was using every trick in the book to hang in there and negate Azumah.

Azumah continued to be outmanoeuvered by Hernandez; he was aggressive but rarely effective. It was a masterful performance from Hernandez. He moved this way and that, side to side, and held on when it suited him. It was clear Azumah needed a knockout to retain his title. Frequently, his swinging punches missed the target, yet at the end of the tenth, he nailed Hernandez in the neutral corner. However, as he stepped back to adjust his range for the follow-up, the Mexican slipped out of the corner and the chance had gone.

When the two came out for the final round, all Hernandez had to do was stay out of trouble. As he had since round seven, Hernandez danced, jabbed, and held on. He was slow to break on Cole's instructions, and when he did, he backpedalled quickly across to the other side of the ring, eating up valuable seconds. When the final bell sounded, both failed to hear it and continued to throw punches until Cole stepped in. The two embraced and headed to their corners to await the scores of the judges.

Not surprisingly, as soon as MC Mark Beiro announced that it was a split-decision, the jeers rang out. Judge Gale E. Van Hoy scored the bout 114–113 in favour of Azumah. Hernandez shook his head in disbelief. Azumah was unmoved. Judge Alfred Asaro scored it 115–113 for Hernandez. The two boxers embraced as Beiro drew the drama out of the situation, finally reading out the score of Richard Davies, who saw it as 118–110 in favour of the new world champion, Genaro Hernandez. As his corner hoisted him into the air, Azumah applauded. Hernandez accepted the applause of his supporters, and Azumah went to his corner and retrieved the world championship belt that he had worn into the ring. He made his way across to the victor and tried to strap it around his waist. Hernandez stopped him. He then told Azumah, "You came a champion. You'll leave a champion. I want you to wear it out of the ring." It was a class act and a sign of the respect Azumah had garnered over the past thirteen years.

This was not a pretty fight to finish on. Azumah certainly did not confirm that it was his last when he said afterwards, "Who knows? Maybe I'll come back again. With God, all things are possible. Sometimes this world goes up and down. You lose some things; some things get better. I'll go home and think about what I'm going to do."

After the fight, Hernandez revealed, "I was frustrating him. I hit him with a couple good body shots at the beginning of the fight, and I was hoping that would affect him a lot. It just didn't do it, but we managed to keep him at a distance. We had to fight him like you fight a bull—play around, grab him, push him around, hold on as long as we could. We had to be smart."

There was no doubt he did all that and did outsmart Azumah, a fact that the now ex-champion acknowledged post-fight. "I know I lost the fight. He was a good challenger, and I wish him all the best of luck and hope he can be a good champion like I was," he said.

Despite acknowledging who won the fight, a question still hangs around the late punch in round seven. Azumah could well have been disqualified under WBC rules for the late blow; there can be no argument of that. Hernandez, to his credit, opted to fight on to win the belt the way it was intended to be decided.

"Of course, he had time to recover. You had to give him time to recover because it was an illegal punch," referee Lawrence Cole says. "I didn't deduct a point from him, but due to it being an illegal activity, you had to give him time to recover. It really made it a dramatic fight because Azumah was closing distance. He was able to close space on Genaro, and he made it a very dramatic fight, which I think with hindsight the score-cards were seven to five rounds. It was a very close fight.

"I do remember it was the eleventh or twelfth round—and I'll never forget it because I stepped in between them—Azumah was closing space and Genaro would hold him. It was a bit of a near fight as a referee, so instead of just pushing hands and making them work out, I was breaking them completely and making them step back. Due to that, it was giving the advantage to Hernandez.

"One time, when I stepped in to break them, and I always look at fighters and both their heads to see if they have an accidental head-butt, I actually got in the line of sight of Azumah, and there did not seem like there was much white in his eyes! It was cold, steely black that looked completely through me. I would describe it as like looking at a lion as he is pacing in a zoo, looking at you like you are his lunch. The irony is that is not the person you see. That was just him focused when he was fighting; only then did he act that way. No, he is a gentleman, and you don't see that side of him. He is always very calm and very respectful."

Azumah did not make excuses after the fight, but even after all these years, he questions the delay after round seven and its impact on the outcome. "I knew how he would fight," he says. "My plan was to keep the pressure on and take his punches. I knew after seven or eight rounds, he would get tired and then I would take him out. He was getting tired. In the seventh, I hit him. He went down and he did not want to get up. He just wanted to rest until he recovered and got his stamina back. If he had not had that rest, I would have beaten him. Yes, he got up and he won the fight, but had he not had that rest, he would not have beaten me."

XV

GOING HOME

Azumah Nelson returned to Ghana, no longer the world champion, but still adored by the people of this now economically more stable West African country. He had been the nation's beacon of hope during the dark, tough days and had played his part in putting it on the map. He had brought the people of Ghana great joy. He had represented them on the world stage with style and humility. So strong had his influence been, and so respected was he in the sporting world, that not only did he ensure that people knew Ghana as an African nation, but the minute one mentioned the country, his name was automatically linked to it.

Social scientist Willis Harman, in his book *Global Mind Change*, stated, "Leadership requires a values orientation that should be accepted, adopted, and then translated into a vitalising vision." By aligning his government with Azumah's success, then-president J. J. Rawlings was able to remind a nation during difficult times of how important values were. Azumah was the man the government could look to when it needed to reassure the nation that Ghana could compete on the world stage. Rawlings's time as president polarised many, but no one can deny he played a major part in helping Ghana become the most politically stable and prosperous nation in West Africa. What is interesting, when one considers his links to the president and his government, is that Azumah never polarised the population. He is much loved by all.

"There was something that I respected and appreciated about him personally. I don't know whether people seem to perform well when they are

251

performing in front of a home crowd. They try to use the psychology of the atmosphere to beat you down in such a way that it brings the worst out of you while providing the best psychological atmosphere for their nation," Rawlings says. "What I noticed about Azumah was that when the odds were stacked against him, that was when he was at his best. And it was proven through what happened against Fenech in Australia.

"He demonstrated the true spirit of a boxer," he continues. "In football, when you are in trouble, most players pass the buck or pass the ball. In boxing, there is no one to pass it on to. You can't pass the buck in a boxing ring, and to have held the title for that long also demonstrates the fighting spirit of the man. He is, in a way, self-made. Others who tried to rely on other environments didn't last that long. Most champions do not last as long as he did, and he did so because of his own personal and internal spiritual, mental, and physical discipline—all three, the state of his mind and spirit. He made sure that his physical performance did not fall behind the strength of his mind and spirit. Winning the championship, the environment did not change his mindset. If he made money, it did not change him."

According to longtime friend Peter Zwennes, "As a Ghanaian, he made you very proud because whenever you travelled outside the country and it came to boxing and sport, people would say, 'You are from Azumah's Ghana? How is Azumah?' Of all our world champions, he is the most likeable. He has endeared himself to practically everyone.

"D. K. Poison was our first world champion, but he was a very quiet person. He kept to himself and did not like the limelight, especially after he lost his title. You would not see him at boxing tournaments. You would not see him in public places. Ike Quartey, after Azumah, was brash. People felt he was—if I talk bluntly—he was disrespectful in a way. But Azumah was always very modest, very likeable. He made the country proud wherever he went. Anytime he fought, you found even the other side praised him. He fought a lot of Mexicans, and I think they have very kind words to say about him. He became the torchbearer for Africa. We did not have many champions at that time in any division, and he was the sole champion. So in all of Africa, everyone was looking up to him to lift the flag of Africa. They all knew Azumah would do them proud.

Nigerians, everybody was proud that he represented Africa in boxing circles."

Jacob Zwennes endorses his brother's sentiments. "His nature and his character are very laid back, very respectful, and he never puts himself above anyone. When people approach him, he always has time for them. He is very inviting," he says. "As opposed to most Ghanaian boxers who come to America and have a fight and then head home, he stayed on and marketed himself well. He has been a great ambassador for our country. He was a key figure at a very important time in Ghana's history. He made the people proud, but more importantly, he made them happy."

Nii Amakai Amarteifio, who was with Azumah when he won his first world title and who worked closely with him in his role as sports minister in the government of the day, has no doubt as to the impact this man has had in Ghana. "He has personal traits that combine with his feats, with his achievements, that make him a role model. He has been a good role model for the young people of this country, and I hope and I pray that for the rest of his life, he remains an icon, a role model—someone who will inspire confidence in people who come from his background. Not just those people, but also anyone who believes that discipline, perseverance, and humility have just rewards, and that is what he tells everybody. He represents triumph over adversity, overcoming social circumstances, and those openings were as tough as the openings in the ring, and of course, that victory was a victory for society.

"He became an icon. He showed to the young people that it was possible to become a huge somebody from a little nobody. He inspired them; he gave them hope; and suddenly everybody wanted to be Azumah Nelson. That was wonderful. To give so much hope, to give so much inspiration to a poor country, especially the young people, is wonderful.

"There is, however, a negative side to it. You see, Azumah having been champion, at the top, for many years, he was naturally a very confident young man. He could dance like Muhammad Ali; he could lower his guard and still batter his opponent. He knew he should tuck in his chin and protect it, but he was so confident he could afford to float like a butterfly.

"But the young ones did not know he'd done it the way it should be done before, and only now can he relax. They did not know him then, and they only saw him when he was Muhammad Ali, playing to the crowd, dropping his guard. They did not see that he learned how to defend himself before that, and we need to tell our next generation of boxers this, and he can help us with this.

"Azumah opened the gate to big money in boxing for the first time, and now nobody wants to learn the trade. Nobody wants to be a good apprentice, and it was because he was a good apprentice that he succeeded. People only see the success side. They do not see how he succeeded. They did not know him when he was an apprentice, and he was a good apprentice. If we do not bring back amateur boxing, it will be a long time before Ghana sees another Azumah Nelson."

Not surprisingly, as a thirty-nine-year-old former world champion, not too many offers to fight came in. He was yesterday's champion and yesterday's hero in this cruel and sometimes ruthless business. Yes, his name would live on as that of a great world champion, but he was no longer the main attraction, no longer the headline act; that honour and responsibility now fell to younger men.

Almost a year after he lost his title to Hernandez, a proposal for one more fight came to Azumah: to meet old foe Jesse James Leija. In three bouts, both fighters had won once and there had been one draw, so this would be the decider. Neither held a world title and both had failed in their attempts to become lightweight champion, Azumah losing to Pernell Whitaker and Leija to Oscar De La Hoya. In addition to settling who would be the overall victor, on the table was the vacant IBA junior lightweight title, which was, many thought, the main attraction.

Why else would Azumah take this fight? Was he really like so many champions before him, not able to tell when it was time to hang up his gloves? It was simple in his mind. "It was the money. They made me a good offer, and I took it for the money," he says. "The titles did not mean anything. IBF, IBA—I don't like this title. I like to fight the tough fighters in the WBC, the real champions. It was not about the title; it was purely business."

So on July 11, 1998, just eight days before his fortieth birthday, Azumah returned to Leija's hometown of San Antonio, Texas, and to the

Alamodome, the scene of their first meeting, to face off in a fourth encounter. Both were aiming to win that elusive lightweight title and move ahead on their personal ledger. The fight, billed as "The Festival of Champions" by Top Rank, featured seven former world champions, and Azumah was the headline act. Also on the card were Gabriel Ruelas, Troy Dorsey, Gregorio "Goyo" Vargas, and Tracy Patterson.

"I was still nervous," Leija recalls. "You have to remember the fight before he had stopped me. So I was nervous for the fourth fight, but I was on my plan and I was not going to lose to anyone that day. Being in the ring with Azumah Nelson three times already, I knew what to expect. I knew how hard he hit, and I knew how tough a fight it was going to be, but I physically prepared myself. Plus, we fought at a heavier weight, and I was more comfortable at that heavier weight."

Despite saying that all these years later, there were still some who thought that Leija looked drawn at the weigh-in the day before the fight and must have struggled once again to make the weight. Time would tell if this was true, as it would undoubtedly affect his performance in the middle or latter rounds. Azumah may have trained well, but on the evening of the fight, in the dressing room, he encountered something new. "My hands started swelling," he recalls. "Before we have even started boxing, before we got to the ring, my hands started to swell."

For this fight, the man in his corner was none other than Gabriel Ruelas's former trainer, Joe Goossen. With Jose "Buffalo" Martin having passed away, Azumah had to find someone else to work with, and he chose Goossen. This meant that rivals Ruelas and Nelson trained and even sparred together at Goossen's Van Nuys gym. Both were ex-world champions now, and both were looking at a chance to win back the title.

To some, it seemed a strange move, but not to Azumah. "I chose them because they have something important, love, and those who have love have a fear of God, and that is very important to me," he says. "People don't understand the boxing game. It is a game—we fought each other, yes, but it's a business. For everyone in this game, I have love and I have friendship. These are my people. We are a family and we must look after each other."

Once again, Azumah came to the ring smiling, this time not bare-chested as he had been in their last fight, but in a poncho in Ghanaian fabric. Leija looked relaxed as he made his way to the ring to the strains of a Mariachi band waiting for him inside the ropes. When his robe came off, there was no doubt that Azumah was in great shape for his age, but the question on everyone's lips was whether he was in good enough shape to win what commentators were calling the "trilogy in four parts."

Both fighters were busy in the opening round, each aware of what the other could do. As it had been at the start, most of the action was in the centre of the ring in round two, with Leija flicking out his jab and Azumah up on his toes, switching to southpaw and looking to lure Leija in so that he could unload his right hand. "Get a bit busier with that left hand," Goossen told Azumah between rounds. "You're looking good on your legs, but you gotta start punching him a bit more with that left. He's looking to throw that right hand, and he's looking to protect himself from your right hand. You gotta sucker him into that left hook." Azumah's face was a picture of concentration. He nodded now and again to what Goossen had to say, but one felt he was already working out in his own mind how to fight this fight.

After four rounds, it was still a very even affair. Azumah was throwing more punches, but Leija was landing more, even though Azumah was landing the heavier blows. It was a very strategic fight, as one would expect—after all, they had met three times previously—but the partisan crowd was not so appreciative of that fact. They made their support clear every time Leija landed a solid punch, and sometimes even when he didn't. By round five, it was clear it was going to take something special to sway the judges to vote against the crowd. It was also clear that Leija was growing in confidence, and it looked like the student was giving The Professor a lesson.

Goossen warned Azumah between rounds six and seven that he was falling behind and that he needed him to do more in each round to close the gap. The Professor nodded. He came out and was far more aggressive than he had been in the sixth. He landed some good body shots before Leija fought back. Azumah then stunned the American with a solid left hook to the head. Suddenly, he was finding his range; suddenly, there was some leverage behind his punches; and suddenly, they were landing with power. Leija had a final flurry before the bell, which may have convinced the crowd it was his round when really it had to be Azumah's.

He continued in the same vein in the eighth and had Leija breathing heavily, following some powerful body punches, but in the final ten seconds of the round, he walked into a right hand from Leija. With the crowd baying for a knockdown, he somehow managed to stay on his feet until the bell sounded.

Despite the urgings from Goossen in his corner throughout round nine, it was Leija's round. Again, he may not have thrown the most punches, but he threw and landed the most effective punches and also managed to evade many of Azumah's. The tenth was also Leija's round. The fight stats had Azumah having landed 218 of 579 punches and Leija 193 of 460, but it was Leija who was definitely controlling the bout.In the eleventh, The Professor kept moving forward, looking for openings to land that crucial punch to steal the fight, but Leija kept rolling with the punches, bobbing, weaving, and moving. Then with one minute and ten seconds left on the clock, the two clashed heads. Leija pulled away and half-turned his back to Azumah. Referee Lawrence Cole stopped Azumah from following him and punching. He waved Leija to continue, but the fighter gestured to the referee and said something. Again, Cole stepped in and stopped Azumah from punching. There was a definite welt on Leija's head. Cole walked over to look at it; there was no bleeding so he ushered the two to continue. The clock had eaten up ten seconds, though—ten crucial seconds for Azumah, who needed a knockout to win.Remembering the incident, Cole explains what happened. "James fought really good for the first six or eight rounds and then started petering off. There was an accidental head-butt in the eleventh, and I remember James looking at me, wanting me to stop the fight, and I'm like, 'No, I have to stop it for a reason,' and he's like, 'I'm cut,' but I go, 'But it's not bad enough.'

"The irony is a few years later, I'm working a fight with James and Micky Ward and he gets cut, and the cut ends up being three or four inches long. I end up stopping the fight, which at the time was a controversial stoppage. It was stopped based on a head-butt, so it went to the scorecards and James won that fight. The fight with Azumah was not that bad, so you make the fighter continue. In the fight with Micky Ward, it

wasn't very deep, but it was getting worse and worse as the fight continued. You are not just worried about the blood impairing the vision, but
that the laceration gets so bad that it could end up finishing a fighter's
career."

Despite the lump and a trickle of blood, it was Leija who finished the
round on top, once again stinging Azumah with a flurry of punches that
managed to find their target. The bell sounded for the final round, the
crowd chanting Leija's name as the two touched gloves. Could Azumah
find a knockout blow the way Salvador Sanchez had in the fight that put
him in the boxing limelight? Or would this be his last round of boxing?
One thing was for sure: He wasn't going to die wondering.

A good right hand jolted Leija halfway through the round as Azumah
tried to apply the pressure. Leija looked to hold on whenever he could.
At one break, he pushed out his mouthguard in order to suck in more air.
With a minute to go, he fought back, and his local supporters found voice
to cheer him home. Azumah kept pressing forward, unleashing punches
to the head and the body, but the crispness and sharpness of old just
wasn't there. The two flailed away in the dying seconds, and when the bell
sounded, they fell into each other's arms. Leija then held his arm aloft,
acclaiming victory.

When the decision was announced, it was no surprise that Leija was
the winner by unanimous decision. Post-fight, Leija put his victory down
to his conditioning and the fact that he had made Azumah work harder
in the earlier rounds than he was used to.

Looking back all these years later, Leija is proud to have fought
Azumah on four occasions. "It was like being punched by three or four
arms, and every punch hurt like crazy," he says. "You just never knew
what to expect from Azumah. He'd sometimes lure you in, make you
make a mistake. Sometimes he would push you harder than you wanted
to be pushed. He was a great, complete fighter, and I am just proud to say
I was in the ring with him for forty-two rounds.

"Sometimes you would see the wildness in his punches, the haymakers,
but they were the ones that caught you because you didn't expect them.
If I were in a street fight, just me and one other person, I would want that
person to be Azumah Nelson. No one at that weight hit harder than

Azumah Nelson. I learned so much from the man, from fighting him so many times. That's where I gained all my experience; that is where I learned to become a true fighter. To me, the proudest point in my career was fighting Azumah Nelson."

When asked post-fight in the ring if this was the end of the line, Azumah hesitated and then said, "I don't know if I'm going back. We'll see." Azumah had won two and lost three of his last five fights, when he had lost only two in the previous forty-one professional fights. It certainly looked like he had reached the end.

"I had a problem with my hand from the fifth round, but I had to keep going," Azumah says, looking back on that fight. "I thank God that Leija does not have a heavy punch. If he did, he would have destroyed me, but he cannot hurt me with his punches. God is my strength, and he obviously wanted it to be this way. He protected me. I did not get hurt and I thank him for that."

This fight did indeed end up being Azumah's last professional fight apart from the rematch with Fenech, which was more an exhibition intended to raise money for his foundation. Azumah received the accolades his career warranted very late. Unfortunately for him, in the early part of his reign as world champion, when he did get television coverage in the U.S., the fights often did not last long. His bouts with Sanchez and Gomez for the world title were only available on cable and syndicated audiences in the States. NBC was in London when he knocked out Pat Cowdell in one round, as well as when he humiliated Danielo Cabrera. CBS was there for the Suarez fight, but it was not until the Fenech bout in Las Vegas that he finally came to the public's attention.

Ferdie Pacheco, talking to *World Boxing* magazine in 1989, was quoted as saying, "What's happened to Azumah Nelson is that he's fallen through the cracks. He's always been a good attraction, but not a great moneymaking attraction, so Don King was always paying more attention to people like Larry Holmes and Tyson, getting them the fights."

In retirement, though, his achievements have been recognised with a number of well-earned awards. He was elected into the International Boxing Hall of Fame on January 8, 2004, and inducted on June 13 the same year. This was the fifteenth induction, and he was hailed as the first

African to be afforded this honour.

He also became a member of the World Boxing Hall of Fame. In 2012, he was one of only twelve boxers to have a watch made in his name in conjunction with Hublot and the World Boxing Council to raise funds for the WBC's charitable initiatives. Azumah stood on stage alongside boxing greats such as Mike Tyson, Sugar Ray Leonard, Lennox Lewis, Larry Holmes, Ken Norton, Tommy Hearns, Roberto Duran, Julio Cesar Chavez, Oscar De La Hoya, George Foreman Sr., and old rival Jeff Fenech.

In 2002, *The Ring* magazine rated him fifteenth in its list of the twenty greatest featherweights of all time. "The Professor could break down his pupils a little at a time, and then when they were ready to go, he could dismiss them with little danger to himself," the magazine asserted.

According to longtime WBC president Jose Sulaiman, back when it all started, Salvador Sanchez had confided in him. "Salvador Sanchez was tough, and he said to me that Azumah was the toughest he had ever met. Azumah was a great champion; he was the best without a question. For him to be the champion of the WBC was a sincere pride because the best champions—and I do not want to say it but I must—the best champions are the WBC champions."

Azumah, by his own admission, was far from perfect. In some people's eyes, he did box on too long, but not in his own. "I have to advise myself when to retire," he says. "I thank God that Leija is not one of the tough guys I fought like Martinez, Villasana, or Fenech, the guys who punch hard. Every time I fought him, I had problems, either with my hand or my eyes, but I said if anyone beat me twice, I will retire. If I fight you once, I have to beat you in the second fight. So if you beat me twice in a row, I must retire."

So retire he did. Not surprisingly, there was no press conference, no public announcement. Azumah simply did not climb through the ropes again. Looking back on his career, he sees that he made many of the same mistakes that world champions before him had made, and mistakes many who follow will also make.

"I am no different from the other boxers," he explains. "But my problem is I am faithful and I love people, and I want to make sure everyone is happy. That is the mistake I made, and a lot of other boxers are like me. Bad people, they come and take the money you give them and they run away. When they have spent it, they come back. You don't quarrel with them because you are wise now. If you are not wise and learn, these people will destroy you. It hurt me that I thought I am doing good, that I am helping them, trying to take them out of poverty and away from their problems. It may look like I am stupid, but I learn fast and these people taught me so much.

"I didn't go to school. Sometimes I put things in people's hands. I try to take care of people, give business to people with less than me. I gave some of them money to try and help them. If you have been to school, you are intelligent and you learn how to make the money work. I never had that opportunity. Even my wife said sometimes, 'I don't like it. You're giving all the money to people you don't know.'

"Yes, I have trusted too many people. I trust people to be like myself. I won't cheat you. I won't do bad to you. I thought people would be the same as me, but not everyone is like that. Peggy, my wife, told me that and she was right. Friends come in and pretend that they love you, and you don't know they are pretending. But when you go down, they all run away. But if you know God, if they go away, you know that they will come back again. You are wise now, and they cannot get to you and destroy you."

Lifelong friend Obi Oblitey thinks he understands why Azumah continues to try and help those who maybe do not deserve his help. "He has had bad people try and use him," he says. "If God loves you, you have to help, and that is why Azumah always helps everyone. He believes God loves everyone, and so if someone does not like him and he knows that, he will still try to help them—even if they can't look him in the eye. God loves everyone. He does not want to upset God."

"I love Ghana and I love Africa. It is my home," Azumah says. "I did not stay in the States to live because God did not bring me to this world to live outside of Africa. He brought me into this world to be of service to Africa and to Ghana and to live here. I love Africa and my country, and I am happy here. I would not want to live anywhere else. When I fought, I did not view it as pressure when I knew the people were watching me and wanting me to win. I felt it was my duty that I had to win for my people because I do not want to let them down. I always felt that if I have to die, that was the only way that anyone can beat me.

"When I was fighting in America, I stayed in Ghana and started my training in Ghana. This was important, as it proved that I can stay here in Africa and rule the world. This was very important. It proved a point that whatever you are, whatever you want to achieve, you can do it from Ghana, from Africa. You do not need to leave. We have hardships in Ghana and Africa, but I cannot see the reasons why we have the hardships. God has blessed us so much. We can use our lands to be richer, and we have cocoa, timber, gold, and oil. We have all these things, but we are suffering.

"I think African people are more proud of their nation than the Western world. We know unity. The sad thing is that many of our people pretend they are with you, when really they are looking to put you down. Those who put God first do the right thing, but many people in Africa are guided by the devil. Our problem is envy.

"There are pretenders, people who laugh with you but not in their hearts. If a white boxer is fighting, they will support the white boxer. In Africa, and in Ghana, there were people who, when I am going to fight, they would go and do spiritual things against me to make me lose the fight. They envied me and they tried to make me lose. I only have good intentions for you, so why do you have bad intentions for me? It is because they were jealous. That is not good. They will pay for that jealousy, jealousy that made them do something wrong, and their children will pay if they don't.

"If you love your children, you will never do these things because you will not want them to pay. Do you want your family to suffer because of what you do? That is why we must have wisdom: to live, to see what is good and what is bad, and understand that the cup that you use to measure will one day be used to measure you.

"If you ask me any place I prefer to fight, it doesn't matter. Fighting is my business. If you want to fight in the room right now, I will, but if you ask where I like, I don't have a favourite. I just come and do my business and go. This world and its big cities are not fantastic to me. There are people who have achieved something, and they raise themselves up as special, but they are not special. It was God who gave them that blessing. He made you famous for the poor people, for those who are not happy, so that through you, you can make them happy. You raise yourself to create a standard. When they call out, 'Hello, champ,' all they want is you to wave back, acknowledge them, or stand and say, 'How are you?' You make their day when you do. You need to think about these people when you are famous—if that makes them happy, it is easy to give up your time to do that. I was there; I came from them; and I know their suffering. It makes me cry sometimes, so I try to love all people.

"I love all the boxers, and I want every one of them to be well, especially the people I fought. I want to see how they are feeling now that we have finished fighting, and if they are not doing well, if they are in trouble, if there is anything I can do to help them. Through them, I became who I am. If I didn't fight them, I do not become who I am. If someone is not feeling well and there is something I can do, I want to help. When I see them, I ask if they are okay, feeling okay, if everything is good in life. I want to make sure everything is okay. The punches we are taking are not good, and I pray that no one gets hurt. When they are well, I feel happy, but when they are not, I feel sad.

"When I saw Muhammad Ali, I cried. I asked myself some questions. Here is the greatest boxer of all time, and he looks like that today. It is very sad. We have to know and think. The beginning is not as important as the end. We must remember that," he adds.

One example of Azumah helping a fellow boxer came in 1999. Azumah was in London to watch a fight at the York Hall. British bantamweight Francis Ampfofo picked him up at the airport and was taking him to the fight. On the way, Ampfofo called former world champion, Charlie Magri, to say he would be late for the opening of the pub Magri had taken over, the Queen Victoria in Mile End. When Azumah heard of the opening, he insisted on attending to support a fellow boxer. Many of the greats of British boxing were there—Alan Minter, John H. Stracey, and John Conteh to name just a few—but when Azumah walked in, everyone stepped back to welcome him.

He walked up to Magri and told him how good a boxer he had been.

It made Magri's night. Despite winning the WBC flyweight title, he had never received the recognition he deserved, as in his first title defence he lost to Frank Cedeno of the Philippines. His loss could have been avoided; unfortunately, in the lead-up to the fight, he had a blind boil in his ear, and although the doctor advised against boxing, his management and the promoters pushed him into the ring. He paid a heavy price.

In Ghana, some boxing was shown on local television, and that was how Azumah had been able to watch Charlie Magri fight. The government paid for his own world title fight to be beamed into Ghana, and Azumah witnessed what that victory meant to his fellow countrymen and made sure that all of his fights were shown live on television in his homeland. "I paid for most of the fights for my people to see. I want them to be happy," he says. "I want all African people to be happy. I did it so they can forget about the problems they had during the fight and enjoy it. It was very important to me that they see my fights and I make them happy."

This is just one of the reasons he is so loved still in Ghana. He is a national treasure. If he is in his car in traffic, and one always seems to be in traffic in Accra, he will be spotted behind the wheel of his car. "Champ!" a cry goes up and a hand is raised in recognition. Others look in the direction of the wave, and suddenly there are more cries of "Champ!" Within seconds, his car is surrounded. He never loses his patience. He smiles and raises a hand in acknowledgment, and if they are putting themselves at risk in the heart of the traffic, he tells them to be careful.

If he is on foot, it only takes moments before he is surrounded. Never does he run to escape his adoring compatriots. Instead, he will shake their hands; he will listen to what they say; and he will talk quietly to them as he slowly makes his way among them to his final destination. Here is a man who feels the love of the people and returns that love by sparing time to treat each with dignity and respect, for he remembers the time when he was one of them, battling on the street day after day to try and make ends meet. That is why he never shuns anyone, why he always has time, and why he is so loved in Africa, not just Ghana.

Many who are born with little or nothing yearn their whole lives to have everything, or if not everything, a larger slice of the pie. Azumah never did. Whatever he earned, he wanted to share. Being able to provide for others was his reward, his justification of a job well done. It was never about himself. They say that no man who has gone hungry ever forgets that feeling, and certainly he gives the impression that every day truly is a gift from God. He was given a talent, a talent that he identified at a young age, and he used that talent to help himself and those around him, as well as those who had helped him and some who did not even know him.

Ghana may not have a royal family, but at home, Azumah is king. The ordinary rules of life do apply, but at times, it appears that they do not. He was given the gift of the ability to deliver when his country needed uplifting. When the eyes of a nation were fixed on him and his exploits, he did not fail. He delivered and he gave them hope. That success gave him the same heroic status as fictional superheroes who always seem to be there at the right time, who always deliver when everyone is watching. They always come through, and Azumah always came through for Ghana and the people of Africa, and in such style and with such humility that he gave the people dignity and a reason to be proud.

It is said that the best education a man can get is through the school of life. There may not be any final exams to sit through, or even any graduation, but there are few tougher seats of learning. Some measure success in money or material trimmings, but ultimately, the best barometer is how your life has touched others. Within the school of life, there are many faculties, but there are few who honour their students with the title, "Professor." Azumah Nelson is one such beneficiary. From the humblest of beginnings, he conquered the world, and his own nation fell in love with him and expected him to deliver and embody their dreams.

Throughout the journey, he has never lost sight of his nation, his friends, or his love of God, and through all his successes and heartbreak he has managed to maintain his humility. He has never forgotten those early days on the street when success came his way. He never wants to forget them, for they contributed to his success, made him who he is today, and helped him to savour the enjoyment of the good times so much more.

As he walks through a hotel lobby in the U.S., Mexico, or Australia, there is a murmur that builds as the people around him recognise the short, stocky man with the overhanging brow and eyes of steel that twinkle like a child's when he knows he has been recognised. It is an excited and welcoming twinkle that is both warm and inviting.

As soon as one person plucks up the courage to talk to him, word spreads like a fire through a cornfield, and soon he is surrounded. Never does he lose his poise or become rude. He will stop and listen to their memories of his fights, and thank them humbly for their kind words and for taking an interest in his career. Often he will engage in conversation and debate issues or correct a fact that with the passing of time has been distorted. When it comes to his fights, he can replay every one in his mind as if it were yesterday.

It was therefore no surprise that a Mexican waiter in Las Vegas should recognise him and leave his station to shake his hand. After all, Las Vegas took over from Madison Square Garden as the boxing capital, and it was his fight against a Mexican in "The Garden" that made the boxing world take notice of Azumah Nelson. In a twist of fate, it was a Mexican, Jesse James Leija, who robbed him of his world title after ten years as champion. He reclaimed it from another Mexican, Gabriel Ruelas, only to finally lose it to yet another, Genaro Hernandez.

They say that great fights define great boxers, and that is no doubt why Azumah's name is mentioned in the same breath as the likes of two boxers he greatly admired, Marvellous Marvin Hagler and Julio Cesar Chavez, as well as many other great boxers.

Boxing changed dramatically during Azumah's career, especially in its accessibility to fans and other fighters, as Azumah explains. "When I started boxing, there was no video film. It was harder—you just sparred and trained with the other boxers. If you are fighting a southpaw, you found someone who is a southpaw who may run, and you train to put pressure on him. If not, then you climb in the ring and in the first round, you study him—how he moves, how he fights—and then you get the chance to put in place your plan to beat him.

"Technically, boxers were better in those days because there were no DVDs. The boys today are luckier than us, as they can see their opponents' fights and learn what they have to do before they get in the ring. It would've helped if we had DVDs in my time, and it would have advanced me as a boxer.

"When I went to the USA, in Don King's camp, I could get film and watch. It made my fights easier, as I had seen my opponent's power punch, his moves, and I know he cannot change. He will not do anything different. You remember when they drop a hand and you watch the tape carefully. He has a good right, so you start thinking how to stop his right hand. You make sure you focus on the right not getting you because as soon as it hits, you will go down. If you have not seen the tape, he can knock you out because you do not know the signs that show he is ready to throw the right hand. The tapes make you a better boxer because you see things and remember them, and then in the ring, you have to box to be sure that he cannot hit you with a big right."

Remarkably, apart from taking on the number-one contenders, Azumah always fought in everyone else's backyard. He fought and beat numerous powerful punchers, and if they disputed the result, he always gave them a second chance. With the exception of Leija, he gave them all a boxing lesson the second time around, and that is why he is The Professor. Only the wise who beat him the first time never gave him a second chance.

Leija acknowledges the achievement of Azumah always fighting in his opponent's home country. "Back then, you had to fight the number-one contender, and you had to fight them right away," he says. "He fought everyone and he beat everyone. He fought everyone in their own backyards and beat them, and he wasn't afraid to go anywhere and fight. That says a lot about a fighter. You do not see that happening these days. They protect fighters like crazy nowadays. He didn't care where he fought, and as I said, the fans can't fight you in the ring; they can only cheer. He was an incredible fighter. There will never be another Azumah Nelson."

The curtain may well have come down on his career in San Antonio, Texas, but he will always be remembered in Las Vegas, a city where the life of a great heavyweight had come to an end, a boxer whom he had watched through grainy black-and-white film, a boxer who had such an influence on this young aspiring boxer in Bukom.

Azumah Nelson conquered the world at a time when his country was at its lowest point. He gave the people of not only Ghana, but the whole of Africa something to be happy about, something to be proud of, and gave them the belief that black Africans, and especially Ghanaians, could stand shoulder to shoulder with the rest of the world. Maybe more importantly, he made the rest of the world start to respect Africa and its athletes.

Joe Louis was a man who did so much to unite America in his fights with German heavyweight, Max Schmeling, and who through his humility helped white America change its view of the black man. At Joe Louis's funeral in 1981, the Reverend Jesse Jackson gave this eulogy to the champion: "With Joe Louis, we made it from the guttermost to the uttermost, from slave ship to championship. Usually the champions ride on the shoulders of the nation and its people, but in this case, the nation rode on the shoulders of the hero."

He could so easily have been talking about Azumah. Azumah's heritage came direct from the slave ships, and he rose from the streets to be the champion of the world. Sure, he rode on the shoulders of his nation, but so, too, did he carry the hopes of a nation on his shoulders, and never once did his knees buckle. When his country needed him to be strong, he did not fail them.

It is not, however, his success that endears him to all, but the way he has handled that success. Throughout his career and his life, through the ups and the downs, he has been constant. He has been a symbol of trust and reliability and has remained a man of the people. He has rubbed shoulders with powerful politicians, movie stars, and the rich and the famous, yet he has never forgotten where he came from or those he left behind. To him, all are equal. His gentleness defies the sport that made the world sit up and take notice of him. He is always polite, thoughtful, and modest. He speaks with a gentility that is at odds with the brash, loudmouthed boxers of today, and that is why so many listen to what he has to say.

Azumah's parents raised him with old-fashioned values, teaching him to respect his elders, to respect the word of the Lord, and to help others. They taught him the importance of respecting yourself and taking responsibility for your actions. Boxing, too, teaches discipline, self-respect, and a winning attitude. It instills the need to push on when it feels as if all is lost. Azumah never viewed boxing as an escape from the life that he had; he has always seen it as a way to use the talent God gave him, which in turn would enable him to carry out his life's mission to help others.

There is no argument that he was a Professor of boxing inside the ring; outside it, he has educated many about Ghana and the continent of Africa. But possibly his greatest gift is the life he has lived—a life that has been a lesson in humility.

THE LAST WORDS

"It was special to both be from Africa and world champions at the same time. We are the only two boxers from Africa to be inducted into the Boxing Hall of Fame. Stan Christodoulou is there as a referee and judge, but Azumah and myself are the only two fighters, so we have that unique record. I respect him and I am sure he respects me, as we had titles at a tough time for boxing.

"He will always be known as a great WBC champion; a guy who knocked them all out; a guy who was a tremendous fighter. To beat a legend like Jeff Fenech as well shows just how great a fighter Azumah Nelson was."

Brian Mitchell
WBA Super Featherweight Champion 1986–1991
IBF Super Featherweight Champion 1991

"My first fight was on the undercard of Jeff Fenech vs. Azumah Nelson, their second fight, in Melbourne on March 1, 1992; this is was the beginning of me. What tremendous work he did against Jeff Fenech. It had been very, very close—the first fight—but in the second, he did a very good job and knocked Jeff out in the eighth round. Of course, we were disappointed because we were in a different corner, but boxing is not only about what's in the ring. It's about who you can be outside of the ring—the best you can be outside of the ring.

"I have met Azumah many times since then, and the first thing he

271

always does is smile. Anywhere he goes, he has a huge smile, and this shows a nice, great character, and people like him."

Kostya Tszyu
IBF Light Welterweight Champion 1995–1997
Interim WBC Light Welterweight Champion 1998–1999
WBC Light Welterweight Champion 1999–2004
WBA Light Welterweight Super Champion 2001–2004
IBF Light Welterweight Champion 2001–2005
Undisputed Light Welterweight Champion 2001–2004

"Azumah and I grew up in the same era where when we took on all comers; we couldn't pick and choose any fighter. If they said that was who we had to fight, that was who we had to fight. Boxing today is a little different; it's changed. There are too many organisations, and basically you don't fight any real good champions today. It's not fair to boxing or fair to the fans; they can't really remember the champions' names, as they don't stay there that long.

"I used to love to see him fight. A warrior—that is what I would call him. I believe people won't forget him because he fought so many great champions and he showed what being a real champion is all about."

Marvelous Marvin Hagler
WBA Middleweight Champion 1980–1987
WBC Middleweight Champion 1980–1987
IBF Middleweight Champion 1983–1987

"He was strong—very, very strong—and a committed fighter. He showed that if you put in the hard work, it'll pay off. Azumah Nelson was one of those fighters who would rather lose with class than win with no class. He will be remembered for his professionalism."

Marlon Starling
WBA Welterweight Champion 1987–1988
WBC Welterweight Champion 1989–1990

"He had a style that reminded me of me. He threw a lot of punches and was a very busy fighter. I was really surprised when I first watched him, and he threw those punches and moved, and threw some more punches and moved again. He came out with a lot of stuff, and I don't know where he got it from. He fought from his heart, and that is what you have to do to be a champion.

"His legacy is: You can come from nowhere and get somewhere."

Aaron Pryor
WBA Light Welterweight Champion 1980–1983
IBF Light Welterweight Champion 1984–1985

"Being a referee is not an easy job; we think differently than the fans as officials, but I look at Azumah Nelson as an individual who was one of the toughest, most skillful, and most dangerous fighters at the featherweight division. Azumah Nelson today still represents himself like a champion. He is a very humble individual; he is like a role model for individuals.

"I wish other fighters around the world would try to copy him because Azumah is an individual who has been going through his life as someone who cares, who wants to better the people from his country and individuals from all walks of life around the world. He continues to be the people's champion."

Joe Cortez
Referee in over 170 World Title Fights

"He was one of the greatest champions the WBC has ever had, and he is not only a boxing champion, but a champion in life. Azumah Nelson, to me, is the greatest fighter born in Africa. He is close to the people, and he is devoted to the service and being good to people. I have the highest regard and respect for him."

Jose Sulaiman
President of the World Boxing Council

"Azumah has a quality that you have to understand: Because of his background, he relates to the poor and still hasn't forgotten where he came from. To me, it's a very good quality."

Dr. Oko Kwatekwei
Former Manager

"He was an incredible fighter. His endurance through the fights, through the years; being on top of his game for so many years; being the top pound-for-pound fighter for maybe ten years—it's unusual for a man to do that. Besides all that, he is a great person. There will never be another Azumah Nelson."

Jesse James Leija
WBC Super Featherweight Champion 1994

"Azumah Nelson launched his star with that loss against Salvador Sanchez; the decision could have gone either way. But the thing is, Azumah Nelson came on to be a great, great fighter. More importantly, he was loyal. I love Azumah."

Don King
Boxing Promoter

"It was always difficult for Azumah, being the opponent as he was, never really heavily supported by a big fanbase. But he was always there and always gave his all. He had the tenacity to overcome adversity. He just persisted over and over again; when most guys would have quit and had enough, he just kept moving forward. I think that's what makes him a great man. I always admired that about him—he's an incredible fighter but a better person."

Lawrence Cole
Boxing Referee

"That guy is a great human being. Look at everything he does. If your son could be like him, or your father, your uncle, you would be very, very proud of knowing that person. As a person, second to none; as a fighter, second to none. But he was part of a team that sometimes performed like a circus. They got in the ring and thought that they were going to win irrespective of whether they won or not."

Jeff Fenech
IBF Bantamweight Champion 1985–1987
WBC Super Bantamweight Champion 1987–1988
WBC Featherweight Champion 1988–1989

"Azumah was the greatest-ever featherweight to lace on a pair of gloves, in my opinion. He was so impressive in that fight against Sanchez with just fourteen days notice; if the fight had been fought over twelve rounds as they are today, he would have wound up as world champion then.

"Boxers today are nothing compared to the guys of twenty, thirty years ago, and it's good to see a guy like Azumah in the Hall of Fame. It is not a coincidence that he is called The Professor; he was a general in the ring, a warrior. He had great defence; he could take a shot and he could fight you or he could box you. That is what you got with Azumah, a complete boxer."

Carl King
Former Manager

"Azumah is a legend, a great fighter. He was the greatest in our era; there was no easy route to a world title back then."

Jim McDonnell
Commonwealth Games Silver Medalist
European Featherweight Champion
Beat three out of five world champions in his division,
boxing twice for the world title

"I am yet to find a Ghanaian boxer who can combine fighting and boxing like Azumah Nelson; he was equally well-endowed. He had a skill for boxing and a heart for fighting. He recognised the impact of his victory on the people; the inspiration it brought to the young people; the hope and the happiness it brought to the people of this country. So whatever he could do to keep it like that for as long as it lasted, he was going to do his bit. I am very glad for this young man."

Nii Amakai Amarteifio
Former Ghanaian Minister of Sport

"Nothing rattles the guy, nothing. You just don't see fighters with that kind of focus."

Angelo Dundee
Trainer to Muhammad Ali, George Foreman, and Sugar Ray Leonard

"I thank God that he will always try and do something to help others; he has done well. Azumah, he respects everyone. Everyone likes him because he didn't start to talk roughly to people. He is kind and he is beautiful. I am proud of him."

Madam Comfort
Mother

"Azumah loved boxing, and apart from that, he had his own talent; my father was a tailor so we all go that line. When he was young, Azumah would fox to get things for the family. He would do everything to get something for the family: sell coconuts, buy anything and sell anything. He would do anything for the family. He always tried to help the family become better."

Mensah Nelson
Brother

"He was a good reflection of the spirit of the Ghanaian—a highly disciplined and very determined person."

Former President of Ghana J. J. Rawlings

"All my life is a miracle."

Azumah Nelson
Professor of Boxing

THE AZUMAH
NELSON FOUNDATION

Throughout his career, Azumah was always looking for ways to help his people in Ghana, and that goal has not changed since his retirement from boxing. In 2008, he set up the Azumah Nelson Foundation, a not-for-profit organization in Ghana.

The foundation is aimed at providing social services to the poor and needy through the use of sports and education. Additionally, it will provide vocational training to the disadvantaged in society. According to Azumah, "The project will also serve as a youth leadership training centre to help the youth in Ghana realise the potential that God has given them."

The foundation has the full support of the Ghanaian government, and together they have initiated steps to construct sports complexes for sporting disciplines such as boxing, volleyball, table tennis, and badminton in various parts of the country as part of efforts to identify and groom talents in those sporting fields, and also to win that elusive Olympic medal.

"Professor" Azumah Nelson aims to become a positive mentor for the disadvantaged youth of Ghana and, ultimately, Africa. The goal of the foundation is to create opportunities using the medium of sport to educate youth and enhance their future social status.

The Azumah Nelson Foundation will design and implement functional education and effective personal development programs with academic and social standards that will mentor targeted children into well-rounded and meaningful members of their community as well as contributors both to national and continental development.

Part of the proceeds from this book will go to the foundation. We thank you for your purchase and the part you have played in helping the foundation and Azumah.

Should you want more information on the foundation or wish to make a further contribution, please do so by visiting the foundation website, www.azumahnelsonfoundation.org.gh.

CPSIA information can be obtained at www.ICGtesting.com
Printed in the USA
BVOW02s1356121114

374734BV00001BA/171/P